555 FAMILIES

A Social-Psychological Study
of Young Families in Transition

URBAN STUDIES SERIES

General Editor: George S. Sternlieb

The Affluent Suburb: Princeton by George S. Sternlieb, Robert William Burchell and Lynne Beyer Sagalyn

The Zone of Emergence: A Case Study of Plainfield, New Jersey by George S. Sternlieb and W. Patrick Beaton

The Ecology of Welfare: The Housing Crisis of Welfare Recipients in New York City by George S. Sternlieb and Bernard P. Indik

Landlords and Tenants: A Complete Guide to the Residential Rental Relationship by Jerome G. Rose

555 Families: A Social-Psychological Study of Young Families in Transition by Ludwig L. Geismar

555 FAMILIES

A Social-Psychological Study of Young Families in Transition

LUDWIG L. GEISMAR

ta

Transaction Books
New Brunswick, New Jersey
Distributed by E.P. Dutton & Co.

To Shirley

Acknowledgments

This book is based on data collected by the Rutgers University Family Life Improvement Project. The study as a whole, including the present analysis, was generously supported by the United States Social and Rehabilitation Service under HEW Grant No. 190.

The author is greatly indebted to the 555 young families who participated in the first phase of the project and to the 175 families who graciously consented to be interviewed repeatedly over a five-year period. Without their ready and open response to our request to share the story of their lives, this study could not have been undertaken.

This research also would not have been feasible without the skillful and conscientious work of our full-time interviewers, Audrey Green, Sara Holzer and Jackie O'Brien. The interviewing and coding efforts of Sara Noddings, Joan Odes, Neil Monroe, June Garelick, Lucia Correll, Renee Weiss, Iola Caplan, Louise Black, Myung Kyo Han, Suzanne Morfit, Margaret Morrissey, Amey Nelson, Judith Perlman, Fred A. Sigafoos and Karmela Waldman — all former graduate students in social work — are gratefully acknowledged.

To four colleagues go my particular thanks for contributing to the present volume. Professor Bruce Lagay, formerly assistant director of the Family Life Improvement Project, was in charge of interviewing operations, including the training of research interviewers. Professor Ursula Gerhart, the project's associate director, guided the team of coders and also did the bulk of interviews with Spanish-speaking respondents. I am especially indebted to her for her contributions to the research described in Chapter 14 and Appendix 2. Mrs. Harriet Fink handled the computer analysis, supervised coding and did much of the statistical work. And Professor Isabel Wolock assisted with diverse aspects of data collection and processing.

The data analysis was aided immeasurably by the reliable coding procedure carried out by Zona Fishkin, Dorothy Jaker, Patricia Lagay and Judy Schwartz, and the whole research endeavor relied on the conscientious secretarial work of Adele Verzatt, Louise Cerretani, Alix Cuilla, Katria Harris and Leona Thomas. The editorial work of my wife, Shirley, was an indispensable aid in producing the final manuscript.

To Dr. Leontine Young and to the staff of the Child Service Association I wish to extend a special vote of thanks for providing the research project with a home in an atmosphere conducive to scholarly pursuits.

I am indebted to Scarecrow Press, Inc., for permission to cite information from Chapters 2 and 6 of *Early Supports for Family Life: A Social Work Experiment* (copyright 1972 by Ludwig Geismar) and to the *Public Opinion Quarterly* for allowing reproduction of the article by Bruce Lagay, "Assessing Bias: A Comparison of Two Methods."

A faculty fellowship from the Rutgers Research Council and special administrative arrangements by the dean and faculty of the Rutgers Graduate School of Social Work freed me from my teaching duties during the academic year 1970-1971 and made the writing of this volume possible.

Contents

Appendices

Preface

This is a study of young families living in a large city on the eastern seaboard of the United States. It includes a cross-section of young parents (some of them single mothers) with a newborn first child — parents who are working and planning to meet added responsibilities and to adjust to the demands of a growing family. We had a number of purposes in mind: first, to learn how families function during this formative period of the family life cycle; second, to explore the ways in which attitudes and behavior are related to parents' backgrounds, the families' social class and their ethnic group; and, finally, to gather knowledge about changes in family functioning during this early phase of family life and to pinpoint the most important factors in such change.

At the heart of this inquiry is our desire to understand what makes families function well or poorly, become stable or disorganized, produce well-adjusted or maladjusted offspring. Such knowledge has implications beyond the field of family study, for the family is a central institution whose well-being is closely related to the welfare of man and society. The family furnishes the intimate environment that sustains most individuals and is the chief socializer of the young. It exercises, directly or indirectly, a great influence on most aspects of human life. As a way of living that almost every individual engages in at some time in his life, the family represents the human group most widely affected by social conditions.

Research on family functioning takes on added significance in a period of rapid social change, because family behavior and attitudes not only reflect but also contribute to such change. Whether the issue is school integration, equal rights for women or a guaranteed minimum income, the family climate of opinion and the predisposition of family members toward action or inaction constitute powerful forces in social and political activity.

Our research relies on a panel method of study to investigate in depth a representative sample of young families during a three- to four-year period. This inquiry is part of a larger endeavor, the Rutgers Family Life Improvement Project, in which families were studied over time to test the effect of preventive services on their social functioning. The volume at hand is not concerned with the special intervention program conducted by the project but views families within the context of services and resources provided regularly by the community.

We selected the longitudinal method, wherein change in the same families is studied over time, as best suited for documenting family development and pinpointing factors related to family disorganization. Longitudinal family life-cycle research is a relatively undeveloped area of study, largely because of the time and cost involved in its execution. Yet such research may hold the key to precise knowledge about the changing character of family needs, tasks and relationships, and the ability of family members to function according to their aspirations and the expectations of society.

A special challenge was provided by the research setting — a community immersed in social upheaval. Here was the opportunity to examine the family's ability to cope with problems attendant to rapid transformations in the urban environment. Because of the diversity of the population studied, we were able to examine how family characteristics such as low social status, unwed motherhood or race, are related to one's chances for good health, adequate housing and satisfactory family relationships.

1.

The Study Setting

The setting for this study is Newark, the largest city in New Jersey, located eight miles west of lower Manhattan. Newark had a population of 405,220 in 1960, but dropped to 382,000 according to the preliminary 1970 census returns. The city, which was founded by Puritans in 1666, experienced its largest population growth between 1850 and 1920, increasing from 38,894 to 414,524. Population fluctuated in the following half-century, with the losses slightly exceeding gains. Between 1950 and 1960 the city's population declined 8 percent while suburban areas registered a 25 percent gain.

Newark is a center for transportation of all kinds — highway, air, sea and rail — and a major distribution point for domestic and overseas goods. Among its industrial products are chemicals, electrical equipment, paints, machinery, leather goods, processed meats and malt liquors. The city also serves as a financial, retail and wholesale center, and houses the home offices of several large American insurance companies. Major institutions of higher learning within its boundaries include the Newark College of Engineering, and the Newark branches of Rutgers University and of Seton Hall University. Municipal government is the mayor-council type, under which executive, administrative and legislative power is divided among the mayor, the business administrator and the council, respectively. The mayor-council government was approved by a referendum in 1954, replacing the commission form which had existed for 37 years.

The most dramatic demographic change in Newark since 1940 is the changing ratio between black and white inhabitants. The U. S. Population Censuses for 1940, 1950 and 1960 give the following percentages for the black population: 10.5, 17.1 and 34.4. The corresponding figures for whites, including Spanish-speaking inhabitants, are 89.5, 82.9 and 65.6. A Rutgers University sample survey lists the 1967 Newark population as

52.2 percent Negro, 38.3 percent white and 9.5 percent other, most of whom are of Puerto Rican origin.[1] In other words, at the end of the 1960s English-speaking whites were clearly a minority. In the space of less than 30 years the black population had risen to an absolute majority.

Newark has one of the largest urban renewal programs in the nation. In 1960 it ranked seventh in terms of total federal funds received and third, behind New Haven, Connecticut and Norfolk, Virginia, in per capita spending for cities of comparable size.[2] Roughly 12 percent of Newark's inhabitants live in some form of public housing, which makes the program one of the nation's largest on a per capita basis.[3] During the late 1960s the city was saturated with community organization programs designed to reduce unemployment and poverty.

Newark's woes have been experienced by many other American cities: business is migrating to outlying areas; real estate taxes are rising steeply; inner-city housing is deteriorating; the crime rate is going up; the more prosperous are fleeing to the suburbs; and the poor are isolated in inner-city ghettoes. All of these factors are closely interrelated. The exodus of business, which finds economically more advantageous settings outside the city, puts a disproportionate tax burden on the remaining residents. This, in turn, gives added impetus to the migration of the economically successful to suburbia. This migration is also racially selective; discrimination in real estate reinforces the segregation fostered by the economic and political systems. The city, faced with a loss of revenue, is forced to cut back on expenditures for education, health and welfare, and the poor and members of minority groups suffer. A combination of factors, including the social characteristics of those left in the city, the concentration of poverty and deprivation, the lack of opportunity for advancement, the frustration caused by the absence of hope and opportunity, gives rise to a climate in which racial tension, social disorganization and deviant behavior thrive.

The data provide dramatic testimony to the city's critical socioeconomic situation. Newark relies on its property tax to raise $7.00 out of every $10.00 of total revenue, while cities of comparable size in other states raise $4.00 out of $10.00 in this manner.[4] Forty-eight percent of Newark families earned less than $7,000 per year in 1967,[5] compared to 41 percent in the nation as a whole. Nationally, the percentage of persons earning under $5,000 is 25.1, for Newark, 38.4. And of those earning less than $5,000, 42.3 percent are black and 28.5 percent are white. Unemployment affects 9 percent of Newark's civilian labor force, about twice the percentage for the country as a whole. In employment as in income Newark Negroes are at a disadvantage, with an unemployment rate of 11.5 percent compared to 5.9 percent for whites.[6]

Housing is a special problem in Newark. Its Model Cities application describes 40,000 of the city's 136,000 housing units as substandard or dilapidated.[7] Public housing, proportionately in greater supply than in most U. S. cities, provides essentially inferior accommodations. High-rise projects are clustered in a small area in the Central Ward, and their residents are crowded into densely populated, vertical silos with little surrounding grass or open space.[8] Most high-rise projects are in the ghetto and house a high proportion of nonwhites, while older, low-rise apartments have mostly white residents. Housing segregation is characteristic of Newark as a whole; in 1960 the six peripheral wards were at least 80 percent white, while the Central Ward was 84 percent black and three other center city wards were between 40 and 60 percent black.[9] A tally of the number of persons per city household shows that one- and two-person households are generally white and four- and more-person households are black or Puerto Rican. This pattern occurs in the inner city as well as the peripheral residential areas.[10]

Newark's public schools had about 69 percent Negro and 7 percent Spanish-speaking pupils in 1966, a rise of 14 percent and 3 percent respectively, over the preceding five years. The high percentage of black students in the city's schools compared to blacks in the city's population indicates that Newark's black population is predominately young. Board of Education statistics reveal staggering educational problems which are graphically reflected in the following data on pupil performance on standardized tests:

1. For Grade 3, in October 1966, the Newark reading median was 1.9 while the national norm was 3.2.
2. For Grade 6, in October 1966, the Newark reading median was 4.0 compared with the national norm of 6.2.
3. IQ medians were substantially below the national norms for Grades 3 and 6.
4. In Grade 7 the Newark average on the Stanford arithmetic test was 5.1 compared with a national norm of 7.2.
5. The reading and IQ medians for Newark show that by present standards well over half of the secondary school pupils are or will be functionally illiterate at the end of high school if the existing trend continues.
6. On standardized tests pupils in predominantly white schools score almost a full grade higher than those in nonwhite schools.
7. The gap between Newark and national levels of performance widens as the student moves up in grades.[12]

Newark's cumulative high school dropout rate was estimated at 32 percent for the period 1962-1966. It may well have been higher, for each year 28 percent of the students transfer to another school, and information about individual pupils is lost.[13] There is little doubt that dropouts and incomplete transfers rarely find work and generally end up in the streets.

The health problems facing the city are enormous, as the following passage from the Newark Model Cities application indicates:

> According to the latest statistics (1966 data), Newark has the highest maternal mortality and VD rates in the country; highest infant mortality rates in the nation, and the highest rate of new TB cases for all cities. Newark ranks seventh, among ten leading cities in the country, in the total number of drug addicts....The most recent report on a national sample of 302 cities tested for air pollution by the U. S. Public Health Service rated Newark ninth highest. Out-of-wedlock births gave Newark a rate three and one-half times the national rate. The overall birth rate is second highest among major cities.[14]

The city's difficult economic situation and its shifts in population composition are vividly reflected in the patterns of expenditures for social welfare, including federal, state and local programs. Aggregate figures are $62,666,625 for the year 1960, $101,344,445 for 1964 and $142,089,075 for 1967, representing a 126 percent rise over a seven-year period. The welfare burden is dramatically illustrated by the fact that, "in the fiscal year 1965, the per capita expenditures for categorical aid programs were seven times as great in Essex (the county in which Newark is located) as in Bergen County (an adjacent, more suburban county), while the per capita ratables in Bergen were 137 percent those of Essex."[15]

The present study was carried out during the period 1964 to 1969 while Newark was undergoing a series of social and political crises, the most serious of which was the racial riot of July 1967, resulting in 26 deaths (24 of the dead were Negroes), about 1,000 injured and over $10 million worth of property damage. Some 1,055 businesses, mostly concentrated in or near the ghetto areas, and 29 residences housing 85 families took the brunt of the losses. The riots had been preceded by a number of crises. There was controversy over the location of the New Jersey School of Medicine and Dentistry, a dispute over the selection of a secretary to the Board of Education, reaction to alleged police abuse at the home of a Black Muslim and increased activity of militants.[17] These were primarily disputes between the black and white communities, although some (like the location of the new medical school building) resulted from a clash of interests between lower-class populations and the Establishment.

The Governor's Select Commission on Civil Disorders reports "a pervasive feeling of corruption" in the city at the time of the riots.[18] As evidence the report cites a series of grand jury presentments and indictments on charges of bribery and graft at various levels of city government, statements by high officials that "there is a price on everything at

City Hall," and the views of many Newark citizens indicating a lack of confidence in the administration and the police department.

The charge of widespread corruption received additional support when former Mayor Hugh Addonizio (two-term mayor, 1962-1970) was convicted with other officials for conspiracy and extortion in the summer of 1970. When Addonizio was sentenced, the *New York Times* (September 20, 1970) ran a feature article in which correspondent David K. Shipler made these points, among others, about the problems of city government:

1. Aides of Kenneth A. Gibson, the first black mayor of Newark, elected in the spring of 1970, have discovered that virtually every contract signed by the city in recent years was inflated by 10 percent to allow for kickbacks to city officials.
2. Corruption was made easier by lack of personnel in city agencies. There are few middle-managers who would dilute the power of the top officials. And the city's Department of Public Works, which controls millions of dollars for sewers, roads and so forth, employs not a single licensed engineer — although it once had 20 to 25 — to guard against fraud and error by private contractors.
3. In its last few months the Addonizio administration let certain private contracts lapse, stalling work on construction projects and depriving the city of certain privately rendered services. Federal funds were also cut off from several programs, leaving the city without the funds to pay some employees when the new mayor took office.

Newark is a city gripped by the agonies of rapid or accelerated social change, in which the welfare of the central city receives low priority. The result is severe problems in employment, health, welfare and other public services. The demography of Newark and its many problems are invariably reflected in the structure, behavior and life styles of the families studied. Housing, work, social life and recreation take place, for the most part, within the confines of the community. The nature of the city's services greatly affects the well-being of the families, and chances for improved living and social advancement are determined, in large measure, by local opportunities. And while the overall effect of the city environment upon the lives of the young families may not be directly measurable in the present study, there is ample evidence of the close interdependence between the nature of the family and the character of the community in which it resides.

NOTES

1. Jack Chernick, Bernard P. Indik, and George Sternlieb, *Newark, New Jersey, Population and Labor Force*, New Brunswick, N.J.: Rutgers — The State University, Institute of Management and Labor Relations and University Extension Division, December 1967, p. 2-8.

2. Harold Kaplan, *Urban Renewal Politics: Slum Clearance in Newark*, New York: Columbia University Press, 1963, p. 3.

3. Thomas Brooks, "Newark," *The Atlantic* 1969, 224 (August) 4-12, p. 4.

4. *Report for Action: Governor's Select Commission on Civil Disorder*, State of New Jersey, February 1968.

5. Chernick, Indik, and Sternlieb, *op. cit.*, pp. 28-29.

6. *Ibid.*, p. 11.

7. *Report for Action*, p. 55.

8. *Ibid.*, p. 56.

9. Nathan Wright, Jr., *Ready to Riot*, New York: Holt, Rinehart, and Winston, 1968, pp. 38-55.

10. Unpublished data analyzed by Professor Bernard Indik of Rutgers University.

11. *Report for Action*, p. 77.

12. *Ibid.*, p. 77, cited from *Report of City-Wide Testing Program, Grades 3, 6, 7, October 1966*, Newark: Department of Reference and Research, Board of Education, Newark, N. J.

13. *Model Cities Application, Newark, N. J.*, Part 2 (a), pp. 2-3.

14. *Ibid.*, pp. 22-23.

15. *Report for Action*, p. 85, cited from Bert Hunter, *Who Pays for Public Assistance in New Jersey?*, Newark, N. J.: Council of Social Agencies, February 1967 (mimeographed, Table III).

16. The Report of the Governor's Select Commission on Civil Disorders states that no exact records were kept on many of those treated. *Report for Action*, pp. 124-125.

17. Nathan Wright, *op. cit.*, p. 7. The items were cited by the writer from a report of the state police. The author, a black leader and authority on urban affairs, views the above as a valid, though incomplete, list of factors contributing to the civil disorders.

18. *Report for Action*, p. 20.

2.

Study Perspective

Organisms have long been analyzed and explained in terms of their life cycle. In the study of human beings we may also seek to describe the span of time that marks their existence — the period from emergence (birth) to termination (death). Usually we have in mind two conditions when we speak of life cycle: that it pertains to an experience or occurrence that is not unique but repeats itself over and over again, and that the period specified is marked by a series of episodes or events. The human life cycle, for instance, is frequently characterized by birth, puberty, courtship, marriage, childbirth, menopause, senescence and death. The use of the life-cycle concept in the study of the family stems from a recognition that, like the individual, its life span is a series of diverse experiences called stages, which have a unique character and exert special influence upon situations and objects associated with them.

In the 1930s a group of rural sociologists used the life-cycle concept to analyze the economic life history of the peasant family.[1] Subsequently, other scholars employed the concept to organize family data in terms of the ages of children, and the expansion and contraction of the family group.[2] In the 1950s life-cycle analysis was helpful in studying consumer behavior[3] as well as many other social and behavioral science variables.[4] A recent application of life-cycle research is Reuben Hill's landmark study using a three-generation sample of Minnesota families to explore the relationship between life-cycle stages and the decision-making process.[5]

There are many ways of organizing the life cycle, depending upon the particular theoretical perspective of the researcher. A well-known effort is that of Evelyn Duvall, who enumerates eight stages, ranging from "couple without children" to "retirement to death of one or both spouses."[6] In the Duvall scheme the variable that differentiates one stage from another is the children's age, particularly the oldest child's.[7] Other

investigators also make age of the oldest child the fulcrum of their classification system, although their grouping differs in other respects.[8]
Roy Rodgers, recognizing the problems posed by child spacing, broken
families, number of children and other family differences, devised a
more complex system of stages based on four family positions: husband-
father, wife-mother, oldest child and youngest child.[9] The Rodgers'
method of organizing the life cycle, which may be considered the most
advanced, yields not eight but 24 distinct categories or role complexes,
and these account for the ages of the youngest child, the oldest child, the
group of children collectively, as well as the death of a spouse.[10]

Evelyn Duvall has also postulated a series of specific developmental
tasks corresponding to life-cycle stages, and to these she has applied
Havighurst's definition of "...a task which arises at or about a certain
period in the life of an individual, successful achievement of which leads
to his happiness and success, while failure leads to unhappiness in the
individual, disapproval by society, and difficulty with later tasks."[11]
Duvall's study details developmental tasks for each family role and life-
cycle stage.[12]

What all these approaches have in common is the recognition that
family life is marked by "successive patterns within the continuity of
family living over the years."[13] The differences in patterns, which can
also be identified by structure, express themselves in differences in
family functions and family goals. Thus, life-cycle stages can be examined in terms of the relationships, activities, attitudes and values
which characterize each period. Such a perspective is offered by the social functioning approach, for it views the family as a social system
which carries out certain socially assigned functions. The family is a
system by virtue of the fact that its constituent parts — members and
social roles — interact and bear a definable relationship to one another.
Function and functioning refer to the actions or interactions of these
constituent parts, which in one form or another contribute to, fail to
contribute to, or even hinder the continuity of the system. Social functioning as a perspective derives many of its formulations from the so-
called structural-functional approach in family sociology. Harold Christensen has identified this approach as a major theoretical framework in
the study of the family.[14] Briefly, "it is concerned with whether any
given element is either functional or dysfunctional to the total system,
determined by the extent to which it either adds to or subtracts from
the system's operations."[15] The guiding propositions of the structural-
functional approach are:

    1. Certain functional requirements must be satisfied if a social sys-
       tem, in this case the family, is to survive at a given level.

2. The family, like other social systems, performs individual-serving as well as society-serving functions.
3. In every society the family performs some of the basic functions — such as reproduction and the socialization of the young — that are necessary for the survival of that society.[16]
4. Family structure defines the parameters within which the family is able to function or carry out socially assigned tasks in pursuit of common goals.

The activities and processes which make the operation of the system possible include reproduction, biological and psychological maintenance, socialization and social control.[17] While different scholars might agree on the basic nature of the foregoing group of functions, they would differ, in keeping with their own theoretical framework, as to the way in which they would be organized and labelled.[18]

The present approach views family functions within a framework of observable tasks, roles and relationships, definable and open to evaluation. This approach is conducive to empirical comparisons among families in terms of some overall criteria of performance. Our goal is to characterize families according to the ways in which they attain or fail to attain the culturally prescribed objectives for family life. Several characteristics of the method defined here facilitate this goal. Each family is described by a profile of social functioning composed of eight discrete areas to be discussed in detail in Chapter 5. The area of individual behavior and adjustment brings together the social roles of each family member. Family relationships and unity, and care and training of children deal with family functions or tasks related mainly to relationships among family members. Social activities and use of community resources cover relationships with persons in other social systems, such as schools, clubs, churches, recreational resources and social agencies. The areas of economic practices, health conditions and practices, and home and household practices deal with so-called instrumental functions, i.e., behavior designed to maintain the family as a biological and physical unit.

The preceding areas or area groups furnish us with the analytical tools for comparing individual families and groups of families with each other. Up to this point, however, only the horizontal dimension, namely the areas in which comparisons can be made, have been outlined. Missing as yet is the vertical dimension, the nature or quality of social functioning, on which comparisons are to be made.

The structural-functional approach is concerned with whether given elements make the system work better or worse, add to its stability or its instability, prolong or shorten its life. Any evaluation of the nature

of family functioning must be given in terms of whether social functioning denotes sufficiency or insufficiency in individual roles, relationships
and tasks of family members. But the meanings of sufficiency and insufficiency remain to be clarified if the vertical profile dimension is to enable us to classify types or areas of social functioning.

The social scientist is naturally hesitant to apply standards of classi-
fying or rating which are superimposed from the outside. He would
ideally categorize and evaluate people on the basis of their own scale of
values and norms rather than on his or someone else's, but two problems
bar this approach: population groups differ in what they consider desirable, which forces the researcher repeatedly to revise his norms to fit
each group studied; and deviant groups certainly would not be identified
as such since they would not consider themselves so by their own standards and norms.

There is another option: formulating criteria which the researcher
decides are widely accepted in a particular culture and using them to
code or rate observed behavior. This was done in a number of previous
research efforts, and since these studies have been reported in the sociological and social work literature,[20] we will not review them here.
These past efforts have comprised the following, however:

1. A study of many social work case records to learn what clients and
   workers consider desirable behavior.
2. A seminar with experienced social workers who had established
   good working relationships with seriously disorganized families on
   the subject of criteria for justifying professional intervention.
3. A systematic analysis of self-administered questionnaires in which
   heads of families expressed goals and priorities for family living
   and community action.
4. A perusal of laws and statutes furnishing legal definitions of child
   neglect, cruelty, unsuitable home and other terminology utilized in
   court procedures to remove children or take other restraining action against a family.
5. A review, with the aid of a legal expert, of so-called illegal behavior
   that tends to be tolerated versus behavior that is generally subject
   to prosecution.
6. An analysis of the literature on child rearing and mental health
   practices focused on behavior that is generally considered functional versus behavior considered dysfunctional.[21]

The final product of this extended and collaborative effort was a 15-
page schedule for rating family functioning in eight areas and 25 subcategories on a seven-point scale.[22] The following are the dimensions on
which ratings of each family were carried out: The first, the *health-*

welfare dimension, seeks answers to the questions of whether behavior contributes to or is harmful to the physical, social and emotional well-being of family members, and whether it is personally satisfying and commensurate with a person's potential for social functioning. The second dimension, termed *conformity-deviance*, asks whether laws are observed or violated, and whether behavior is in harmony or in conflict with the mores and standards of a community or a family's status group.

At this point it should be helpful to look jointly at the two frames of reference for research on family life, the life-cycle approach and the social-functioning perspective, in order to comprehend how they can furnish an analytic focus for the study of young families. Duvall states succinctly how each life-cycle stage can be differentiated from every other according to the individual and collective roles, tasks, responsibilities and expectations of family members.[23] Duvall also enumerates and describes roles, tasks and related variables and how these are related to successful family development. Life-cycle research can also begin with an assumption of differences in roles and tasks and proceed to an examination of the ways in which these affect a specific aspect of a family's social functioning. Thus, it may be asked how a different constellation of roles and responsibilities such as that found in families headed by unwed mothers, for example, affects the family's ability to function in a manner that promotes health and well-being, yields satisfaction and minimizes conflict and deviant behavior.

The foregoing question can be posed as pure research, for the sake of knowing the dynamics of social functioning over the span of a family's life cycle. The question can also be raised in relation to applied research goals, namely, to learn the implications of different levels of social functioning for planning and action, consonant with the values of society. The present report is weighted in favor of the former, although there is an occasional reference to implications for social policy.[24]

This study spotlights the formative period of family life following the birth of the first child. The childless period of marriage is viewed by many couples as an extension of courtship or the honeymoon. Relations between partners, economic and social responsibility and the division of labor have not been fundamentally altered. With the arrival of the first child the power structure changes, along with the division of labor and the interpersonal relationships of the parents.[25] New patterns which are established in this period will prevail during the major portion of their life together.

If the woman has been working, as is a prevalent pattern among newlyweds, and she leaves the labor force, she becomes more dependent upon her husband. The heavy demands of child care remove her from contact with fellow workers and limit her opportunities to participate in social and recreational activities. Motherhood tends to engender social isolation and increased need for support by the husband. [26]

The shift from work outside the home to full-time homemaking brings corresponding changes in domestic tasks. After the mother regains her strength following birth, she will tend to take over more of the housework while the husband will share fewer of the tasks. For years to come the wife may be the chief housekeeper while the husband will be the only wage earner. [27]

The baby's presence inevitably alters the husband-wife relationship. They no longer can enjoy unlimited companionship, especially outside the home, and the intensity of their relationship is likely to be reduced. The attention of both parents is diverted to the child, and the husband may often feel that he is being neglected. [28] New parenthood also involves an expansion of tasks and responsibilities, disruption of routines, particularly those of sleep and recreation, and loss of mobility — all related to the care of the infant. [29]

The patterns of family life which evolve set the pace for the life style that will prevail while there are dependent children in the home. Although roles, tasks and responsibilities will change as the family moves from one life-cycle stage to another, they will be more like each other than like those which marked the early childless stage of marriage.

If the period immediately following the birth of the first child may be termed the establishment phase, in which new patterns of living are laid down, the subsequent timespan could be referred to as the institutionalization phase. In this period new routines become the accepted pattern, characterizing life during the rearing of the first child and subsequent offspring.

Stage 2 in the Duvall scheme is characterized by an oldest child under 30 months, and stage 3 occurs when he is between two and one-half to six years of age. What is the significance of these stages for the social functioning of the family? The basic hypothesis underlying this longitudinal study is a decline in the quality of family functioning during the early stages of the family life cycle. Having children and rearing them requires major adjustments for the new parents (or the mother, if she is unmarried). In American society marriages are consummated, for the most part, on the basis of romantic love and the companionship of the marital partners, rather than on aptitude for family living and parenthood. Young people select their marriage partners on the basis of compatibility; they are quite unaware of the demands of later married life and unable to predict the changes which will occur in themselves and their partners in response to these demands. Children call for resources and skills on the part of the young couple for which they are relatively unprepared, and these demands multiply as the children grow older. Coupled with the cultural and economic pressures is what Alice S. Rossi has termed "irrevocability,"[30] the belief that the marital relationship is compelling and responsibility for the offspring unalterable.

Sociological studies during the past three decades uniformly point toward increasing difficulties during the course of married life, at least during the first decade. Most of these studies use happiness as a criterion of change in family life. Lewis M. Terman, for example, concluded in 1938 that marital happiness declines after about seven years, only to rise again and reach a new low after 16 years of married life.[31] A sample of families studied originally by Burgess and Wallin was followed up 20 years after marriage by Dentler and Pineo, who discovered that intimacy had been reduced and shared activities had decreased.[32] Blood and Wolfe, using cross-sectional analysis with a sample of over 900 wives at different life-cycle stages, found that love and marital companionship declined in each child-rearing stage.[33]

Eleanor Braun Luckey found marital satisfaction negatively related to the number of years of marriage.[34] Using personality variables on the Leary interpersonal checklist, she found that a person tended to describe his spouse less favorably as the life cycle progressed. Harold Feldman found that children tend to reduce the interaction of spouses, and that both the intimacy and intensity of the marital relationship decline over the years.[35]

A systematic survey of the literature by Rollins and Feldman on the relationship between marital satisfaction and life-cycle stages yielded 12 studies with samples ranging in size from 120 to over 15,000.[36] Marital satisfaction was invariably highest at the beginning of the family life cycle but the low points varied from the childbearing period (stage 2) to the middle years to the retirement period (stage 7).[37] Actually eight out of the 12 research projects summarized listed stage 5, when the oldest child is between 13 and 20 years of age, as the lowest or one of the lowest stages in the family life cycle. Rollins and Feldman, in their study of 852 couples married for more than five years, report that wives are most dissatisfied with marriage during the childbearing and child-rearing stages, while husbands are least satisfied when anticipating retirement. Both report a loss of "positive companionship experiences" as the life cycle progresses, with only a slight improvement in the later phases.[38]

Wesley R. Burr recently investigated six types of marital satisfaction.[39] The data, which cover the attitudes of 147 middle-class couples, indicate a broad relationship between the experiences reported by husbands and wives. Although different types of satisfaction do not show identical curves over the course of the family life cycle, there is a general decline in all types of satisfaction between the time the oldest child is under six years old and the time he is between six and 12.[40] Afterwards, there is a predominantly rising though zigzagging pattern of satisfaction. A curvilinear trend with decreasing marital dissatisfaction during the early stages followed by a leveling off and a rise during the later stages was also found in the work of Gurin, Veroff and Feld.[41]

One study clearly challenged the notion of a decrease of marital satisfaction over the life cycle. Bradburn and Caplovitz made a questionnaire survey of a probability sample of 2,006 persons in four Illinois communities and found that marital tensions decreased over time with only minor changes in the degree of marital happiness.[42]

A cross-sectional study by Geismar, comparing young families at two life-cycle stages, revealed that families function better after the birth of the first child than they do when one or more children are in the middle school years (grades 6 to 8). Although the two random samples differed in social and ethnic composition because of the city's age-linked migration patterns, the difference in functioning between life-cycle stages continued to exist when social class was controlled.[43]

By and large, the aforementioned life-cycle studies do not support a widespread notion that Duvall's stage 2, the childbearing period, is a time of crisis in the life of the parents.[44] The crisis notion has also been challenged by Jacoby,[45] and the belief has gained ground that the process of parenthood, though requiring fundamental adjustments from the marriage partners, is also rewarding. Harold Feldman, for instance, found that couples rate the first year with the infant as more satisfying than subsequent stages in the family life cycle.[46]

A multidimensional investigation of family change covering factors such as satisfactions, husband-wife relationship, mobility, occupational roles, community participation and others was undertaken by Jan Dizard in a 20-year follow-up study of the Burgess and Wallin sample of 1,000 engaged couples.[47] The predominant change reported by the author is described as an emotional "deadening" of the husband-wife relationship. "Decreasing husband-wife happiness and permanence," the author found, "is disproportionately common in those marriages which move toward a greater degree of role differentiation."[48] The middle years of marriage, in contrast to the beginning ones, are characterized by greater husband-wife disagreement over the performance of familial tasks and increasing dominance by one of the partners.[49]

All in all, the research is heavily weighted on the side of concepts such as happiness, companionship and satisfaction, and although there is no reason to belittle the importance of such factors in family life, the studies reveal little about the manner in which they are attained by family members. Social functioning analysis is designed to yield such information, to provide tangible data about which roles and tasks are responsible for or contribute to the satisfactions of marital partners. Where appropriate, reference will be made to a few other studies which also address themselves to the more concrete aspects of family behavior as it relates to life-cycle stages. [50]

Since personal satisfaction is one of four criteria for judging the adequacy of family functioning, one would tend to look for a direct relationship between the satisfactions the couple experiences and the overall social functioning of the family group during given life-cycle phases. In applying this reasoning, one would argue that declining satisfactions reflect the degree of success in dealing with the tasks, many of them new, confronting the family after the arrival of the first child. The greater satisfaction Feldman found during the year following child birth may, in fact, represent the early emotional response to the newborn and the initial enthusiasm over the new status the family has achieved by adding a new member. During the process of child rearing, more formidable aspects of parenthood appear for which guidelines are lacking. [51] Books on nutrition and primers on child care fall short of helping parents successfully socialize their children.

Child care becomes more challenging and is more likely to turn into a problem during stage 3, when the child has ceased to be an infant and begins to interact vigorously with his environment, which may already include one or two siblings. The toddler or preschooler is apt to confront his parents with problems of discipline, or various forms of deviant behavior which the younger child does not exhibit.

This third life-cycle stage, usually accompanied by increases in family size, brings with it financial obligations which often exceed the family's earning power. Parents must modify existing roles, assume others, and arrive at new ways of sharing power and responsibility — all of which makes substantial demands upon them. The likely result, according to our hypotheses, is a reduction in the adequacy of family functioning.

This book will examine closely a series of specific aspects of family functioning, such as child rearing, interpersonal functioning, economic practices, community relations and so forth. The study will investigate how factors such as family background, social class and ethnic affiliation tend to affect various aspects of family social functioning. A preliminary discussion in each area will seek to analyze the significance of each inquiry and state, where appropriate, the hypotheses used to guide the particular investigation.

NOTES

1. Pitrim A. Sorokin, Carle C. Zimmerman, and C. J. Galpin, *A Systematic Sourcebook in Rural Sociology*, Vol. 2, Minneapolis: University of Minnesota Press, 1931.

2. Reuben Hill and Roy H. Rodgers, "The Developmental Approach," in Harold T. Christensen (editor), *Handbook of Marriage and the Family*, Chicago: Rand McNally and Company, 1964, pp. 171-211.

3. L. H. Clark (editor), "Consumer Behavior," Vol. 2, *The Life Cycle and Consumer Behavior*, New York: New York University Press, 1955.

4. J. B. Lansing and L. Kish, "Family Life Cycle as an Independent Variable," *American Sociological Review*, 1957, 22 (October) pp. 512-519.

5. Reuben Hill, "Decision Making and the Family Life Cycle," in Ethel Shanas and Gordon Streib, *Social Structure and the Family, Generational Relations*, Englewood Cliffs, N. J.: Prentice Hall, Inc., pp. 113-139.

6. Evelyn Duvall, *Family Development*, Philadelphia: J. B. Lippincott Company, 1957, p. 8.

7. Only the first and last stages as indicated above, as well as the second to the last stage (empty nest to retirement) are characterized by childlessness.

8. Sorokin, Zimmerman, and Galpin, *op. cit.*, p. 31; Harold Feldman, *A Report of Research in Progress in the Development of Husband-Wife Relationships*, Ithaca, N. Y.: Cornell University, Jan. 30, 1961, p. 6.

9. Hill and Rodgers, *loc. cit.*, p. 183.

10. *Ibid.*, p. 189.

11. Duvall, *op. cit.*, pp. 98-99, quoted from Robert J. Havighurst, *Human Development and Education*, New York: Longmans, Green and Company, 1953, p. 2.

12. Duvall, *op. cit.*, pp. 95-524.

13. Duvall, *op. cit.*, p. 4.

14. Harold T. Christensen, "Development of the Family Field of Study," in Harold T. Christensen (editor), *Handbook of Marriage and the Family*, pp. 3-32.

15. *Ibid.*, p. 21.

16. Summarized by Jennie McIntire, "The Structure-Functional Approach to Family Study," in F. Ivan Nye and Felix M. Berardo (editors), *Emerging Conceptual Frameworks in Family Analysis*, New York: The MacMillan Company, 1966, pp. 52-77; pp. 63-64.

17. Adapted from William J. Goode, "The Sociology of the Family," in Robert K. Merton, Leonard Broom, and Leonard S. Cottrell, Jr. (editors), *Sociology Today*, New York: Basic Books, Inc., 1959, pp. 178-196, pp. 178-179.

18. For a summary of the most important conceptual approaches, see McIntire, *loc. cit.*, pp. 66-71.

19. Christensen, *loc. cit.*, p. 21.

20. L. L. Geismar and Beverly Ayres, *Measuring Family Functioning, A Manual on a Method for Evaluating the Social Functioning of Disorganized Families*, St. Paul, Minn.: Family Centered Project, 1960; Ludwig L. Geismar, *Family and Community Functioning*, Metuchen, N. J.: The Scarecrow Press, Inc., 1971; L. L. Geismar and Michael A. La Sorte, *Understanding the Multi-Problem Family, A Conceptual Analysis and Exploration in Early Identification*, New York: Association Press, 1964; L. L. Geismar, Michael A. La Sorte, and Beverly Ayres, "Measuring Family Disorganization," *Marriage and Family Living*, 1962, 26 (February) pp. 51-56; L. L. Geismar, "Family Functioning as an Index of Need for Welfare Services," *Family Process*, 1964, 3 (March) pp. 99-113; Gordon E. Brown, *The Multi-Problem Dilemma*, Metuchen, N. J.: The Scarecrow Press, Inc., 1968, pp. 107-189.

21. A good example of such an effort is reported in Catherine S. Chilman, *Growing Up Poor*, Washington, D. C.: U. S. Department of Health, Education, and Welfare, Welfare Administration, 1966.

22. Gordon E. Brown, pp. 165-179. A revised version of this schedule is contained in Geismar, *Family and Community Functioning, op. cit.*

23. Duvall, *op. cit.*, pp. 95-476.

24. For the latter approach see Ludwig L. Geismar, Bruce Lagay, Isabel Wolock, Ursula C. Gerhart, and Harriet Fink, *Early Supports for Family Life: A Social Work Experiment*, Metuchen, N. J.: The Scarecrow Press, Inc., 1972.

25. Robert O. Blood, Jr., *Marriage* (second edition), New York: The Free Press, 1969, p. 439.

26. Robert O. Blood and Donald M. Wolfe, *Husbands and Wives: The Dynamics of Married Living*, Glencoe, Illinois: Free Press, 1960, p. 43.

27. Blood, Jr., *op. cit.*, p. 439.

28. *Ibid.*, pp. 439-440.

29. *Ibid.*, pp. 440-445.

30. Alice S. Rossi, "Transition to Parenthood," in Jeffrey K. Hadden and Marie L. Borgatta (editors), *Marriage and the Family, A Comprehensive Reader*, Itasca, Illinois: F. E. Peacock, Publishers, Inc., 1969, pp. 361-376.

31. Lewis M. Terman, *Psychological Factors in Marital Happiness*, New York: McGraw Hill Book Co., 1938, p. 177.

32. Robert A. Dentler and Peter C. Pineo, "Sexual Adjustment, Marital Adjustment, and Personal Growth of Husbands," *Marriage and Family Living*, 1960, 22 (February) pp. 45-48.

33. Blood and Wolfe, *op. cit.*, pp. 158, ff., 232, ff.

34. Eleanor Braun Luckey, "Number of Years Married as Related to Personality Perception and Marital Satisfaction," *Journal of Marriage and the Family*, 1966, 28 (February) pp. 44-48.

35. Harold Feldman, *Development of the Husband-Wife Relationship*, Ithaca: Cornell University, Department of Child Development and Family Relations, pp. 151-155 (mimeographed).

36. Boyd C. Rollins and Harold Feldman, "Marital Satisfaction Over the Family Life Cycle," *Marriage and the Family*, 1970, 32 (February) pp. 20-28.

37. The two studies that listed stages 2 and 3 as low points did not extend beyond stage 3. *Ibid.*, p. 21.

38. *Ibid.*, pp. 24-27.

39. Wesley R. Burr, "Satisfaction with Various Aspects of Marriage Over the Life Cycle: A Random Middle Class Sample," *Marriage and the Family*, 1970, 32 (February) pp. 29-37.

40. The Duvall stages were not used in this research.

41. Gerald Gurin, Joseph Veroff, and Sheila Feld, *Americans View Their Mental Health*, New York: Basic Books, Inc., 1960, pp. 101-104. See also a survey of recent research on marital happiness over time in Mary W. Hicks and Marilyn Platt, "Marital Happiness: A Review of Research in the Sixties," *Journal of Marriage and the Family*, 1970, 32 (November) pp. 553-574, pp. 564-566.

42. Norman M. Bradburn and David Caplovitz, *Reports on Happiness*, Chicago: Aldine Publishing Co., 1965.

43. Ludwig L. Geismar, *Preventive Intervention in Social Work*, Metuchen, N. J.: The Scarecrow Press, Inc., 1969, pp. 58-68.

44. E. E. LeMasters, "Parenthood as Crisis," in Marvin B. Sussman (editor), *Sourcebook in Marriage and the Family*, Boston: Houghton Mifflin Company, 1963, pp. 194-198.

45. Arthur P. Jacoby, "Transition to Parenthood: A Reassessment," *Journal of Marriage and the Family*, 1969, 31 (November) pp. 720-727.

46. Feldman, *op. cit.*, pp. 21-22.

47. Jan Dizard, *Social Change in the Family*, Chicago, Illinois: Community and Family Study Center, University of Chicago, 1968.

48. *Ibid.*, p. 73.

49. *Ibid.*, pp. 15-21.

50. Feldman, *op. cit.*, Blood and Wolfe, *op. cit.*, and Jan Dizard, *op. cit.*

51. Rossi, *loc. cit.*, p. 372.

3.

How the Families Were Studied

Interviewing and observation have long been the key methods of collecting data in the field of family study. Alone or in combination they enable the researcher to gain factual information, elicit opinions, describe behavior and search for attitudes by comparing expressed views with observed behavior. But to ensure its usefulness, data collection should proceed within a theoretical framework which outlines the scope of the endeavor and guides the testing of hypotheses. In the following pages the methods of data gathering which were applied to the theoretical framework outlined in Chapter 2 are described.

THE INTERVIEWS

Our main instrument for gathering data in this study was the open-ended interview, accompanied by observation, and standardized attitude schedules, taking about 20 minutes of the respondent's time, pertaining to child rearing, marital relations and social integration. We selected the open-ended interview because it is less obtrusive than the closed questionnaire and it covers large amounts of information. The respondents, at least during the initial contact, were young mothers under the age of 30 who had given birth to their first child during 1964 or the first four months of the following year. We visited them in their homes while they were busy with housework or child care; the interviewer, doing her utmost to adapt herself to the mother's routine, if necessary conducted the interview while the woman was cleaning, cooking or feeding the infant. Sometimes the interviewer lent a hand with chores or accompanied the woman on a trip to the park.

The unstructured interview allowed the mother to talk at leisure, according to her own priorities and interests, while the interviewer made notes on a pad of paper. Since between 90 and 150 minutes were required to complete the interview, the respondent had a choice of finishing in one visit or spreading it over two. The attitude scales were filled out by the interviewee herself at the end of the first or second visit, or at another time if she so wished, and were picked up later by the interviewer. Where there was a language problem, however, the scales were administered by the interviewer. Spanish translations of the attitude questionnaires were given to Spanish-speaking respondents, and the open-ended interviews were also conducted in Spanish (by special interviewers) whenever necessary. Perhaps the greatest advantage of the open-ended interview is that it enables the researcher to cover an infinite variety of situations which, if the interview were structured, would necessitate a questionnaire of enormous proportions. The safeguards for adequate subject coverage with the much shorter unstructured questionnaire rest, of course, upon the skill and sophistication of the interviewer, which will be discussed later.

Initial data for the analysis of family functioning were derived mainly from the first research interview. There is a certain hazard in relying on information furnished by means of a single interview because of the superficial relationship between interviewer and respondent. Respondents are likely to withhold sensitive information under those conditions. In our analysis of these initial data we used pertinent information supplied in subsequent contacts.

The young women's isolated social situation, combined with the type of instrument, gave the interview a therapeutic character. Young mothers are confined to their homes after the birth of the first child and they usually feel "cooped up." Unmarried mothers particularly have little opportunity to discuss their problems and concerns. Interviewers in our project discovered what has been observed repeatedly,[1] that a subject will respond favorably to research interviewing if it meets one of his or her real needs.

Observation played an important part in contact with the respondent. The interview schedule called for observational data under most headings. The respondent in the first interview was invariably the mother, but in subsequent panel contacts husbands and other members of the household — whenever the family lived with relatives — were often included.

The main tool for data collection is the schedule for documenting family functioning (see Appendix 2), which is organized into eight areas, covering the history of the parents' families of origin, circumstances leading to marriage, postmarital adjustment and present functioning. The structured questionnaires comprise ten five-item PARI (Parental Attitude Research Instrument) Scales[2] dealing with the values and goals of the mother on child rearing and marital relations, and the five-item Srole Anomie Scale.[3]

Because the interviewing method was unstructured, the interviewers had to be skilled in translating schedule items into language appropriate for the respondent and in guiding the interview flexibly enough to make the respondent feel relaxed while seeking all the desired information. We felt we could find this kind of interviewer by employing college-educated persons with prior interviewing experience to whom we could give special training. Our search for research interviewers centered on social workers with a professional master's degree or with a bachelor's degree and job experience; we also looked for college-trained persons who had worked in survey or public opinion research. Candidates for the job were given a half-day of instruction before being sent out on a trial interview with a family whose name was part of the universe but not the research sample. Candidates with the "best" credentials were in short supply because of a sellers' market in 1964 and 1965, years which marked the start of the War on Poverty. Moreover, some of the best trained workers were reluctant or unwilling to interview in racial ghetto areas where many of the sample families lived. Of 72 job applicants, most of whom went so far as to conduct trial interviews, only 34 were found to be employable and actually worked for the project at one time or another during the first (or interviewing) phase.[4] None of them had master's degrees but with one exception (a high school graduate), all either had bachelor of arts degrees or were seniors attending college. Most were housewives who wanted a part-time job with flexible hours. Nearly all had some prior interviewing experience. Of the dozen or so who administered the first set of interviews, only two worked full time. At least one full-time Negro interviewer was always employed by the project. This was essential for two reasons: black interviewers were generally more ready than whites to work in racially black neighborhoods, and they encountered less resistance from ideologically militant respondents.

THE SAMPLE

We selected a random sample of 555 young Newark families from a universe of 3,585 families who had a first child in 1964 or the first four months of 1965, for a one-point-in-time or cross-sectional analysis of social functioning. A subgroup of 175 cases was used to carry out the change-over-time or longitudinal aspect of the study. How were these families chosen and how representative are they of the larger population of young families?

The original universe of 3,585 primiparae was secured from 16 months of records in the Newark Bureau of Vital Statistics in the Department of Health and Welfare. From the universe of 3,585, a 50 percent random sample of 1,800 families was picked to be interviewed. We attempted to contact and interview 1,453 cases, which means that 347 families were left as a sample pool residue after enough respondents for the experimental and control groups had been found.

How did the 1,453 sample cases shrink to a working group of 555? Repeated efforts, which included a search of new phone directories, gathering change-of-address information from the post office and inquiries in the neighborhood, failed to locate 585 families. We were left with 868 eligible research cases, and contacts with them were established. Of this group a full 255 failed, for several reasons, to meet the sample definition. For example 147 out-of-wedlock mothers had placed their children for adoption; 67 mothers had left the study area shortly after the birth of the baby; 27 mothers had older children who were not recorded in the birth register; and there were 14 cases of infant mortality. Of the remaining 613 cases, 58 or 9.5 percent, refused to be interviewed. Thus, a total of 555 families constituted our working sample.

These families were visited in their homes and interviewed. Members of the working group of 555 families were identified as belonging to experimental or control groups after the initial interviews (the original sample of 1,800 had been randomly divided). This arrangement was in keeping with the project design, which specified that neither interviewer nor family should have any knowledge about a family's eventual place in the project lest such information bias the initial interviews. Before the start of the action phase, 272 treatment and 283 control cases were so identified. Attrition during the course of the five-year study reduced them to 177 and 175 families, respectively. Whatever might be said about the significance of attrition — and we will comment on it shortly — it operated at an almost identical rate in the experimental and control groups.

The longitudinal research concerns itself exclusively with the 175 control-group families. (For a comparison of their characteristics with those of the beginning sample of 555 cases see Chapter 15.) Since this phase of the research was concerned with family change,[5] our interest was focused on modifications in social functioning which resulted from the operation of natural forces in the community.

We had anticipated an attrition rate of approximately 50 percent during the time of the study, hoping in the end to have at least 150 cases each in intervention and control groups. The actual loss rate turned out to be somewhat lower, 34.9 percent and 38.2 percent for the experimental and control groups, respectively. There are two main reasons for the attrition: 1) refusal of the family to cooperate after the initial research interview, dropping out at various states of the research, and 2) moves out of the study area — study area being defined, in the case of the control group, as a radius of about 30 miles from downtown Newark.

An analysis of control-group families reveals that refusals at some point after the initial interview (66 cases) account for 61 percent and moves out of the area (19 cases) for 18 percent of those lost during the course of the project. The remaining 21 percent (23 cases) could not be retained for a variety of reasons: in some cases the family disappeared for unknown reasons; in others, the family broke up and the identity of the research case became uncertain; and in one case, an experimental-group family moved in with a control-group family.

The research design specified that control-group cases would be interviewed at varying intervals, in order to examine the possible effect of interview frequency on our measurements. Accordingly, about one-sixth (45 of the families) were seen three times yearly, one-sixth (45) twice yearly, one-half (143) once a year, and one-sixth (50) at the beginning and at the end of the project only.[6] A statistical test shows that the relationship between attrition rates and frequency of contacts is not significant, and that chance factors are likely to account for the variations noted above. The question of the possible influence of interview frequency on changes in scores was answered largely in the negative.[7]

The greatest problem in the sampling procedure arose from the fact that 585, or 49 percent out of the 1,198 potentially usable research cases in the study sample, could not be located despite our most energetic efforts. Is the sample still representative? In order to explore this question in depth, we carried out a special sample validation study in which a 10 percent random sample of families interviewed was compared with a 10 percent random sample of cases not found. Obviously this necessitated a major "search-and-interview" endeavor (see Appendix 3). Summarized briefly, the intensive search netted valid interviews with 77 percent of the missed cases. Although these families hardly differed on demographic variables from the sample of cases originally located, they did differ significantly on the major dependent variable, family functioning. There is an overrepresentation of poorly functioning cases in the group we had failed to locate. But how do the families originally found and interviewed differ from the universe of the families in the age cohort studied? According to a tenable assumption the two types of families, those originally found and those not found, constitute subuniverses in social functioning. While the true universe is not actually known, an approximation can be obtained by combining the weighted (for their respective Ns) scores for these two subgroups. When the combined group scores are compared with the scores of those originally located (it must be remembered that the combined families are assumed to approximate the true universe), differences in the same direction as in the prior comparison are found, but they do not reach statistical significance (X^2 = 5.59, 2 d.f., p< .10).

Unfortunately, this comparison leaves us with a further unanswered question: Does the 23 percent of the group of missed families that could not be found affect the outcome of the previous comparison? It may well be that a degree of family "invisibility" (this, not mobility, was the major problem, for the special search undertook to interview families wherever they might be) is inversely related to social functioning, which suggests that the 23 percent who were never located had more serious problems than the 77 percent eventually found and interviewed.

Although our attempt to determine the degree of sample representativeness did not yield foolproof answers, the converging evidence strongly points to an overrepresentation of relatively well functioning families and an underrepresentation of poorly functioning cases in the research sample.

RELIABILITY AND VALIDITY

The key variable in this study is family functioning. Other data gathered are, for the most part, factual information or the results of standardized attitude scales; they are discussed under their appropriate chapter headings. The St. Paul Scale of Family Functioning was used to process information on family functioning; its reliability and validity have been reported in several publications.[8] Because data validity, which is more difficult to establish, has not been dealt with extensively, we gave it special attention[9] by comparing the independent views of husbands and wives on the families' social functioning. Reliability testing was undertaken as a preliminary step to checking out the validity of the data.

Family functioning scores varied little, since the study population was composed for the most part of young, normal families; thus the customary approach to validity and reliability testing was unfeasible. Although agreement between two raters on the same or adjacent score positions ran between 80 percent and 95 percent, this criterion was not meaningful since the population's social functioning score variance on the ordinal scale was small.[10] This made it necessary to devise a different validity and reliability testing procedure.[11]

Briefly, in order to test the accuracy of interview data, the researchers designed a six-dimensional scheme covering a variety of family situations and behavior which cut across the eight areas of family functioning. Five dimensions were composed of three subcategories, one dimension was composed of four, making 19 subcategories in all. For each of these, coders were asked to rate family interview data, recorded in the Profile of Family Functioning, in terms of several criteria specified under each dimensional heading. The criteria were of the nominal data variety. The coding scheme is shown in Appendix 4.

Forty husbands and their wives[12] had been interviewed independently[13] as part of a special validity study, and their respective protocols were used for the reliability test. Teams of coders rated them on whether the information furnished in each under the 19 subcategories corresponded to that furnished by their spouse. The reliability ratio represents the number of observations on which the two raters agree divided by the total number of observations.

Reliability ratios ranged from .95 for the physical well-being of husband to a low of .65 for sexual satisfaction. The mean reliability ratio for all subcategories was .80 with a standard deviation of .068. This denoted reasonably satisfactory interrater reliability and enabled the researchers to consider agreement between husbands and wives as an index of validity.

It may be objected that a comparison of husband and wife responses is a test of reliability and not of validity, an argument that would be correct if the marriage partners were employed as conveyors of information on a given subject. They were not research aides, however, but were themselves part of the data that the researchers were evaluating. We did not seek to learn whether they are reliable informers but rather whether the information they furnish is true.

We assumed that agreement between husband and wife responses on such diverse subjects as the well-being of family members, types of satisfactions, the allocation of roles, values and goals, and the nature of decision-making constitutes truth. In the absence of collusion between spouses the likelihood of a high measure of accidental agreement is quite small; and collusion seems unlikely. Generally wives had been interviewed several times before the husbands, and the data gathered from them had covered many more areas than that secured from the husbands.

Appendix 5 shows the agreement ratios between husbands and wives which were based on the same comparisons as those reported for the reliability test. Information on issues reflecting interrater disagreement (comprising 20 percent of the items in the reliability test) was determined by means of an interrater conference. The mean validity ratio is

.80 with a standard deviation of .067 and the range for subcategories is from .68 to .93. State of physical well-being and role allocation was reported with a somewhat higher degree of unanimity (mean ratios of .853 and .876, respectively), satisfactions of family members (mean ratio .733) with a somewhat lower degree than the other variables. Observations on the two variables are based on more or less objectively verifiable phenomena with a high degree of visibility, factors which others have found to be conducive to agreement between independent respondents.[14] Satisfactions, decision-making, emotional well-being, goals, values and beliefs all show a lower ratio of husband-wife agreement, representing variables that are relatively intangible, subject to individual interpretation. The high measure of disagreement (.32) on sexual satisfaction might reflect subject sensitivity. Evidence from other studies on this subject is not uniform,[15] but there is reason to believe that our interviewers often settled for vague, hard-to-code responses rather than probing further into sensitive areas.

Appendix 5 shows that 16 out of 19 agreement ratios were statistically significant at the 5 percent level or better. The mean validity ratios put the present study in line with some of the more trustworthy findings in the literature, although the question of lower data accuracy on abstract and sensitive subjects requires continued research.

NOTES

1. Elizabeth Herzog, Maurice B. Hamovitch, Ludwig L. Geismar, Michael A. La Sorte, and Celia B. Deschin, *Research Interviewing in Sensitive Subject Areas*, New York: National Association of Social Workers, 1963. This is a collection of three articles on the subject with an introduction by Elizabeth Herzog; the articles appeared first in *Social Work*, 1963, 8 (April) pp. 3-18.

2. Earl S. Schaefer and Richard Q. Bell, "Development of a Parental Attitude Research Instrument," *Child Development*, 1958, 29 (September) pp. 339-361.

3. Leo Srole, "Social Integration and Certain Corollaries: An Exploratory Study," *American Sociological Review*, December 21, 1956, pp. 709-716.

4. This phase which lasted about 15 months is to be differentiated from the later action phase when some of the families in the sample were given services.

5. The experimental or intervention program is dealt with in Geismar, Lagay, Wolock, Gerhart, and Fink, *op. cit.*

6. The original Ns called for by the design were 50, 50, 150 and 50. The smaller number of cases that actually materialized in each category reflects first-stage attrition of various kinds.

7. Geismar, Lagay, Wolock, Gerhart, and Fink, *op. cit.*, Appendix C.

8. Geismar and Ayres, *op. cit.*, pp. 21-51; Ludwig Geismar and Jane Krisberg, *The Forgotten Neighborhood*, Metuchen, N. J.: The Scarecrow Press, 1967, pp. 320-321; David Wal-

lace, "The Chemung County Evaluation of Casework Service to Dependent Multiproblem Families: Another Problem Outcome," *Social Service Review*, 1967, 41 (December) pp. 379-389; Gordon E. Brown, *op. cit.*, pp. 107-161.

9. The question of scale validity received its fullest treatment in the Chemung County Study. See Gordon E. Brown, *op. cit.*, pp. 139-143.

10. Geismar and Krisberg, *op. cit.*, p. 330; L. L. Geismar and Beverly Ayres, *Patterns of Change in Problem Families*, St. Paul, Minn.: Family Centered Project, 1959, pp. 3-6, pp. 39-41. Previous populations had been composed of older, substantially more disturbed families whose social functioning scores were characterized by means close to the theoretical midpoint of the scale and relatively large standard deviations.

11. For details about the nature of this problem and ways of solving it, see Geismar, Lagay, Wolock, Gerhart, and Fink, *op. cit.*, pp. 35-45.

12. The 40 couples were selected randomly, but because of efforts to complete the interviews during a two-month period and also to avoid offending a few mothers who objected to their husbands' inclusion in the project, randomness of the sample was compromised.

13. Husbands and wives were seen separately, in their homes when no other adult was present. There were three exceptions to this arrangement — husbands who had to be seen in other locations in order to accommodate to their schedule.

14. Leonard Weller and Elmer Luchterhand, "Comparing Interviews and Observations on Family Functioning," *Journal of Marriage and the Family*, 1969, 31 (February) pp. 115-123; Hugh J. Parry and Helen M. Crossley, "Validity of Responses to Survey Questions," *Public Opinion Quarterly*, 1950, 14 (Spring) pp. 61-80.

15. Alexander L. Clark and Paul Wallin, "The Accuracy of Husbands' and Wives' Reports of the Frequency of Marital Coitus," *Population Studies*, 1964, 18 (November) pp. 165-173; J. Richard Udry and Naomi M. Morris, "A Method for Validation of Sexual Data," *Journal of Marriage and the Family*, 1967, 29 (August) pp. 442-446.

4.

Social Characteristics of the Young Families

We first contacted the 555 study families when the children were still infants with limited physical mobility and rudimentary communication skills. With few exceptions mothers were at home, engrossed in child care and housekeeping or sharing chores when the young family resided with parents or in-laws. Some mothers went to work (or school in a few cases) shortly after the birth of the baby and arranged for substitute child care. Nearly 5 percent of the mothers either found work or returned to a previous job within three months of childbirth; slightly over one-fifth did so within a year.

The research population was 61 percent black, 35 percent white and 4 percent Spanish-speaking, mostly Puerto Rican. In comparison with the estimated Newark population in 1967[1] whites and Spanish-speaking individuals are somewhat underrepresented, possibly because the children of white unwed mothers are often placed for adoption, and because we did not have enough interviewers who were fluent in Spanish.

The religious makeup of the sample is 34 percent Catholic, 58 percent Protestant, 3 percent Jewish and 5 percent mixed, with husbands and wives professing different faiths. Religion was not used as a separate variable in this study because of its high correlation with race. Seventy-seven percent of the white study population is Catholic while 91 percent of the black families are Protestant.

Median ages at marriage are 19 years for women and 22 years for men. White women are, on the average, a year older than Negro women at the time of marriage, whereas Negro and white men differ less in this respect. Thirty-nine percent of Negro women and 27 percent of white women marry under the age of 18. For men 32 percent of the Negroes and 23 percent of the whites marry under 18.

The only truly common denominator among the study families is the young mother and her dependent child. Other characteristics denoting family structure and social position vary greatly. In about one-third of the cases at the beginning of the study the fathers are absent. Except for about 2 percent of families that have already experienced separation or divorce, the father's absence is explained by the fact that the children were born out of wedlock. Ninety percent of unmarried mothers do not maintain their own home but live with parents or relatives.

The young families, whether headed by one or two parents, have a variety of living arrangements. Nearly half live in apartments in private multiple dwellings; about 40 percent in private duplexes; 7 percent in public housing; while fewer than 5 percent live in single houses. Sixty percent of the families reside in primarily residential surroundings, 8 percent in predominantly industrial-commercial areas and 32 percent in mixed residential-commercial-industrial neighborhoods.

Slightly under two-thirds of the young families are completely self-supporting; the remainder depend upon part-time work, various degrees of help from relatives and public assistance, or a combination of these. Occupationally only about one-fifth of the families[2] belong to the white-collar class, while a nearly equal proportion (18 percent) are headed by unemployed men who are either without occupations or chronically on public assistance. Semiskilled blue collar and service workers head one-fourth of the sample families, and unskilled workers are at the head in 17 percent of the cases. In the remainder of the families, slightly over one-fifth, the heads are skilled blue-collar workers.

When one-third of the families begin their life cycle without a father in the home, sociological analysis of the urban family cannot be exclusively concerned with the two-parent unit even though that happens to be the modal structure and represents the pattern most in line with professed American values. The high ratio of young families headed by unmarried mothers is one of the significant facts of urban life in the 1960s and 1970s.

Even this proportion of young unmarried families does not include situations where the child was not kept. The illegitimacy rate for primiparae in the universe was 43 percent, and was less than 2 percent lower in the original random sample of 1,453. The substantially lower rate of 31 percent in the study sample of 555 families can be explained by the fact that at least 147, or 10 percent of the original random sample of mothers with a first child, gave their babies for adoption.[3] Current adoption procedures precluded any possibility of studying these children in their new social environment.

The proportion of illegitimate births has been steadily rising in Newark over a decade and a half. Their percentages relative to all live births in that city are as follows: 1950 — 6.1 percent; 1955 — 8.5 percent; 1960

— 12.0 percent; 1965 — 21.3 percent; 1966 — 24.6 percent.[4] The steepest rise occurred during the five-year period preceding the beginning of our research. Newark's trends in illegitimacy are not an isolated phenomenon but parallel the nationwide growth of out-of-wedlock births. The increase exceeds the overall national trend, as is shown below, but may not be out of line with illegitimacy rates in other areas undergoing rapid social change.[5]

In the United States as a whole the illegitimacy rate per 1,000 unmarried women and the ratio per 1,000 live births has been rising between 1950 and 1965. The rate of illegitimate births by women between the ages of 15 and 44 rose from 14.1 to 23.5. The corresponding rates were 6.1 and 11.6 for whites and 71.2 and 97.6 for nonwhites.[6] Ratios, after having been relatively stable in the 1940s,[7] reveal a similar trend, rising from 39.8 in 1950 to 77.4 in 1965. The parallel white and nonwhite ratios rose from 17.5 to 39.6 and from 179.6 to 263.2, respectively.[8] It should be noted, nonetheless, that the steady increase in illegitimacy between 1940 and 1957 for the United States as a whole slowed during the period 1958 to 1965.[9] United States data have begun to be classified by metropolitan and nonmetropolitan areas only since 1962. The period from 1962 to 1964 revealed a more rapid rise in the former than the latter. The proportion of out-of-wedlock births varied from a high of 20 percent in Memphis, Tennessee, to a low of 1.3 percent in Provo-Orem, Utah. For specified urban areas which have been collecting statistics since 1955, the illegitimacy ratio shows increases in most places during the subsequent ten-year period. Among nonwhite births the proportion classified as illegimate was as high as 50 percent in a number of areas.[10]

The evidence from 35 reporting states in both 1955 and 1964 is that about half of all out-of-wedlock births are first births, a proportion approximately double that of all illegitimate births. Among white illegitimate births, first births make up nearly two-thirds of all such cases; while among nonwhite out-of-wedlock births, only 42 to 44 percent of all reported cases are first births. For both racial groups second and subsequent children make up successively smaller proportions of the total number of illegitimacies. Newark's 43 percent rate of illegitimate first births probably is half the total number of children born to unmarried mothers in the city and double the rate of all illegitimacies.[11]

The 171 unmarried mothers in the study are 94.2 percent black, 2.9 percent white and 2.3 percent Puerto Rican, with 0.6 percent of mixed Negro-white descent. Three-fourths belong to the bottom socioeconomic status group, called here class 6 on the modified Hollingshead status scale and composed largely of persons with minimal formal education and no job skills.[12] The distinct underrepresentation of white out-of-

wedlock (OW) births[13] is, to a large extent, the result of adoptive place-
ments which greatly favor white babies since there is a larger demand
for them than for black children. Part of the discrepancy is also explained by the fact that class 6 is heavily represented among young Newark families. This is the status group to which most of the unmarried
mothers belong and in which unwed motherhood is mainly concentrated;
it has three times as many blacks as whites. The unmarried mothers and
their children have four types of living arrangements: 71 percent live
with their own parents; 14 percent reside with others of the mother's
relatives; 10 percent live alone; and the remaining 5 percent live with
relatives of the OW father and friends.

Contrary to the stereotyped view of the unmarried mother, about
half maintain an ongoing relationship with the father of the child, extending over a year or more.[14] Moreover, nearly one-half of these mothers receive at least some financial support from the father of the child,
or subsequent children if the woman bears more out-of-wedlock offspring.

The foregoing data on families headed by unwed mothers bring home
a point made earlier: out-of-wedlock families represent a considerable
and probably growing proportion of American urban families. They are
charged with most of the tasks assigned to two-parent families, and
have many of the same needs and problems. However, critical differences in structure and patterns of living make it necessary to treat the
OW family as an independent variable whose influence needs to be examined in relation to nearly every facet of this research.

The educational backgrounds of men and women in the study population are similar. In each instance the modal group is made up of high
school graduates (36 percent of the men and 38 percent of the women).
Fewer than 5 percent (4 percent of the men, 5 percent of the women)
have less than an eighth grade education. By contrast, 13 percent of the
men and 7 percent of the women have attended college, but of these only
one-third graduated with at least a bachelor's degree. Blacks, especially
men, are considerably less educated than whites. For instance, 43 percent of the white mothers and 37 percent of the black mothers graduated
from high school. For fathers the respective percentages are 45 and 27.
Eleven percent of white and 5 percent of black mothers have at least
some college education. This is also true for 24 percent of white male
heads of families; but only 7 percent of the Negro males heading sample
families have ever attended college. The group of black unwed mothers
includes only a little more than half the number of high school graduates than black mothers as a whole have; and, correspondingly, nearly

twice as many OW mothers (30 percent) compared to married mothers (17 percent) never went beyond the ninth grade.

The deprived economic situation of the study families is reflected in the low income distribution which shows that one-fifth earn less than $3,000, roughly one-third earn under $4,000, and over two-thirds have incomes below $6,000. Only about 6 percent of the study families have annual incomes of $10,000 or more. Eight percent of the project families are fully supported by public assistance and another 7 percent receive partial support. Study families, according to this income distribution, are poorer than Newark families as a whole,[15] and the difference may be assumed to reflect the higher prevalence of one-parent families and the younger ages of the heads of households in the sample. Negro incomes are substantially below those of whites, with 31 percent of the former compared to 3 percent of the latter earning under $3,000 a year. The proportions for those earning under $6,000 are 79 percent and 53 percent, respectively. The strikingly disadvantaged position of unmarried mothers[16] is shown by the finding that 68 percent of them have earnings under $3,000 and 97 percent under $6,000 a year.

Barely over one-half of the parents in the research sample are natives of Newark or vicinity. A Negro-white comparison, however, presents a sharply contrasting picture,[17] with 73 percent of white fathers and mothers but only 45 percent of black fathers and mothers listing Newark as their place of birth.[18] Unwed mothers do not differ greatly in this respect, with 52 percent reporting Newark or vicinity as the place where they were born. Of greater significance is the fact that more than one-third of the parents in the study have lived in Newark less than ten years. This is true for fewer than one-quarter of white heads of families, while 45 percent of black fathers and 43 percent of black mothers report having come to the city within the last ten years. A full 25 percent of the parents have been in Newark less than five years. In this respect, too, Negro families are more heavily represented among these most recent newcomers. Thirty-two percent of black fathers and 30 percent of black mothers compared to 14 percent of white fathers and 16 percent of white mothers indicate that they arrived in Newark within the last five years.

At the time the first interviews were being held, only about three-fifths of the parents' family of origin (58 percent of maternal and 61 percent of paternal families) were reported to be intact. Twenty-two percent of maternal and 18 percent of paternal families of origin had been broken by divorce and separation, and 16 percent and 19 percent, respectively, were no longer intact as a result of death. Fewer than 5 percent in each case reported out-of-wedlock situations in the homes of the parents. The latter percentage, it should be remembered, does not represent the incidence of illegitimate births in the families of orientation but rather the status of the grandmother at the time one of her children became a parent. Unwed mothers report a higher frequency of parental homes in which the grandmother had never married (8 percent of their families as against 4 percent of the families of married mothers). The proportions for broken maternal and paternal families, when separation or divorce were listed as a cause of breakup, are more than twice as high for black as for white families (maternal: black 27 percent, white 12 percent; paternal: black 29 percent, white 11 percent). The proportions are very similar (four percentage points apart) when death is cited as the cause.

The married parents in the study families were, with few exceptions, married under church auspices. Sixty percent were married in either a church or synagogue; 24 percent were united by clergymen in another setting; and 16 percent had civil ceremonies. Civil weddings are about equally common for Negroes and whites, but nearly all the whites who married under religious auspices had weddings in a church or synagogue, while fewer than half of the blacks (44 percent) who chose religious ceremonies had them performed in a house of worship.

A formal engagement preceded the marriage for a bare majority (56 percent) of the couples. Of these, three-fourths were engaged for a year or less. Negroes and whites differ in this respect: 56 percent of the Negroes but 32 percent of the whites marry without having been formally engaged; engagements longer than one year mark the marital career of 19 percent of the whites but only 9 percent of the blacks.

Membership in community organizations has been found to be highly related to family life-cycle stage, and participation in organizations and associations is reported lowest during the early child-rearing stage.[19] Social status, likewise, is noted as a factor related to formal group membership.[20] We found that families in this research are not joiners. At the beginning of the study the highest participation was registered in church clubs (13 percent of mothers and 12 percent of fathers) and sports clubs (11 percent of fathers). Membership in social, civic, political, civil rights and professional organizations is confined to less than 10 percent of the parents, with the exception of labor unions, in which 29 percent of the fathers hold membership. Church attendance patterns vary widely, with 28 percent of the parents attending frequently, 19 percent attending rarely and 25 percent never attending. In just over one-fourth of the families one parent attends frequently or seldom, with the other staying away entirely or coming along on rare occasions. No sharp differences between blacks and whites were noted, except for the fact that church attendance is less often a joint affair for blacks. The unmarried mother stays away from church considerably more frequently (43 percent never go to church) than the married mother (about 27 percent never attend).

The youth of the study families is reflected in their limited use of community resources. The type of agency used by the largest number of families is public health services such as well-baby clinics, visiting nurses, and city outpatient clinics and hospitals. Sixty-two percent of the total study group use these facilities and resources, and Negro families do so much more extensively (82 percent) than whites (25 percent). Nearly all (92 percent) of the unwed mothers avail themselves of the services of health agencies. Eighteen percent of the study group use public assistance, with many more clients from black families (26 percent) and unwed mothers (48 percent) than from white families (3 percent). The only other community service used by over one-tenth of the total group dealt with employment; public employment agencies serve 12 percent of the study population. There are some differences in the extent to which blacks and whites avail themselves of the services of social and recreational agencies, and these differences will be discussed in Chapter 13.

The study families which were drawn in the research sample clearly reflect Newark's social situation in their socioeconomic makeup. They are predominantly a working-class/lower-class group; they are poor, even poorer on the average than Newark residents as a whole, because of the widespread absence of fathers and the youth of heads of households. Their formal education is limited. One-third of the families are without a male head at this early stage of the family life cycle.

With few exceptions the families are starting life as tenants in multiple dwellings, a far cry from the American dream of home ownership with ample outdoor play room. Many of the families are in unfamiliar surroundings, since only half of the parents are natives of the city, while most of the remainder are relatively recent newcomers to the city. Like young families in general and lower-class populations in particular, the project families are not joiners, nor do they avail themselves of community resources to any substantial extent. The latter is true because of generally good health and, with still-limited financial obligations, modest need for resources.

The structural and demographic characteristics described in this chapter indicate a socially handicapped status. We must question the meaning of this status for the families' social functioning — their ability to carry out socially expected tasks aimed at maintaining or enhancing the well-being of their members. We will discuss these issues in the next chapter.

NOTES

1. Chernick, Indik, and Sternlieb, *op. cit.*, pp. 4-5.

2. Excluded from this analysis were 37 families in which no husband was present and the mother was financially dependent solely upon her family of origin.

3. Out-of-wedlock cases were about equally represented in the cases interviewed and cases not found, as was shown by Lagay's sample bias study. For details see Appendix 3.

4. Anna P. Halkovitch, "New Jersey's Illegitimate Births," *Public Health News*, N. J. Department of Health, 1968, 49 (January-February) pp. 15-22.

5. U. S. data on metropolitan areas were not available for the 1950s.

6. Alice J. Clague and Stephanie J. Ventura, "Trends in Illegitimacy," in Jeffrey K. Hadden and Marie L. Borgatta (editors), *Marriage and the Family, A Comprehensive Reader*, Itasca, Illinois: F. E. Peacock, Publishers, Inc., 1969, pp. 543-559, 549-551.

7. Rates doubled from 7.1 to 14.1 in the 1940s, reflecting a substantial increase in all births, legitimate as well as illegitimate. Ratios, however, disregard the absolute rise and provide a relative measure of the extent of illegitimacy.

8. Clague and Ventura, *loc. cit.*, p. 551.

9. *Ibid.*, p. 545.

10. *Ibid.*, p. 554.

11. The total proportion of illegitimate births in 1965 was 21.3 percent. Halkovich, *loc. cit.*, p. 20. Allowance must be made for the fact that all mothers in the sample were under 30 years of age, but national figures show that nearly 90 percent of out-of-wedlock children are born to mothers in that age group.

12. This measure represents an adaptation by William Wells of the Hollingshead Index of Social Position which is based on the education and occupation of the head of the household. The six class system, in contrast to the Hollingshead five class breakdown, permits a sharper status differentiation among lower-class populations such as those making up the present study. Williams Wells, "Index of Social Position," Rutgers University, 1962 (unpublished paper). The Hollingshead Index of Social Position is described in August B. Hollingshead and Frederick C. Gedlich, *Social Class and Mental Illness*, New York: Science Editions, John Wiley and Sons, Inc., 1964, pp. 387-397.

13. During the period for which the sample was drawn (1/1/64-4/30/65) the Newark illegitimacy rate for first birth was 23 percent for whites and 55 percent for nonwhites. Of children born out-of-wedlock, 20 percent were white, 70 nonwhite, and for 8 percent race was not recorded.

14. Clark Vincent reported that 55 percent of his sample of 850 unmarried mothers reported either "a love relationship of some duration" or "a close friendship relationship" with the father of their baby. Clark E. Vincent, *Unmarried Mothers*, New York: The Free Press, 1969, p. 83.

15. The 1967 Rutgers population study showed 16.5 percent of Newark families earning under $3,000 and 58.4 percent — as against 74.2 percent of study families — making less than $7,000 per year. See Chernick, Indik, and Sternlieb, *op. cit.*, p. 28.

16. No assessment of income was available for 34 unmarried mothers because they had no budget separate from that of the families they were living with.

17. This was borne out by the Rutgers Population Study. The percentages listed as having always resided in Newark were 44.5 percent for whites, 17.4 percent for Negroes and 2.1 percent for others (mostly Spanish speaking). Chernick, Indik, and Sternlieb, *op. cit.*, p. 7. The proportion of migrants is higher in the total Newark population than in the sample for the former, due to its larger share of older residents, offers a greater potential for including persons who moved. Differences may also be due to the fact that the present study, in contrast to the Chernick survey, included among the natives persons who were born in the vicinity of the city.

18. In each group differences between fathers and mothers were only fractions of a percentage point.

19. John F. Schmidt and Wayne C. Rohrer, "The Relationship of Family Type to Social Participation," *Marriage and Family Living*, 1956, 18 (August) pp. 224-230; p. 229. Jan Dizard, *op. cit.*, p. 43.

20. For a summary of studies see John Mogey, "Family and Community in Urban-Industrial Societies," in Harold T. Christensen (editor), *Handbook of Marriage and the Family*, Chicago: Rand McNally & Co., pp. 501-534, p. 518.

5.

Early Functioning and Relationships

Our goal in reporting on the social functioning of a sizeable and reasonably representative group of young urban families is to understand how these families get along as social units, faced as they are with the responsibilities of rearing children and providing physical and emotional care for all family members. Meaningful reporting requires the conversion of tens of thousands of items of information into data patterns that can be interpreted according to some norm. The theoretical scheme sketched in the second chapter affords an opportunity for such an interpretation. These are basically two types of norms which can serve as guideposts for comparisons. Theoretical norms are based on the postulation of certain criteria or standards as being good or bad, acceptable or unacceptable, adequate or inadequate. Statistical norms employ the same frame of reference as the theoretical norms but use actual empirical data as a point of reference.

There is limited opportunity to use statistical norms because the technique of measurement which is employed here has been used mainly with clinical populations, particularly with agency clients who are poor and socially handicapped. Nonetheless, to the extent that such data serve as a meaningful point of reference, we will draw upon them for purposes of comparison. Theoretical norms, on the other hand, use the total scale limits of the measurement. Under that system scores on family functioning are interpreted according to position on a continuum ranging from adequacy (reasonable conformity to laws and norms and physical, social and emotional well-being) to inadequacy (deviance of a law-violating nature, and behavior and/or situations which constitute a clear threat to individual as well as group welfare).

The analysis of the families' social functioning rests on a fourfold use of quantitative data: total family functioning scores and the overall mean of area mean functioning scores;[1] area or main category scores;

subcategory scores; factor scores utilizing a factor analysis of the sub-category scores.

1. *Total family functioning scores* are the most comprehensive index of family behavior and change, but they are not necessarily the most meaningful. In earlier work with multiproblem families the distribution of area scores fit the Guttman model of scalability, and accordingly, the total scores took on a predictive value relative to area scores.[2] Social functioning area scores of the young families in the present study are skewed toward the adequate end of the continuum, and the distribution does not meet the requirements of Guttman scalability. This means that in analyzing the levels of social functioning before us, we are dealing with more than a single dimension. That supposition is borne out by the factor analysis reported below. However, the individual areas making up the total scores are significantly correlated with each other as well as with total scores (see Appendix 6), indicating that we are dealing here with an array of roles and tasks which are interrelated. The total score, therefore, furnishes an approximate index of a family's overall character of social functioning, but it does not by itself accurately reflect performance in given areas except in cases of total adequacy or inadequacy (which are quite rare). Total scores, however, can be made more meaningful by correlating total score groups with types of social functioning as reflected in the families' task and role performance in given areas.

2. *Area or main category scores* serve to pinpoint individual role and social task performance by eight areas,[3] each of which denotes a dimension of behavior that has been conceptually and operationally defined. These scores represent a numerical rating that is a composite of weighted subcategory ratings. The weighting follows specific guidelines which take into account the relative importance of the subcategories.[4] Area scores represent ratings of fairly abstract behavior, such as care and training of children, or economic practices.

3. *Subcategory scores* are the most basic units of observation and measurement in the study of the social functioning of young families. There are 25 subcategories distributed over the eight main categories, with five of them contained in two main categories each, four and three of them contained in one category each, and two in four. Each one of the subcategories represents fairly specific and concrete forms of behavior — for instance, the relationship among siblings in the family, the physical care of the children or the management of the family's money. Main and subcategory scores will be discussed below under a common heading.

4. *Factor scores* are indicants of the common dimensions underlying the subcategories of functioning. Obtained by means of factor analysis, they represent a form of data reduction based upon the determination of

clusters of subcategories. Factor analysis offers an opportunity to view parsimoniously a large number of indices in terms of a limited number of dimensions, particularly where efforts at building a single score index based on a hypothesis of unidimensionality has proved unsuccessful.

In the present chapter the analysis will be concentrated on characteristics of the total group rather than on intra-subgroup comparisons. The latter will be given special treatment in subsequent chapters.

The study of young families has not received much emphasis in family sociology. Pierre de Bie and Clio Presvelou, in a survey covering the European and American literature on young families for 1960-68, conclude that "the discrepancy between the scarcity of valid sources and the abundance of statements on the traits, status, future trends and social measure for young households needs to be stressed," and "empirical research has on the whole been aimed at testing theories of mate selection, hence preventing the formulation of new hypotheses of the correct structuration [sic] of questions related to the young families as such."[5] The authors found the couple and the marriage to be the most frequently studied subjects, with relatively little importance being assigned to the nuclear family.[6] A first notable international effort to highlight issues related to the young family was the 1969 International Seminar of the International Scientific Commission on the Family, which was devoted to "Images and Counter-Images of Young Families."[7] Most research dealing with young families is either descriptive or comparative in nature, i.e., younger and older families are compared, using longitudinal or multiple cross-sectional studies. In both types of studies the emphasis is upon happiness, satisfactions, love and companionship, while adjustment, decision-making, distribution of power, division of labor and performance of family tasks are much less important. Therefore, attempts to postulate in advance differences in types of family functioning among young families cannot be bolstered by prior knowledge based upon extensive research. Any hypotheses guiding the analysis in this chapter are drawn primarily from a limited number of studies (see Chapter 2) and from observations and insights gathered from a variety of sources, including our own prior studies.

Examinations of the data on the young families' social functioning will be guided mainly by two hypotheses: (1) young families as a group function at a high level of social adequacy, with malfunctioning confined to a relatively small minority; (2) the problems of these families, such as they are, tend to be concentrated in instrumental (denoting behavior directed toward the maintenance or improvement of physical family environment and obtaining the means to attain basic goals) rather than in expressive (representing behavior aimed at achieving basic satisfactions and goals of a social, emotional and spiritual nature) areas of behavior.

Both suppositions spring from a contention in the literature, more implicit than explicit, that young people who voluntarily join in marriage possess traits that make for reasonably congenial coexistence, at least at the onset of their family career. If the marriage works it is most likely to do so in the beginning when husbands and wives are playing roles that resemble the marital role images they brought to the union. During the early stage of marriage, according to Dizard, the husband's sphere of activity overlaps with that of the wife, and there is a rather high degree of agreement on values and behavior, with lines of communication open so that differences and disagreements are settled as they occur.[8] Of course, this line of reasoning does not apply to families headed by unmarried mothers, and there are substantial differences in social functioning between them and two-parent families, as will be shown later. Nonetheless, the functioning of unwed mothers generally appears to indicate that a fair measure of concern was exhibited by their families of origin, leaving only a small minority of one-parent families to be characterized as truly problematic.

Expectations of more problematic functioning in instrumental areas than in expressive areas stem from the knowledge that the study families are distributed over the lower half of the status scale because of our choice of setting. In that position, job, income and housing leave much to be desired. Furthermore, expressive behavior was the basic cement that initially drew people to each other and held them together, and its positive influence is likely to be reflected in the Family Functioning Profile during the early childbearing stage.

OVERALL SOCIAL FUNCTIONING OF THE YOUNG FAMILIES

If social adequacy is taken as a criterion for judging the role and task performance of the 555 study families during the year after the birth of the first child, only 12 percent can be rated adequate throughout (total score of 56, representing a rating of 7 in eight areas of family functioning). These are the families which, on the basis of interviews and observations, are judged free of major problems and able to cope successfully with minor difficulties. Adequacy does not denote rigorous conformity or stress-free living. Rather, it means that the families so rated are behaving within the limits of the law as well as the mores of their neighborhood subculture, and that norm-violating behavior, if present, has no negative consequences for family members or the community. Adequacy also signifies an ability to handle day-to-day problems or stresses either within the family or through the use of community resources, without damaging family morale or welfare.

At the other end of the continuum are about 10 percent of the families with total scores of 40 or less, having an average rating of 5 (above marginal) or below, and invariably some ratings of 4 (marginal) or less in the separate areas of functioning. These families are characterized more by insufficiencies in functioning than by social deviance, particularly in the economic and housing areas, although problems in individual roles and interpersonal relations are frequently present.

If a score total of 48 representing an average rating of 6 (near adequate) is taken as the cutoff point, we find that 63 percent of the population lies above that point. Conversely, just over one-fourth (27 percent) of the families function less well, with scores between 48 and 41, but above those in the bottom group, who have problems in several areas.

Unfortunately, comparative data on the social functioning of young families as measured by the present technique are lacking. Nevertheless, an approximate idea of their relative adequacy can be obtained by comparing overall mean scores. (Total scores are not useful because other studies employ nine[9] rather than our eight categories of family functioning.) Thus, the overall mean score for the present study is 6.14 (slightly above the near adequate level) in contrast to the overall mean scores of 3.85 (slightly below marginal) and 4.5 (between marginal and above marginal) for two groups of seriously disorganized lower-class families[10] and equivalent scores of 5.54 and 5.72, respectively (between above marginal and near adequate), for a metropolitan and suburban sample of families receiving AFDC (Aid to Families of Dependent Children).[11]

The crudeness of the comparisons does not obscure the fact that the functioning of a random sample of young families is, on the average, at a much higher level than seriously disorganized families and somewhat higher than welfare families which, as a group, were characterized by stability and a low rate of deviant behavior.[12]

Short of establishing scalability, one way to infuse more meaning into total scores is to show their systematic relationship to area scores by means of grouping and cross-tabulating both indices. The grouping of families by total score values was accomplished by dividing the distribution into four approximately equal groups (the numbers of the four groups varied slightly from true quartiles because the dividing lines were set up to avoid splitting cases with the same scores between different groupings).

The four groups and the designations are shown in Exhibit 5.1.

EXHIBIT 5.1: DISTRIBUTION OF STUDY FAMILIES BY TOTAL FAMILY
FUNCTIONING SCORE

TOTAL SCORE GROUP	Score Range	No. of Families	Percent of Cases
High (H)	56 - 54	166	30.0
Medium-High (MH)	53 - 50	146	26.2
Medium-Low (ML)	49 - 46	110	19.8
Low (L)	45 - 13[a]	133	24.0
Total		555	100.0%

[a] The lowest total score encountered was 13. There were eight families with scores below
32 which represents an average of marginal (4) ratings.

We shall now proceed to look at each score grouping in terms of the
distribution of its main components, the areas of family functioning.
For each group, main categories characterized by various degrees of
malfunctioning will be listed ordinally.

1. The High family group is characterized by such a degree of social
adequacy that its proportion of cases showing less than adequate functioning in any area is small. Marginal or more problematic functioning
does not occur, and ratings on main categories denoting near adequate
(6) or above marginal (5) functioning are given to fewer than 5 percent of
the cases in the areas of family relationships and unity, individual behavior and adjustment, care and training of children and use of community resources. Problematic functioning of a limited scope (above marginal and near adequate) occurs in health conditions and practices (24
percent), home and household practices (22.9 percent), economic practices (16.3 percent), and social activities (14.5 percent). In short, the adequately functioning families of the so-called High group do not face any
major functioning problems, and the minor difficulties are chiefly concentrated in the instrumental areas of health (here the problem revolves
mainly around practices) and housing (where the issue is mainly the
adequacy of facilities rather than the nature of housekeeping).

2. The Medium-High group is also free from truly problematic functioning; the two minor exceptions are home and household practices and
economic practices, where 6.8 percent and 0.7 percent of the families
registered scores of 4 (marginal and below). However, near adequate (6)
and above marginal (5) functioning is frequent or predominant, as shown
in the ordinal array of main categories and the percentage distribution
of Medium-High cases functioning below the adequate level.

The Medium-High families, when compared to the High group, present a somewhat greater frequency of less-than-adequate but better-
than-marginal social functioning. Health and housing, the two instru-

EXHIBIT 5.2: FAMILY FUNCTIONING OF MEDIUM-HIGH GROUP BY AREAS

AREA	FAMILIES FUNCTIONING BELOW ADEQUATE LEVEL
Health conditions and practices	68.5%
Home and household practices	67.1
Individual behavior and adjustment	53.4
Economic practices	52.8
Social activities	52.1
Family relationships and unity	40.4
Care and training of children	29.5
Use of community resources	14.4

mental areas in which the High group encounters some problem functioning, also occupy top positions in the Medium-High group. In addition, slightly over half the families are rated below adequate in the areas of individual behavior and adjustment, economic practices and social activities. In other words, those families functioning inadequately in roles and tasks find that instrumental problems figure somewhat more prominently than difficulties in social relationships. Still, seriously problematic behavior in any area is the exception for families functioning at Medium-High levels.

3. The Medium-Low group of families presents a profile that is largely free of serious malfunctioning. Marginal or lower level functioning occurs with a measure of frequency only in home and household practices (17.1 percent), and in low proportions for four other areas (family relationships and unity, 8.1 percent; social activities, 3.6 percent; economic practices, 2.7 percent; and health conditions and practices, 0.9 percent). However, family functioning at the near adequate (6) and above marginal (5) levels has now become the modal pattern in all main categories with the exception of use of community resources. The percentage distribution of Medium-Low families below the adequate level is shown below.

EXHIBIT 5.3: FAMILY FUNCTIONING OF MEDIUM-LOW GROUP BY AREAS

AREA	FAMILIES FUNCTIONING BELOW ADEQUATE LEVEL
Individual behavior and adjustment	91.0%
Home and household practices	86.5
Social activities	82.9
Health conditions and practices	82.0
Economic practices	78.4
Family relationships and unity	78.4
Care and training of children	64.0
Use of community resources	48.6

The rank order distribution by problemicity of main category has not changed drastically from the Medium-High to the Medium-Low group (Spearman rho = +.79). The main difference between the two distributions is the greater frequency of moderately troubled functioning in all areas, particularly in family relationships and unity, individual behavior and adjustment, care and training of children, and use of community resources (denoted by a percentage rise of over 30 points but not necessarily a shift in ordinal position). Problems in the relationship areas and of an expressive nature are more common among the Medium-Lows than the Medium-Highs, although instrumental difficulties continue to be more prominent. (It should be remembered that the individual behavior and adjustment category is a composite of both instrumental and expressive roles.)

4. The Low group of families presents a somewhat more complex picture. Truly problematic behavior, represented by scores of 4 (marginal) or less, is characteristic (affecting one-fourth or more of the cases) of the five areas of home and household practices, economic practices, individual behavior and adjustment, family relationships and unity and health conditions and practices. The distribution by two score groupings is given below:

EXHIBIT 5.4: FAMILY FUNCTIONING OF LOW GROUP BY AREAS

AREA	FAMILIES FUNCTIONING BELOW ADEQUATE LEVEL	FAMILIES FUNCTIONING AT MARGINAL LEVEL AND BELOW
Individual behavior and adjustment	98.5%	34.1%
Health conditions and practices	97.7	25.0
Economic practices	97.0	37.1
Home and household practices	96.2	55.3
Social activities	95.5	13.6
Family relationships and unity	94.7	33.3
Care and training of children	90.2	16.7
Use of community resources	71.2	9.1

The change in rank order of problems from the Medium-Low to the Low group is again relatively small (rho = +.81), but shifts from the former to the latter do not indicate a greater relative prominence of difficulties in expressive and relationship areas. If anything, a slight trend in the opposite direction is indicated, suggesting the saliency of the poverty problem among young families exhibiting relatively poor functioning. When the Lows are viewed from the perspective of pervasiveness of problems as well as severity, it becomes clear that housing and making a living dominate the picture. Although the rank order positions of individual behavior and adjustment and family relationships and unity have not shifted in the Lows relative to their place among the Medium-Lows, there is a substantially greater occurence of disturbed (marginal and below) functioning in the former group, amounting to percentage changes of 34 and 25, respectively (data not shown).

The consistently low ordinal position of care and training of children and use of community resources, along with the relative absence of severe problems in these categories among the Low families, reflects, above all, the early life-cycle stage of the study family units. The period immediately following the birth of the first child does not present any major child-rearing difficulties because the child does not yet respond as a social being. At the same time, use of community resources is not much of a problem because the families have limited requirements.

The relative level of problems in the eight categories of functioning in the four family groupings (High, Medium-High, Medium-Low and Low) can be compared by computing the Kendall's coefficient of concordance. This measure is an index of sameness versus difference in each category's position among the four social functioning groups. The coefficient of concordance (W) is +.96, is statistically highly significant (X^2 = 26.88, 7 d.f., $p < .001$) and denotes a high degree of stability of rank or relative position for the eight areas of family functioning in the four score groupings. This means, in effect, that increasingly severe malfunctioning as represented by successively lower total score groupings is expressed by relatively comparable increases in problematic functioning in all areas.

Total score groupings were found to be relatively powerful tools in the analysis of family functioning. This is indicated by the very strong correlation between total score groupings and main category scores (gamma coefficients ranging from +.80 to +.95 with a mean value of +.86) and the high statistical significance of these relationships (X^2 values ranging from 206 to 445, which at 6 degrees of freedom are significant much beyond the .001 level). An important finding concerning the overall functioning of young families is that successive degrees of greater malfunctioning tend to signify more extensive problematic functioning in all areas rather than serious problems in only a selected few. The character of malfunctioning in young, urban, predominantly lower-class families is more instrumental than expressive, although problems in role behavior, which combines expressive and instrumental aspects, are widespread in the two lower social functioning groupings.

FAMILY FUNCTIONING AS EXPRESSED IN
MAIN AND SUBCATEGORIES

We arrived at areas or main categories of family functioning by conceptualizing social functioning in terms of the more concrete and specific types of behavior identified under the subcategories. The area scores are composite ratings based upon judgments that are theoretically defensible and guided by a specific procedure. An area is a collective term, covering functioning pertaining to situations and activities which have a common objective such as rearing children or maintaining the home.

EXHIBIT 5.5: THE SOCIAL FUNCTIONING OF PROJECT FAMILIES AS REFLECTED IN AREA AND SUBCATEGORY MEAN SCORES AND STANDARD DEVIATIONS

AREAS AND SUBCATEGORIES	N[a]	Mean	S.D.
Family Relationships and Unity	555	6.13	1.12
Marital relationship	455	5.96	1.27
Parent-child relationship	555	6.61	0.76
Sibling relationships	31[b]	6.71	0.63
Family solidarity	554	6.22	1.15
Relationships with other household members	235	6.19	1.10
Individual Behavior and Adjustment	555	6.06	1.07
Father	457	6.08	1.32
Mother	555	6.05	1.01
Children—older (ten and over)	—	—	—
younger (under ten)	547	6.98	0.13
Care and Training of Children	555	6.40	0.84
Physical care	555	6.53	0.86
Training methods and emotional care	552	6.43	0.81
Social Activities	555	6.16	0.91
Informal associations	551	6.15	0.92
Formal associations	160	6.55	0.53
Economic Practices	555	6.03	1.07
Source and amount of income	548	5.97	1.11
Job situation	411	6.49	0.88
Use of money	487	6.46	0.87
Home and Household Practices	555	5.67	1.44
Physical facilities	553	5.32	1.63
Housekeeping standards	553	6.21	1.23
Health Conditions and Practices	555	6.12	0.91
Health conditions	552	6.55	0.66
Health practices	552	6.09	0.96
Use of Community Resources	555	6.58	0.72
School	530	6.75	0.61
Church	266	6.75	0.44
Health resources	554	6.58	0.79
Social agencies	215	6.45	0.86
Recreational agencies	138	6.83	0.39

a. N denotes the number of ratings where the number is lower than 555; missing cases generally indicate that information was not appropriate or, in some cases, unavailable.

b. Based on only 31 cases where the family had twins or a second child had been born at the time of the interview and the relationship of toddler to newborn was rated.

The subcategory, on the other hand, is a variable to be taken into consideration when evaluating the larger objective which is delineated by the area or main category. In considering the care and training of children, for instance, it is pertinent to ask about the physical as well as the educational and psychological aspects of the care.

The various subcategories of a given area need not be characterized by similar levels of functioning, nor do they necessarily intercorrelate at the same level with the total score or with the other subcategories. The question of empirical communalities will be dealt with in the next section of this chapter. Our present discussion is concerned with depicting the project families' social functioning in terms of the more concrete types of behavior that the subcategories designate, and the relative contributions of these subcategory ratings to the main area scores. This is shown in Exhibit 5.5.

An examination of area and subcategory scores shows that our sample of young families tends to function at or close to the adequate level, with about two-thirds of the cases distributed roughly within the space of one scale step. The profile of family functioning is shallow (see Exhibit 5.6)

EXHIBIT 5.6: THE PROFILE OF YOUNG FAMILIES' SOCIAL
FUNCTIONING

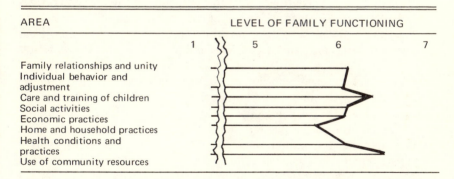

AREA	LEVEL OF FAMILY FUNCTIONING

— in contrast to that of seriously disorganized lower-class families in which there are sharper contrasts[13] — with the two instrumental areas of home and household practices and economic practices being slightly more disturbed than the rest.[14] The lowest average rating is assigned to physical facilities in housing (5.32), clearly a reflection of the Newark housing situation. In a large measure this subcategory rating also contributes to the comparatively low rating for home and household practices (5.67). Ratings of greatest adequacy characterizing the use of community resources reflect the following situations: non-use or limited use (especially recreational and social agencies and the church); positive use (as in the case of health resources); or non-use (except for a few parents continuing their high school education) but a favorable attitude toward the schools. A high measure of adequacy also characterizes the care and training of children. Adequacy here, as stated earlier, signifies the absence of problems at a time when the child is too young to display emotional or social difficulties, a fact further documented by the practically adequate (6.98) rating of the role behavior of the child.[15]

The generally high degree of adequacy in most main and subcategories should not obscure the fact that a number of scores pertaining to home and household practices, the physical facilities in the home, the housekeeping standards, the behavior of the father and the marital relationship, show a wide scatter (as indicated by a large standard deviation of the mean). This is evidence that certain families rate substantially lower than others. The identification of characteristics associated with lower ratings will be the subject of subsequent chapters.

FAMILY FUNCTIONING AS INTERPRETED BY FACTOR SCORES

Up to this point quantitative analysis of data on family functioning has revolved around the so-called built-in units of measurement which correspond to the conceptual model that has guided the total investigation. Thus, the social functioning of the project families has been assessed in terms of: subcategories, the smallest units of standardized observation; areas or main categories, combining groups of conceptually related subcategories; and total scores, representing a summation of area scores. There is yet another way of summarizing findings, namely, by determining through factor analysis the empirical clusterings or factors among subcategories. The goal is twofold. First, this method tests the theoretical proposition underlying the measurement effort which states that the main dimensions of family functioning are expressive, instrumental and role behavior. The first purpose, then, is a form of hypothesis testing. Second, this approach facilitates parsimonious data reporting which may be empirically and, hopefully, theoretically justified. Factor analysis, as was pointed out earlier, is a most meaningful form of data reduction, particularly where a hypothesis of unidimensionality (as tested by Guttman scaling) cannot be supported. Factor scores, the product of factor analysis, constitute a set of components of a compound variable — in this case the social functioning of young families — whose relationship to hypothetically related variables can be meaningfully tested.

The principal component method (using orthogonal rotation of factors and merimax solution) was used here to determine the underlying factors among the subcategories. (The rotated factor matrix is shown in Appendix 7.) For purposes of this factor analysis 21 out of the maximum number of 25 factors were utilized. Sibling relationships and behavior of older children were omitted as not applicable to the present study. Also excluded from the analysis were individual behavior of the child, because of the negligible variance, and use of recreational agencies, because of the small number of ratings (138). It was decided to set the cut-off point for assigning subcategories to factors at +.50, and the assignment was done on the basis of the highest loadings.[16] The five factors all with eigenvalues above 1.00[17] and their respective subcategories with loadings are shown below:

EXHIBIT 5.7: FACTORS OF FAMILY FUNCTIONING BY SUBCATEGORIES AND LOADINGS

FACTORS	
Factor 1[a]	Interpersonal-Expressive Functioning
Marital relationship	0.72
Parent-child relationship	0.76
Family solidarity	0.78
Relationship with other household members	0.60
Individual behavior—father	0.58
Individual behavior—mother	0.78
Training methods and emotional care of children	0.73
Informal associations	0.66
Factor 2	Instrumental Functioning
Physical care of children	0.72
Physical facilities of home	0.52
Housekeeping standards	0.64
Health practices	0.79
Use of health resources	0.84
Factor 3	Economic Functioning
Source and amount of income	0.66
Job situation	0.82
Use of money	0.55
Use of social agencies	0.50
Factor 4	Formal Relationships
Formal associations	0.63
Use of church	0.75
Factor 5	Health conditions
Health conditions	0.65

[a]Use of school with loadings of less than ± .50 was dropped from the analysis.

The factor groupings of subcategories follow rather closely the previously discussed conceptualization, based on theoretical premises, of expressive, instrumental and role functioning. The first factor or dimension constitutes behavior aimed at attaining gratification and basic satisfactions, while the second factor is a collection of subcategories dealing with system maintenance and improvement. The empirical factor groupings differed in two respects from those which were theoretical.

1. What was earlier identified as individual role behavior, combining expressive as well as instrumental roles, did not emerge as a separate factor, but was found clustered in the interpersonal-expressive category. The explanation undoubtedly lies in the fact that expressive rather than instrumental behavior dominated the evaluation of the individual behavior and adjustment subcategories, although one of the roles, that of the father, also appears with a heavy loading on economic factors — a finding which points up the economic significance of the father role.

2. Economic functioning did not, as one might have expected, emerge with high loadings in the instrumental column. Instead, its highest loadings formed a natural third grouping, together with the subcategory use of social agencies. The presumed common denominator is economic behavior, which seems obvious with regard to the first three variables — subcategories of economic practices — but less so with regard to use of social agencies. Emergence of that variable under the economic factor suggests that most transactions involving the study families and social agencies centered upon meeting their economic needs.

The last two factors, composed of two and one subcategories, respectively, are quite self-explanatory. Factor 4 represents formal social relationships under the auspices of church, labor unions, sports clubs, social and civic organizations. Factor 5 emerged as a one-variable item whose content is characterized by the subcategory health conditions, covering essentially the general state of health (problems as well as positive aspects) of the study families.

One distinction between the "conceptual" groupings identified as areas or main categories of functioning and the factor analytic dimensions is that the latter combines functions more in terms of the socio-economic nature of the activity such as meeting interpersonal needs, taking care of the physical aspects of family living, and performing economic functions. The former, by contrast, brings together roles and tasks with a common but specific objective such as caring for the children, maintaining the home or protecting the health of family members.

Results of the factor analysis support most of the conceptual distinctions made in the main categories of family functioning including the broad differentiation between expressive and instrumental functions, although role behavior, which was hypothesized to represent a separate dimension, did not emerge as such. Nonetheless, reasonably high loadings on other factors (economic for the father, instrumental for the mother) point to the mixed nature of parental roles.

The next step in the factor analytic approach was the creation of factor scores for each one of the 555 study families. Because the first three factors comprised 85 percent of the subcategories and factors 5 and 4 were composed of one and two variables, respectively, on which information was already available, we decided to use only the first three factors — interpersonal-expressive, instrumental and economic functioning.[18] The social functioning of every family on each of the three factors or dimensions is characterized by a separate factor score[19] which will be used in subsequent analysis. Factor scores on the interpersonal-expressive dimension ranged from 15 to 70 (mean = 62.3, S.D. = 8.42), on the instrumental dimension from 10 to 70 (mean = 61.5, S.D. = 8.95), and on the economic dimension from 15 to 70 (mean = 62.8, S.D. = 7.81). In the analysis to follow, scores per dimension will be expressed in terms of four approximate quartile groupings.[20]

The correlations between total scores per family and their major factor scores are high and statistically significant, as was to be expected on the basis of factor analysis results. The variations in the strength of association are small, with factors 1, 2 and 3 showing (gamma) coefficients of +.91, +.85 and +.77, respectively, in their relations to total family functioning scores.[21]

In line with the hypothesis for this chapter, the means and standard deviations for the three factors corroborate the earlier observation that the social functioning profiles of normal young families reflect a relatively high measure of adequacy and present no sharp differentiations among areas of functioning. The factor distribution, like that of the main categories, gives some support to the other previously stated hypothesis that instrumental functioning is likely to be more disturbed than expressive or relationship functioning.[22] The lack of differentiation in the social functioning of this group of young families is, as we had a chance to observe earlier, a reflection of their youth and normalcy, since we did not select a clinical population for study. Nevertheless, distributions presented in this chapter obscure some pronounced and significant differences along status, ethnic and kinship lines, as will be shown in subsequent chapters.

This chapter has analyzed the young families' relationship patterns with the aid of several statistical indices which will be utilized throughout the book. The four methods of data presentation by total, main category or area, subcategory and factor scores represent alternative ways of reporting information which differ in degree of generality vs. specificity as well as content focus. At the same time the statistical analysis has served as a means of validating the basic soundness of the conceptual framework employed in this study.

NOTES

1. Used as an alternative to total score when comparisons are made with samples from other studies which employed a different number of categories.

2. Geismar, La Sorte, and Ayres, *loc. cit.*

3. The ninth area, relationship to the intervention worker, is not used here since it is only applicable when evaluating programs of service.

4. Geismar and Ayres, *Measuring Family Functioning*, p. 66 ff.; the revised version of the above manual entitled *Family and Community Functioning, op. cit.*

5. Pierre de Bie and Clio Presvelou, "Young Families: A Survey of Facts and Guiding Images in the European and American Literature," *Journal of Marriage and the Family*, 1969, 31 (May) pp. 328-338; p. 333.

6. *Ibid.*, pp. 331-332.

7. Jan Trost and Ada Brutus-Garcia, "Special Report: The ICOFA Second International Seminar on 'Images and Counter-Images of Young Families,' " *Journal of Marriage and the Family*, 1970, 32 (February) pp. 132-133. Clio Presvelou and Pierre de Bie (editors), *Images and Counter-Images of Young Families*, Louvain, Belgium: International Scientific Commission on the Family, 1970.

8. Dizard, *op. cit.*, pp. 6-7.

9. The other studies were related to intervention programs and utilized the subcategory use of the social—or intervention—worker as a separate area of social functioning.

10. Geismar and Krisberg, *op. cit.*, p. 330. Geismar and Ayres, *Patterns of Change in Problem Families*, p. 39.

11. Ludwig L. Geismar, "The Social Functioning of the ADC Family," *The Welfare Reporter*, 1963, 14 (July) pp. 43-54; p. 52.

12. *Ibid.*, pp. 50-54. It is a well established fact that the procedure for establishing AFDC eligibility frequently screens out the more deviant elements among those in need of welfare aid, and this is reflected in the relatively high measure of adequacy among the families in this sample.

13. Geismar and Ayres, *Patterns of Change in Problem Families*, p. 5.

14. This is also in contrast to the lower-class, socially disorganized family whose more disturbed function is concentrated in areas marked by interpersonal family relationships.

15. The deficit between the rating of 6.98 and 7.00 represents nine cases of babies showing "upset" behavior, generally of a gastro-intestinal origin.

16. One subcategory, use of school as a community resource, which had +.43 as its highest loading, was not assigned to any factor. The lower loading on this variable may be a reflection of the fact that we were not measuring actual behavior — because of the young age of the children at the start of the project — but only the attitude of the parents toward school.

17. The eigenvalues of the five factors in succession were 8.90, 1.87, 1.32, 1.18 and 1.03.

18. In order to overcome the problem of missing information on some of the variables, we decided to use mean scores for the subcategories under each factor. The actual family factor scores are the subcategory means multiplied by ten to avoid the use of decimals.

19. The development of factor scores utilized the principle of unique assignment of variables to factors rather than multiple assignment. Only variables with loadings of +.50 were used in this process. Subcategories were assigned on the basis of their highest loadings. Where loadings were similar or within a range of 0.00 to +0.03, variable assignment was guided by efforts to enhance conceptual fit, i.e., support of the hypothesis underlying the factor analysis. This provision applied only to one variable, individual behavior of the father, which was almost equally loaded on factors 1 and 3 (0.577 and 0.598) and consequently put under factor 1. This assignment could also have been justified on the basis of a widespread practice among statisticians of assigning variables with similar loadings to the first factor on which they are heavily loaded.

20. There is a slight variation from exact quartiles because, as mentioned before, the cut-off points were chosen so as to avoid splitting cases having identical factor scores between different factor subgroupings.

21. Chi squares were 547.89, 453.74 and 351.45 with nine degrees of freedom, all highly significant.

22. It should be remembered that the conceptual and factor groupings are not fully identical and that the latter excludes economic variables from the factor instrumental functioning.

6.

Social Class and Ethnic Patterns

What are the effects of socioeconomic status and ethnic group membership, two important structural variables, upon family functioning? Our inquiry deals with the differences associated with membership in social status groups and with being either black or white. Analysis of the social status variable will rely on the modified Hollingshead Index of Social Position referred to in Chapter 4. Notwithstanding some differences in operational definitions, social class indicates: one's place in the economic hierarchy as a result of occupation and income; one's style of life as expressed in education, type of housing, material possessions, social contacts; and the status derived from the foregoing factors as well as from nativity, descent and ethnic group membership. Although traditionally social science has made a distinction between social class and status group this study follows the lead of Hollingshead and others in using the two concepts interchangeably. Family sociologists, aware of the far-reaching impact of these characteristics on family life, have used social class as a variable in the analysis of family structure, child rearing, husband-wife roles, family planning and so forth. Donald G. McKinley has stated that "probably no variable or measure developed in sociology is as predictive of so many phenomena as is social class,"[1] and this observation no doubt led him to select social class as the focal variable in his analysis of family life.

Being a Negro in the United States also has far-reaching socioeconomic consequences because it means living in a society which has not accorded equal rights to blacks or, for that matter, to a number of other racial minority groups. The heritage of slavery and exploitation has resulted in the establishment of adaptive living patterns which have had a historical impact and continue to affect the lives of Negro families.[2] The disadvantaged social position of the black is, of course, most directly reflected in his social class membership. As a member of a particular class he is exposed to many of the forces, influences and opportunities, or lack of such, that affect whites. The question posed by our research is whether class membership constitutes an all-encompassing force levelling every other observable difference between black and white family life or whether residual differences, the product of bio-psychosocial factors operating in the past, exist independently of social class membership.

Both ethnic group and social class membership confront a family with a given social structure or an array of largely predetermined roles which either facilitate or hinder its ability to function. This becomes quite obvious once we realize that being born into black society affects one's chances for education, housing and employment, and that in normal economic times the majority of families remain in the same social class position from one generation to the next.[3]

THE EFFECT OF SOCIAL CLASS

Although figuring very prominently in family analysis, the social class factor has not received a great deal of attention when social functioning as defined in this volume has been studied. Investigators have focused instead on the relationship between status and such functioning-related factors as family stability,[4] family problems and crisis,[5] marital dissatisfactions[6] and marital adjustment.[7] The converging evidence indicates that social class is indeed a major force affecting family welfare and that lower status tends to be correlated with more disturbed functioning, particularly in the economic and instrumental areas. We expected that the data on the social functioning of our young study families would support these generalizations and that differences would be more pronounced in material spheres than in relationship areas. The basis for the latter argument is the contention that during the early phases of the family life cycle, when romance provides some of the cement for family stability, the deleterious effect of lower-class existence is not so sharply reflected in relationships and expressive social functioning as it is in the economic dimensions of functioning which are the keystone of social status.

The social class distribution[8] of the 555 study families as based on the two-factor modified Hollingshead Index of Social Position is as follows:

EXHIBIT 6.1: SOCIAL CLASS DISTRIBUTION OF STUDY FAMILIES

CLASS	N	Percent
1	9	1.7%
2	7	1.3
3	27	5.0
4	55	10.2
5	241	44.6
6	201	37.2
Total	540[a]	100.0%

[a]Information on 15 families was not complete and precluded social status classification.

The predominantly lower-class character of the study sample, a reflection of the Newark population as a whole, is well demonstrated by the above distribution. In order to simplify both analysis and results, the class factor will be dealt with from this point by grouping families in the top four classes into one category called Class 1-4, composed of 18.2 percent of the families.

Some of the salient correlates of class membership are summarized in Exhibit 6.2, which presents the relationship of social status to gross family income, and to the education of father and of mother. These data leave no doubt that lower status is expressed in family income as well as educational level. Economic deprivation takes its most dramatic form in Class 6, where only 18 percent of the families have gross incomes over $5,000 per year as compared to 77 percent of Class 1-4. The education of each of the parents viewed for the group as a whole is marked by substantial similarity, with some contrasts shown only in the top status

EXHIBIT 6.2: RELATIONSHIP OF SOCIAL CLASS TO GROSS FAMILY INCOME AND EDUCATION OF FATHER AND MOTHER

	PERCENT OF FAMILIES IN SOCIAL CLASS		
Annual Gross Income	1-4	5	6
Under $2,000	0.0%	4.8%	30.4%
$2,000-4,999	21.1	37.7	37.0
$5,000-6,999	30.0	37.2	13.3
$7,000-9,999	30.0	12.7	4.5
$10,000 and over	16.6	4.8	0.6[b]
Unmarried mother completely dependent on her own family	2.3	2.8	14.2
Total	100.0%	100.0%	100.0%
N[a]	90	228	181

Years of Completed Education	1-4		5		6	
	Father	Mother	Father	Mother	Father	Mother
Fewer than ten grades	4.1%	4.1%	11.6%	12.8%	28.0%	28.5%
10 to 11 grades	5.2	11.2	35.2	33.2	42.6	40.5
Graduated high school	38.5	51.0	41.2	43.2	26.7	26.0
Vocational school	8.3	11.2	3.4	5.4	0.0	1.0
Some college to graduate degree	43.9	22.5	8.6	5.4	2.7[c]	4.0
Total	100.0%	100.0%	100.0%	100.0%	100.0%	100.0%
N	96	98	233	241	146[d]	200

[a]Ns not totaling 555 reflect missing information on one of the variables.
[b]Represents one OW father.
[c]Fathers with a college education in the lowest status groups are unmarried fathers whose education did not enter into the family's status rating.
[d]The lower N for fathers is the result of missing information on absent, mostly OW, fathers.

group where nearly twice as many fathers as mothers had some college education.

Class differences in overall social functioning are shown in Exhibit 6.3. The contrasts are striking and the gamma correlation of +.61 is statistically highly significant. There is a consistent decline in total family functioning as we proceed from the highest status level to the middle and lowest ones. The two most striking observations are the concentration of almost two-thirds of the Class 1-4 cases in the High social functioning group and 42 percent of the Class 6 families in the Low functioning group.

EXHIBIT 6.3: RELATIONSHIP BETWEEN SOCIAL CLASS AND OVERALL FAMILY FUNCTIONING

LEVEL OF FAMILY FUNCTIONING[a]	PERCENT OF FAMILIES IN SOCIAL CLASS		
	1-4	5	6
High	65.3%	33.6%	10.4%
Medium-High	22.4	32.3	19.9
Medium-Low	8.2	18.7	27.4
Low	4.1	15.4	42.3
Total	100.0%	100.0%	100.0%
N	98	241	201

Gamma = +0.61; X^2 = 138.41; 6 d.f.; p $<$ .001.
[a]For an explanation of the levels of functioning total score groupings, see Chapter 5.

The eight main categories of social functioning correlate highly (gammas from +0.38 to +0.71, $\overline{X}$ = +0.54) and significantly (chi squares range from 33.26 to 139.46 with 4 d.f., p < .001) with the families' social status. As anticipated, economic practices shows the strongest association with the class variable (+0.71).

All subcategories but one, individual behavior — child (where 98 percent had been rated as functioning adequately), show a positive relationship to social class. The correlation falls short of statistical significance (at the 5 percent level) in four subcategories: formal associations; use of community resources — church; relationship to other household members; and use of community resources — social agencies. All four have a high ratio of N.A. (not appropriate) ratings, indicating that either resources were not used or the household contained no members other than the nuclear family. Class 1-4 is grossly underrepresented in social agency use (only seven families out of 98, or 7 percent, had sufficient contact to make a rating possible) compared to 46 percent in the remainder of the sample. In addition, only 16 percent of that class report having nonnuclear family members in the household, compared to 47 percent for Classes 5 and 6. Class 6, on the other hand, is underrepresented in its use of formal associations (only 29 or 14 percent of the 201 Class 6 families were engaged in codable formal associations as against 38 percent of the remainder of the study population), while use of church favors the higher status groups only slightly.

Strongly correlated with the social class of the study families are three dimensions of family functioning.

EXHIBIT 6.4: RELATIONSHIP BETWEEN SOCIAL CLASS AND FACTORS OF FAMILY FUNCTIONING

FACTOR	Gamma	Chi Square	D.F.	P
(1) Interpersonal-expressive	+0.50	91.40	6	<.001
(2) Instrumental	+0.53	103.25	6	<.001
(3) Economic	+0.62	145.41	6	<.001

The strength of associations between the dimensions varies among the three factors in the direction one would have expected. The economic factor contains those variables (subcategories) that are closely associated with material adequacy (see Chapter 5 for details), which in turn appears as a close correlate of social class in practically every measurement. Instrumental functioning reflects both capacities and habits of physical care of children, adults and home that generally accompany level of education and the financial ability to perform adequately. Interpersonal-expressive social functioning, though not based as directly as the other two factors on economic capacity, emerges here nonetheless as a significant correlate of the social status of young families.

THE EFFECT OF RACE

Few relationships in the social and behavioral sciences have been more thoroughly documented than that of being black and occupying a disadvantaged social and economic position. The evidence has been presented not only in sociological studies but in census reports, statistics on income, unemployment, education, housing and so forth. It is strongly reflected in our data, as demonstrated in Exhibit 6.5, which shows the relationship between social class and race.

The close interrelationship between the class factor and the character of family functioning, on the one hand, and the strong association between race and social class, on the other, indicates that being black or white has a substantial effect upon the nature of family functioning.

EXHIBIT 6.5: RELATIONSHIP BETWEEN SOCIAL CLASS AND RACE

CLASS	PERCENT OF FAMILIES[a]	
	White	Black
1-3	18.9%	2.2%
4	15.8	7.4
5	50.0	42.2
6	15.3	48.2
Total	100.0%	100.0%
N	190	325

Gamma = +0.63, x^2 = 86.11; 3d.f.; p<.001.
[a]Puerto Rican families and racially mixed marriages are omitted from this analysis.

Exhibit 6.6 reveals that race is almost as closely correlated with the social functioning of young families as is social status. More specifically, a Negro family is substantially and significantly more likely to function at a lower level than is a white family.

EXHIBIT 6.6: RELATIONSHIP BETWEEN RACE AND FAMILY FUNCTIONING

LEVEL OF FAMILY FUNCTIONING[a]	PERCENT OF FAMILIES	
	White	Black
High	53.6%	17.2%
Medium-High	26.0	25.1
Medium-Low	8.9	26.9
Low	11.5	30.8
Total	100.0%	100.0%
N	192	338

Gamma = +0.59; x^2 = 92.52; 3d.f.; p <.001
[a]For an explanation of the levels of functioning total score groupings, see Chapter 5.

Before inquiring into the significance of this finding, we will explore the consistency with which the overall levels of family functioning reflect corresponding differences among the components of the social functioning dimension. Each of the eight areas or main categories shows moderately high and statistically significant relationships to being white (gammas range from +0.31 to +0.63, $\overline{X}$ = +0.53, chi squares range from 11.08 to 72.51, 2 d.f., p < .01 or better). The category most highly correlated with ethnicity is care and training of children (+0.63), closely followed by home and household practices (+0.62), economic practices (+0.59), and individual behavior and adjustment (+0.58).

Of the 23 subcategories used in this analysis, 20 show correlations in the same direction with the race factor as total score and area scores, and 16 of those are statistically significant while five (health conditions;

relationship to other household members; use of community resources — school, church and recreational agencies) are not. Three subcategories (individual behavior — child; formal associations; and use of community resources — social agencies) do not have a statistically significant relationship to race.

The three factors or dimensions of family functioning are all highly and significantly associated with white status position, as is shown below:

EXHIBIT 6.7: RELATIONSHIP BETWEEN RACE AND FACTORS OF FAMILY FUNCTIONING

FACTOR	Gamma	Chi Square	D.F.	P
(1) Interpersonal-expressive	+0.55	79.32	3	<.001
(2) Instrumental	+0.62	99.27	3	<.001
(3) Economic	+0.51	62.45	3	<.001

The factor scores are correlated to race at a magnitude comparable to their correlations with social class. The chief distinction between the two investigations lies in the finding that economic functioning, which emerged as the highest correlate of class, occupies the lowest position in relation to ethnic status. It appears that while being black has consequences for all dimensions of family functioning, it affects most adversely the manner in which the family physically maintains itself.

The chief merit of the preceding analysis of the relationship between race and family functioning is that it helps us formulate the relevant questions more clearly. Given the significant differences in social functioning between black and white families as expressed in total, area and factor scores (and in subcategory scores where differences are mostly in the same direction but only partly significant), what explains the relatively more adequate performance of white families compared to black families?

Surprisingly little research has been devoted to this issue even though the question of the role of the Negro family has generated a great deal of controversy in recent years, sparked in part by a government publication which came to be known as the Moynihan Report[9] after its main author Daniel P. Moynihan, then Assistant Secretary of Labor. Implicit in this document is one of two dominant social science viewpoints on the subject. Briefly stated, this position is that although the Negro has been adversely affected by economic and social discrimination, his deviance is more than a function of his disadvantaged status; it is the product of a total subculture, propelled and sustained by its own internal dynamic of family role deviance.[10] Thus, the past and present social situations of the Negro do not fully explain his deviant role performance; on the contrary, he has institutionalized norms different from those of the rest of society, norms that operate relatively independently of existing social conditions. Support for the Moynihan argument comes from studies by Bernard and Udry, who used census data to determine the degree of marital instability among Negroes.[11] Both researchers found that at every status level marital instability among blacks exceeds that of whites. The authors concluded that cultural factors must be introduced to explain Negro-white differences.[12] In a similar vein, Axelson found that Negro and white adult males differ in their perception of the working wife and that socioeconomic status and age as test variables do not materially change the differences between the races.[13] In two other studies, attitudes toward parental responsibility for child behavior and opportunities for learning new or different child-rearing practices were found to differ between Negroes and whites even when status and geographic factors are controlled.[14]

A somewhat different point of view is implicit in the writings of Liebow,[15] Billingsley,[16] Rainwater,[17] and Blood and Wolfe,[18] who view differences in the behavior of Negro families as being mainly a consequence of adjustment to conditions of discrimination, low status, powerlessness and the likelihood of failure. In this view, modification of behavior is more closely linked to changes in the social situation rather than changes in subcultural norms.

After studying in depth a sample of Negro males, Parker and Kleiner also rejected the Negro subculture hypothesis. They found that "the family ideals of the lower-status males do not differ significantly from those of higher status groups," and that "social structural factors such as status position and status mobility are not related to any perceived differences in the aspects of family role behavior dealt with in this study.[19] However, the researchers discovered that four social-psychological variables relating to degree of perceived success in life and hope for the future could order data on the discrepancy between the men's actual and ideal role performance, leading to the possible conclusion that Negroes who perceive themselves as relative failures are also more prone to believe that they are failing in their family role performance.[20]

A study conducted by this writer and a co-investigator on the social functioning of inner-city and suburban Negro and white young families led to the conclusion that differences between these groups are largely the result of variations in social class and that most of these differences tend to disappear when class is held constant.[21] We concluded that "it is the delicate interplay among social, economic, and psychological factors rather than the operation of any one of them which determines the social functioning of families in various ethnic groups. [22]

Armed with the results of prior studies and the arguments of a number of thoughtful writers, this investigator hypothesizes that the strong relationship between race and family functioning will become attenuated when the two racial groupings are compared within the families' social strata, or, put differently, when class is held constant. Underlying this hypothesis is the contention that whatever the sum total of social and cultural influences upon family life, social class represents a dominant factor tending to level most of the ethnic differences in family functioning. As in the earlier sections of this chapter, we shall look at Negro-white differences in terms of total area, subcategory and factor scores but for each one of the major social status groupings identified above.

EXHIBIT 6.8: RELATIONSHIP BETWEEN RACE AND FAMILY FUNCTIONING WITH SOCIAL CLASS HELD CONSTANT

LEVEL OF FAMILY FUNCTIONING	Class 1-4 Percent of Families White	Negro	Class 5 Percent of Families White	Negro	Class 6 Percent of Families White	Negro
High	77.3%	41.9%	47.4%	24.1%	24.1%	7.6%
Medium-High	15.2	35.5	33.7	29.2	20.7	19.2
Medium-Low	4.5	16.1	9.4	26.3	17.3	29.9
Low	3.0	6.5	9.5	20.4	37.9	43.3
Total	100.0%	100.0%	100.0%	100.0%	100.0%	100.0%
N	66	31	95	137	29	157
Gamma	+0.59		+0.44		+0.24	
x^2	12.05		21.80		8.13	
D.F.	3		3		3	
P	<.01		<.001		<.05	

Exhibit 6.8 presents total scores for black and white families with social class held constant. Two preliminary conclusions emerge from this comparison. Differences in overall functioning between black and white families continue to exist at a statistically significant level, although the strength of the association between the factors is reduced from the level prevailing in a comparison where class was not controlled. Also, differences between Class 6 families in particular are considerably smaller than overall black-white differences.

Main category differences between Negroes and whites in the three class groupings present a more complex picture, as is shown in Exhibit 6.9. For the three status groupings, Classes 1-4, 5 and 6, all relationships between social functioning and being white are positive, although of these correlations only three in Class 1-4, six in Class 5 and two in Class 6 are statistically significant.

EXHIBIT 6.9: CORRELATION COEFFICIENTS AND STATISTICAL SIGNIFICANCE LEVELS BY AREAS FOR NEGRO-WHITE DIFFERENCES IN FAMILY FUNCTIONING WITH CLASS CONTROLLED

AREA OF FAMILY FUNCTIONING	Class 1-4		Class 5		Class 6	
	Gamma	P	Gamma	P	Gamma	P
Family relationships and unity	+0.22	N.S.[a]	+0.52	<.001	+0.15	N.S.
Individual behavior and adjustment	+0.18	N.S.	+0.50	<.001	+0.31	<.001
Care and training of children	+0.67	<.001	+0.57	<.001	+0.30	N.S.
Social activities	+0.49	<.05	+0.26	N.S.	+0.20	N.S.
Economic practices	+0.26	N.S.	+0.38	<.01	+0.46	.02
Home and household practices	+0.36	N.S.	+0.56	<.001	+0.25	N.S.
Health conditions and practices	+0.54	<.01	+0.43	<.01	+0.19	N.S.
Use of community resources	+0.11	N.S.	+0.01	N.S.	+0.08	N.S.

[a]N.S. means not statistically significant at the 5 percent level at least.

The vast majority of subcategories also show the two variables positively related, but comparatively fewer relationships reach the 5 percent level — five in Class 1-4, 12 in Class 5 and six in Class 6. Of special interest is the fact that in no main category and only in one single subcategory (physical care of the child) was race significantly correlated with family functioning for every status group. This observation suggests that whatever the ethnic differences in social functioning, their magnitude and, to some extent, their direction (in the case of some subcategories) are affected by the class factor.

A summary picture of the relationship between ethnicity and functioning by subcategory can be gained by looking at the gamma coefficients and statistical significance levels for factor scores in Exhibit 6.10.[23] The factor score distribution confirms the deduction drawn from an inspection of areas and subcategories — that black-white differences in family functioning vary by social class. In Class 5, whites function significantly better on every dimension; in Class 1-4, they do so in instrumental areas; and in Class 6, in interpersonal-expressive behavior. None of the three dimensions shows significant differences between Negro and white families in all three classes. Instrumental functioning emerges as the factor most closely associated with race, while economic functioning shows the lowest correlation.

EXHIBIT 6.10: CORRELATION COEFFICIENTS AND STATISTICAL SIGNIFICANCE LEVELS BY FACTOR FOR NEGRO-WHITE DIFFERENCES IN FAMILY FUNCTIONING WITH CLASS HELD CONSTANT

FACTOR	Class 1-4 Gamma	P	Class 5 Gamma	P	Class 6 Gamma	P
(1) Interpersonal-expressive	+0.41	N.S.[a]	+0.45	<.001	+0.29	<.01
(2) Instrumental	+0.46	<.05	+0.58	<.001	+0.34	N.S.
(3) Economic	+0.29	N.S.	+0.36	<.01	+0.20	N.S.

[a]N.S. means not statistically significant at the 5% level at least.

Class 5 differs from the higher and lower status groups in the greater consistency with which black and white families are found to differ significantly in social functioning. However, there is the risk of reading too much into the meaning of these differences that are partly a function of the distribution of cases. Black and white families have a larger total N and are more equally distributed in Class 5 than in the other two classes (see Exhibit 6.8). Gamma coefficients expressing the direction and strength of association among variables do not reveal striking contrasts in the way black and white families differ in the three status groups. Beyond that, the somewhat lower gamma coefficients in the high and low social classes are probably a function of the fact that membership in these classes constitutes more of a leveling force than belonging to Class 5.

One would argue that families in Class 1-4 are part of the middle class which tends to produce an ethic and behavior which powerfully affects blacks[24] as well as whites. Class 6 families, composed mostly of out-of-wedlock (61 percent) and economically dependent cases (26 percent of families with fathers in the home are partly or totally dependent on outside financial aid), also find themselves in a social situation which, one might assume, has a strong effect on the values and the functioning of the family. If the average of gamma correlations serves as a guide [25] (see Exhibits 6.9 and 6.10), this is also the social class in which family functioning showed the lowest association with race.

The argument advanced here proceeds on psychosocial rather than on economic grounds. Data available from this study show that, in terms of income, occupation and the extent of self-support, blacks are more disadvantaged than whites in each status group (for more details see Chapter 12) and the discrepancy is not greater in Class 5 than the other two classes. This is further borne out by the fact that the subcategory source of income (which is a measure of the adequacy of family income) showed moderate correlations to being white in each of the status groups, 1-4, 5 and 6 (+0.58, +0.44, +0.35).[26] The top and bottom social classes seem more likely to produce an overall orientation of either hope or despair, which in turn leaves its imprint on family functioning. Class 5, by contrast, does not point with equal force toward either middle-class living or existence at the lower margin of society; it thus allows one more room for the operation of beliefs and behavior which are the outgrowth of ethnic experience.

On the question of black-white differences in Class 5 versus other social classes, one analysis yielded convincing evidence in support of the hypothesis that racial differences in social functioning become attenuated as class is held constant. Even so, differences in social functioning between Negro and white families do not disappear as the result of introducing class as a control factor but vary considerably in magnitude by category and dimension of family functioning.

There is a natural temptation to explain intraclass variations between Negro and white families in terms of subcultural differences. While this question will be taken up later, this writer believes that such an assertion can only be defended by showing that black-white behavior differences in specific social settings are not due to economic disparities and are correlated with differences in norms. A verification of the subculture hypothesis of family functioning would depend on a demonstration of consistent differences pertaining to ideals, goals and norms for family life. But it is worth observing that a number of investigators who have addressed themselves to the ethnic subculture thesis have expressed skepticism or a negative point of view on this subject.[27] Furthermore, the existence of intraclass economic differences between blacks and whites in our study population would have to be discounted as an explanation of disparities in family functioning before the subculture hypothesis could be given a measure of credence. Our own data (see Chapter 12) furnish evidence that the economic factor is a major determinant in overall family functioning.

NOTES

1. Donald Gilbert McKinley, *Social Class and Family Life*, New York: The Free Press of Glencoe, 1964, p. 258.

2. E. Franklin Frazier, *The Negro Family in the United States*, Chicago: The University of Chicago Press, 1939.

3. Ruth Shonle Cavan, "Subcultural Variations and Mobility," in Harold T. Christensen (editor), *Handbook of Marriage and the Family*, pp. 535-581, p. 567.

4. As an example see August B. Hollingshead, "Class Differences in Family Stability," in Marvin B. Sussman (editor), *Sourcebook in Marriage and the Family*, Boston: Houghton Mifflin Company, 1963, pp. 255-261.

5. Gerson David, *Patterns of Social Functioning in Families with Marital and Parent-Child Problems*, Toronto: University of Toronto Press, 1967. Earl L. Koos, "Class Differences in Family Reactions to Crisis," *Marriage and Family Living*, 1950, 12 (Summer) pp. 77-99. Donald A. Hansen and Reuben Hill, "Families under Stress," in Harold T. Christensen (editor), *Handbook of Marriage and the Family*, pp. 782-819.

6. George Levinger, "Sources of Marital Dissatisfaction Among Applicants for Divorce," in Jeffrey K. Hadden and Marie L. Borgatta, *Marriage and the Family*, Itasca, Illinois: F. E. Peacock Publishers, Inc., 1969, pp. 517-521.

7. The literature on this subject, even as it pertains to social class, is too extensive to be cited. For a well executed study see Julius Roth and Robert F. Peck, "Social Class and Social Mobility Factors Related to Marital Adjustment," in Robert F. Winch, Robert McGinnis, and Herbert R. Barringer, *Selected Studies in Marriage and the Family*, New York: Holt, Rinehart and Winston, 1953, pp. 560-582. See also Jessie Bernard, "The Adjustment of Married Mates," in Harold T. Christensen (editor), *Handbook of Marriage and the Family*, pp. 675-739.

8. For the educational and income correlates of class, see Exhibit 6.1. A brief explanation of the modification of the Hollingshead two-factor scale is given in Chapter 4.

9. Office of Planning and Research, *The Negro Family — The Case for National Action*, Washington, D. C.: U. S. Department of Labor, March 1965.

10. Seymour Parker and Robert J. Kleiner, "Social and Psychological Dimensions of the Family Role Performance of the Negro Male," *Journal of Marriage and the Family*, 1969, 31 (August) pp. 500-506; p. 500. This statement is a formulation of the Moynihan argument by the authors and does *not* represent their ideological positions.

11. Jessie Bernard, "Marital Stability and Patterns of Status Variables," *Journal of Marriage and the Family*, 1966, 28 (November) pp. 421-439. J. Richard Udry, "Marital Instability by Race, Sex, Education, and Occupation Using 1960 Census Data," *American Journal of Sociology*, 1966, 72 (September) pp. 203-209.

12. Regarding the culture hypothesis see also Jessie Bernard, *Marriage and the Family Among Negroes*, Englewood Cliffs, N. J.: Prentice Hall, Inc., 1966, and McKinley, *op. cit.*, pp. 227-230.

13. Leland Axelson, "The Working Wife: Differences in Perception Among Negro and White Males," *Journal of Marriage and the Family*, 1970, 32 (August) pp. 457-464.

14. L. Broom and N. D. Glen, "Negro-White Differences in Reported Attitudes and Behavior," *Sociology and Social Research*, 1966, 50 (January) pp. 187-200. Zena S. Blau, "Exposure to Child Rearing Experts: A Structural Interpretation of Class-Color Differences," *American Journal of Sociology*, 1964, 69 (May) pp. 596-608.

15. Elliot Liebow, *Tally's Corner*, Boston: Little Brown and Co., 1967.

16. Andrew Billingsley, *Black Families in White America*, Englewood Cliffs, N. J.: Prentice Hall, Inc., 1968.

17. Lee Rainwater, "Crucible of Identity: The Negro Lower-Class Family," in Talcott Parsons and Kenneth Clark, *The American Negro*, Boston: Houghton Mifflin Co., 1966, pp. 160-204.

18. Blood and Wolfe, *op. cit.*

19. Parker and Kleiner, *op. cit.*, p. 504, 506.

20. *Ibid.*, p. 506.

21. See Ludwig L. Geismar and Ursula Gerhart, "Social Class, Ethnicity, and Family Functioning: Explaining Some Issues Raised by the Moynihan Report," *Journal of Marriage and the Family*, 1968, 30 (August) pp. 480-487. See also critique of the article by William Parish, Jr., and reply by the authors in "Letters to the Editor," *Journal of Marriage and the Family*, 1969, 31 (August) pp. 429-431. This exchange centered around possible faulty conclusions drawn from data based on a small sample.

22. Geismar and Gerhart, *op. cit.*, p. 487.

23. The two residual factors identified in Chapter 5, formal relationships and health conditions, do not relate significantly to race in any status group.

24. Frazier, *op. cit.* (revised and abridged edition), 1967, pp. 317-333.

25. For Classes 1-4, 5, 6 the mean gammas on areas are +0.35, +0.40, +0.24, and on factors +0.39, +0.46, and +0.28, respectively.

26. For Class 1-4 and 5 relationships were significant at the 1 percent level; for Class 6 relationship was not significant.

27. Parker and Kleiner, *loc. cit.*; Helen I. Safa, "The Poor Are Like Everyone Else, Oscar," *Psychology Today*, 1970, 4 (September) pp. 26-32; Blood and Wolfe, *op. cit.*; Elizabeth Herzog, "Is There a Breakdown of the Negro Family?" in Jeffrey K. Hadden and Marie L. Borgatta (editors), *Marriage and the Family*, Itasca, Illinois: F. E. Peacock Publishers, Inc., pp. 483-489; Liebow, *op. cit.*; Rainwater, *loc. cit.*

7.

Families of Origin and the Kin Network

In this chapter we shall focus upon the young families' relationships with relatives, their families of origin and more distant kin. Early sociological literature on the family did not probe such relationships for it was devoted in large part to proving that urban society required the family to be an independent nuclear unit. It was argued that industrial society, with its demands for high geographic and occupational mobility and general adaptability to the needs of the business-industrial structure, necessitated independence from kinship ties. Furthermore, it argued, many of the functions once carried out by the nuclear and extended family, particularly economic and protective, have been taken over by specialized institutions of society.

According to Marvin Sussman, two types of errors characterize the arguments of these early theorists — errors of both commission and omission. The first is the notion that social structures and relationships break down and deviant behavior develops as a long-term consequence of the transition from rural to urban society. The second is the failure to take into account social change and the adaptability of the family to new conditions.[1] Evidence on these two points had already been provided by anthropologists engaged in kinship studies.[2]

Sussman marshals some impressive empirical evidence, accumulated during the 1950s and 1960s, supporting his thesis that there exists in modern society a viable kin network whose major functions are mutual aid and social activities.[3] Cross-national data from Denmark and Great Britain as well as from the United States reveal that "elderly people in all three countries tend to live in the vicinity of their children..." and "most elderly people in all three countries are in regular contact with at least one of their children."[4]

The major activities of the kin network are social visiting, joint leisure activities, and giving financial aid, goods and a wide range of services.[5]

The flow of support is in two directions, tending to be from parents to children in the early stages of the family life cycle and from children to parents later on. The network is particularly active during ceremonial occasions, such as anniversaries and holidays, and during crisis situations. Kin members can live at some distance from each other and still maintain an active relationship. Although in some instances the kin group controls the decisions of the nuclear family, this is not the norm; the role of the kin network in relation to the nuclear family could be characterized as supportive rather than coercive.[6]

Continuity rather than discontinuity is the characteristic pattern of the relationship between families of origin and their married children. In an analysis of income and the family life cycle, Schorr concludes that beyond the platitude expressed by occupational research to the effect that the father's occupation determines the son's is the more discerning observation that the "father's circumstances determine the son's and the circumstances that surround them both determine occupational choice."[7]

While occupational inheritance is not the rule in the United States, data from a variety of studies indicate that "sons and fathers tend to be in related if not identical occupations more frequently than not."[8] Similar conclusions can be reached with regard to income mobility[9] and educational mobility.[10] Key factors preventing a high rate of movement from one social level to another are the lack of opportunity and the adherence to inappropriate values or sets of belief which are built into the socialization process.

Hyman showed that the judgments an individual makes about the importance of work versus a college education were determined not only by his own class position but by that of his father as well.[11] Reissman believes that the family plays a pivotal role in setting aspirational levels by serving as models and providing guidance and support or discouragement and punishment for the ideas and plans formulated by the child.[12]

Continuity between the two generations of study families is expressed, first of all, by significant relationships in social status between the young families and their respective maternal and paternal homes. This is shown in Exhibit 7.1, where the findings replicate an earlier sample of urban and suburban families who lived in the general area of Newark.[13] Stronger status relationships for maternal than for paternal families in this and the earlier study probably reflect only the lack of status information on absent fathers.

Exhibit 7.1 supports the supposition of continuity between the generations, clearly the modal pattern. However, some of the families of procreation improve their status over that of their parents and others find themselves in a lower position. Of the two trends, the stronger is upward

EXHIBIT 7.1: RELATIONSHIP BETWEEN THE SOCIAL CLASS OF YOUNG FAMILIES AND THAT OF PATERNAL AND MATERNAL FAMILIES OF ORIGIN

SOCIAL STATUS OF YOUNG FAMILIES	Class of Maternal Families[a] Percent of Cases			Class of Paternal Families Percent of Cases		
	1-4	5	6	1-4	5	6
1-4	38.1%	30.3%	31;6%	41.7%	31.2%	27.1%
5	10.0	45.9	44.1	13.1	41.7	45.2
6	5.3	24.2	70.5	24.4	19.5	56.1
N	53	133	192	41	58	74

Note: For maternal families, gamma +0.49; X^2 = 68.30; 4 d.f.; p $<$.001.
For paternal families, gamma +0.31; X^2 = 19.25; 4 d.f.; p $<$.001.

[a]Ns short of 555 represent cases where status information was missing, mostly on family of origin.

mobility from the grandparent generation to the parents', a movement about twice as great as the downward one.[14] It reflects, presumably, an intergenerational increase in formal education which is characteristic of American society as a whole[15] and particularly this population, almost half of whom are migrants from the South and rural areas (approximately 60 percent and one-third, respectively).

Does a substantial measure of status continuity between the generations also imply a high degree of similarity in the social functioning of the families? Put differently, can we infer that the quality of family life as measured by role and task performance in the home of the grandparents has a decisive influence on the nature of the young parents' family life? This area of inquiry, unlike that of status continuity, is poorly researched.

The notion of social inheritance seems deeply imbedded in the minds of psychiatrists, social workers and others in the helping professions. That concept when used in its broadest sense, namely to cover economic opportunities, residential patterns, academic achievement, occupational mobility, delinquency relative to socioeconomic status of the home and so forth, is hard to challenge. When it comes to the specifics of individual or familial functioning, claims about social inheritance are, more often than not, based on clinical data or on a study of disturbed populations alone.[16]

Some evidence on social continuity in family life comes from Kirkpatrick, who compiled studies showing that the happiness of the parents' marriage is related to the marital adjustment of the young couple.[17] In an earlier study with an urban-suburban sample, Geismar showed a high correlation in social functioning between a generation of young parents and their respective families of origin.[18]

There are good grounds for hypothesizing a significant correlation between the social functioning of the families of origin and the young families of procreation. Most individuals are socialized into a variety of roles within the family of origin which, in original or modified form, they will be performing for the rest of their lives. Some role learning is the result of direct teaching, some comes about because of a desire to pattern behavior after desirable models, while much is undoubtedly the result of combinations of these factors. Postulating the importance of the home in role learning is not to deny the effect of outside influences, the opportunity structure and sources such as peer group, favorite reference groups, certain media and others. We hold instead that the character of parental home life, as expressed by such factors as interpersonal relationships, the selection of values and goals, the success or failure with which these were attained, the opportunities available for achieving personal goals and aspirations, and so forth, constitutes a force sufficiently dominant to leave its mark on the nature of the life forged by the young family. One would also anticipate that, in families such as those being studied here, a stronger relationship exists with the maternal homes since in lower status families, many of which are out-of-wedlock cases, the mother is the more dominant influence.

Information on the grandparents lacked the richness of the data on the families of procreation themselves. Such data were necessarily second-hand, obtained from the parents and most generally the mother. Paternal family data were often incomplete for the mother sometimes had no accurate picture of the in-laws' family life.

Coders followed the same procedure in rating the functioning of the families of origin as they did in rating families of procreation with one major difference. Instead of rating each area separately they rated only two broad dimensions, namely, expressive family functioning and instrumental family functioning as defined in Chapter 5. We resorted to this procedure in order to make coding possible even where information on a specific category of social functioning was missing. Maternal and paternal homes were rated on a five-point scale[19] for expressive and instrumental functioning, respectively. For purposes of correlating the social functioning of families of origin and procreation, a combined three-point index for expressive and instrumental functioning was used.[20]

When reading and interpreting findings it should be kept in mind that ratings of the families of origin are not as time specific as those of the young families. The older generation was coded on the basis of a description of life in the parental home prior to the offspring's departure to be

married. The narratives cover the characteristic aspects of the social
and emotional atmosphere, the economic situation and other instrumental aspects of the home without reference to a particular time period.
Therefore, the rating on the social functioning of the families of origin is
based on a broad characterization while ratings of the families of procreation cover the time period immediately preceding the first research
interview. As a result, the generalized ratings on the parental homes are
not subject to distortions arising from atypical events or situations as
are the ratings of the young families. They are, however, more prone to
personal bias since the information is based less on detailed descriptions
of family situations and more on memories of states or events viewed
and interpreted by the young parents.

Exhibit 7.2 depicts the relationship between the social functioning of
the older and younger generation. The ratings for the former use the
combined three-point index for expressive and instrumental functioning.
All point to a substantial association in family functioning between the
two generations. As we hypothesized before, the lower but still highly
significant correlation between the young families' functioning and that
of the paternal as compared with the maternal families may reflect the
reduced influence of fathers in lower-class, maternally dominated
homes. However, the sparseness of data on the paternal family could
affect the degree of association among the variables and therefore be
largely responsible for the lower statistical significance levels registered
for this correlation.

EXHIBIT 7.2: THE RELATIONSHIP OF SOCIAL FUNCTIONING BETWEEN
FAMILIES OF ORIGIN AND PROCREATION

SOCIAL FUNCTIONING OF FAMILIES OF PROCREATION	SOCIAL FUNCTIONING					
	Maternal Families			Paternal Families		
	I^a	II	III	I	II	III
High[b]	54.7	31.0	10.5	57.0	37.6	23.4
Medium-High	26.7	32.8	19.6	25.2	32.5	22.5
Medium-Low	13.0	20.1	23.9	10.4	12.8	24.3
Low	5.6	16.1	46.0	7.4	17.1	29.8
Total	100.0	100.0	100.0	100.0	100.0	100.0
N	161	174	209	135	117	111

Note: For maternal families gamma +0.58; X^2 = 138.63; 6 d.f.; p <.001.
        For paternal families gamma +0.42; X^2 = 45.60; 6 d.f.; p <.001.

[a]Explanation in text.

[b]For explanation see Chapter 5.

With the composite ratings on the functioning of families of origin as
a starting point for testing the degree of intergenerational continuity,

we can now extend this analysis by examining the relationship of the specific dimensions of parental family life, expressive and instrumental functioning, to the specific components or factors of the young families' social functioning. Exhibit 7.3 summarizes correlations between maternal and paternal expressive and instrumental behavior and the three major dimensions and total score of the study families' social functioning.

Exhibit 7.3 reveals the same measure of intergenerational relationship among specific dimensions of social functioning as was found between total scores and two dimensions of parental functioning (Exhibit 7.2). The degree of association is somewhat lower between young families and paternal homes than between the families and maternal homes, presumably for the reasons cited above. There are only minor differences among the three factors of the young families' functioning and their relationship to parental functioning. Maternal expressive and young families' interpersonal-expressive as well as overall functioning are somewhat more closely associated than the remaining variables, suggesting that the social and emotional quality of the mother's home life before marriage had greatest influence upon the lives of her offspring and husband. Beyond this observation there is little evidence of a specific flow of influence from the older generation to the younger. In other words, the nature of parental expressive functioning has about the same effect upon the expressive as upon the instrumental and economic functioning of the children's own families. The instrumental functioning of the older generation affects the three different dimensions of the young families' functioning in a similar manner. One would conclude, therefore, that the intergenerational transmission of familial influences is of a generalized nature and expresses itself in an overall quality of competence or incompetence, as the case may be, in interpersonal relations and the skills required for making a living and running the home.

Social class emerges as a definitive component in parental family functioning. Confining the analysis to the maternal family alone (case attrition in the data on parental functioning in the lower classes [21] was due to the absence of fathers), we find that both the mother's expressive and instrumental functioning were significantly class related (gammas +0.44 and +0.42, chi squares 60.77 and 51.81, with 4 d.f., both significant beyond .001).

Since the young families' race was found to have a substantial effect upon the nature of its social functioning, there is a basis here for inquiring whether being either Negro or white is also related to the social functioning of the maternal family of origin. The question can be answered

EXHIBIT 7.3: THE RELATIONSHIP OF EXPRESSIVE AND INSTRUMENTAL FUNCTIONING OF PARENTAL HOMES TO THREE DIMENSIONS AND TOTAL SCORE OF SOCIAL FUNCTIONING OF THE FAMILIES OF PROCREATION

SOCIAL FUNCTIONING OF FAMILY OF PRO- CREATION Factors	Maternal Expressive			Maternal Instrumental			Paternal Expressive			Paternal Instrumental		
	Gamma	X^{2a}	P	Gamma	X^2	P	Gamma	X^2	P	Gamma	X^2	P
I. Interpersonal- Expressive	+0.59	159.52	<.001	+0.45	93.48	<.001	+0.40	51.67	<.001	+0.28	27.64	<.01
II. Instrumental	+0.46	93.96	<.001	+0.45	92.61	<.001	+0.36	41.57	<.001	+0.38	50.05	<.001
III. Economic	+0.47	103.58	<.001	+0.42	88.30	<.001	+0.40	55.64	<.001	+0.29	31.88	<.01
Total Score	+0.58	132.57	<.001	+0.50	99.90	<.001	+0.44	49.41	<.001	+0.37	37.61	<.001

[a]All factor tables have 12 degrees of freedom while total score tables have six degrees of freedom.

most meaningfully by examining Negro-white differences while holding social class constant. Findings are summarized in Exhibit 7.4.

EXHIBIT 7.4: NEGRO-WHITE DIFFERENCES IN THE SOCIAL FUNCTIONING OF THE MATERNAL FAMILIES OF ORIGIN WITH CLASS HELD CONSTANT

SOCIAL CLASS	Maternal Expressive			Maternal Instrumental		
	Q	x^{2a}	P	Q	x^2	P
1-4	+0.37	2.97	N.S.[b]	+0.36	3.03	N.S.
5	+0.33	6.50	<.02	+0.38	8.93	<.01
6	+0.44	4.74	<.05	+0.56	8.77	<.01

[a]All tables have one degree of freedom.

[b]N.S. means not significant at the 5 percent level at least.

Exhibit 7.4 shows that there are considerable differences between Negro and white families in the functioning of their maternal families of orientation. All relationships are of a low to moderate magnitude in the same direction, but they are not statistically significant for the top status group, Class 1-4. Not too much can be read into the differential significance levels in view of the fact that there were substantial differences in sample size among the three status groups (Class 1-4 — 97, Class 5 — 230, Class 6 — 185), while coefficients of association did not differ greatly in magnitude. These findings roughly parallel those on black-white differences in the social functioning of the families of procreation and provide some indication that white families tend to function more adequately than black families even if allowance is made for the effect of social class.

Up to this point we have amassed substantial evidence on intergenerational continuity in family functioning between the young study families and their families of origin. We have also learned that class and ethnic factors bear a significant relationship to the functioning of the families of the grandparents just as they do to that of the young families themselves. The actual contribution of class and ethnic factors can be gleaned more accurately by examining the intergenerational correlation of family functioning with the factors of class and ethnicity held constant, as is done in Exhibit 7.5.

The evidence from that table quite conclusively supports the notion of intergenerational continuity in family functioning even when the factors of class and ethnicity are controlled. Viewing the combination of gamma correlations and chi square coefficients (for limitations regarding the latter see the footnote to Exhibit 7.5), it is clear that neither race nor class greatly affect the degree to which the social functioning of the maternal family of origin influences the functioning of the family of procreation. Continuity is somewhat more strongly expressed on the expressive dimension rather than the instrumental, suggesting that patterns of social and emotional relations in the mothers' parental homes have a more pronounced influence than the ways in which the house is run, meals served and money brought in. There is also a slight suggestion of greater continuity in white families than in black families, and this difference may reflect lesser intergenerational continuity among Negroes because of higher geographic mobility.

EXHIBIT 7.5: THE RELATIONSHIP OF EXPRESSIVE AND INSTRUMENTAL FUNCTIONING OF MATERNAL HOMES TO TOTAL SOCIAL FUNCTIONING OF THE YOUNG FAMILIES, WITH CLASS AND ETHNICITY HELD CONSTANT

| CATEGORY OF COMPARISON | SOCIAL FUNCTIONING OF MATERNAL FAMILY | | | | | | | |
| | Expressive | | | | Instrumental | | | |
	Gamma	x^2	D.F.	P[a]	Gamma	x^2	D.F.	P
Class 1-4	+0.58	44.17	12	$<$.001	+0.42	15.96	9	N.S.[b]
Class 5	+0.42	36.76	12	$<$.001	+0.34	33.72	12	$<$.001
Class 6	+0.51	51.66	12	$<$.001	+0.43	35.68	12	$<$.001
Class 1-4, white	+0.65	39.99	9	$<$.001	+0.34	27.45	9	$<$.01
Class 1-4, black	+0.45	28.16	12	$<$.01	+0.32	12.88	9	N.S.
Class 5, white	+0.43	33.70	12	$<$.01	+0.39	31.60	12	$<$.01
Class 5, black	+0.37	24.58	12	$<$.02	+0.29	18.96	12	N.S.
Class 6, white	+0.81	18.54	12	N.S.	+0.80	16.30	12	N.S.
Class 6, black	+0.44	29.21	12	$<$.01	+0.33	23.21	12	$<$.05

[a]Significance levels should be viewed with caution since the computer-produced chi square computations were carried out without regard to the usual limitations applying to the use of that statistic.

[b]N.S. means not statistically significant.

So far, the relationship of the family of origin to that of the young married family has been viewed largely in a historical context, enabling us to examine some of the influences that help mold the present and future home life of the young generation. However, in view of the fact that only about 60 percent of the young mothers and fathers have both natural parents living together in the same home while most others have both living parents either separated and living alone or remarried (only 16 percent of the maternal homes and 19 percent of the paternal homes were broken by the death of one parent, while 4 and 2 percent, respectively, are the children of unmarried mothers) the question of continuing contact with kin can be meaningfully raised.

The present analysis groups together contacts with close family or kin, which is defined as parents and siblings of the heads of the study families. Over 90 percent of the family heads had one or more living brothers or sisters. Only 9 percent had no contact or rare contact with kin, as defined above; the reasons nearly always were that none were living nearby. Fifty-four percent of the family heads were in frequent contact, defined as one or more monthly visits, while 37 percent were in continuous contact, meaning they shared living quarters. This high proportion of joint living arrangements reflects the fact that 71 percent of the unwed mothers lived with their parent or parents and a further 8 percent with siblings, whereas only 18 percent of the married couples lived with one of their parents.

While the contacts between grandparents and the young families were oriented toward sociability, recreation, holiday and anniversary celebrations, and the giving of mutual aid, a full 14 percent of the young families, excluding completely financially dependent unmarried mothers, were partly supported from the income of one or both grandparents. This predominantly one-way flow of financial aid is characteristic of the early life-cycle stage[22] and tends to be reversed as the young families become more firmly established while the older ones reach an age marked by greater dependency.

Contacts with more distant kin, such as aunts, uncles, cousins, relatives of in-laws, etc., are almost equally widespread among the study families. Seventy-two percent reported being in frequent contact with one or more of these relatives and 9 percent in continuous contact, indicating again a sharing of living quarters. Here too unmarried mothers account for the bulk (23 out of 37) of such arrangements. Of some interest is the fact that the rate of contact with both friends and more distant kin is similar. About 80 percent of the young parents maintain frequent contacts with friends but only four families were in touch continuously as a result of living together.

There is very little variation among social classes and ethnic groups in the degree to which they engage in social intercourse with friends[23] — the only exception being Negroes in Class 1-4, a scant 61 percent of whom maintain frequent contact with friends.[24] The variability noted earlier in the rate of contact with kin is mainly due to the presence of out-of-wedlock mothers who, tending to live with their families of origin, are in continuous contact with close relatives. Black families whose social status was rated as Class 1-4 are the only subgroup with significantly fewer close kin contacts than other groups (X^2 = 4.68, 1 d.f., p<

.05), and this lack of relatedness matches the absence of close contacts with friends which was mentioned above. Furthermore, the more restricted sociability patterns of high-status blacks also seems to apply, though not at a statistically significant level, to their contacts with relatives other than close kin. We can only speculate upon the reasons for this since the rate of extended geographic mobility of the higher-status blacks is not much different from other groups who have higher rates of contact with friends and kin. They show a much higher rate (14 percent) of movement to new housing within two months after the first child's birth. That rate is only 3 percent for the sample as a whole and for Class 1-4 whites. Twenty-one percent of Class 1-4 blacks moved to a new home within six months of the birth of the first child in contrast to less than half that proportion for the total sample and 6 percent for higher-status whites. Does the relatively low degree of social connectedness for higher-class black families reflect a preoccupation with resettlement after the arrival of the first child? Or does that small rate of contact denote a measure of restraint in social intercourse brought about by the lack of opportunities for contacts in the same status group? Did the higher-class black families have to move greater distances, thus being isolated from friends and relatives, in order to find the kind of jobs and housing they wanted? Our data do not provide the answers. There is some indication, however, that the lower degree of social relatedness of upper-class blacks is not a purely situational matter. Those black families in Class 1-4 who remained in the research project for five years still had, at the end of the study, less contact with close family and friends than the rest of the sample.[25] This would suggest that the more limited social relatedness of top status Negroes may result from intensive preoccupation with immediate family concerns such as economic advancement, home improvement and so forth. But, in spite of differences in the degree of social involvement, the proportion (ranging between 60 percent and 80 percent) of blacks in Class 1-4 reporting frequent and/or continuous contacts with relatives and friends marks this group as anything but anomic.

The study population of young families as a whole can be characterized, first of all, as being closely involved with their immediate kin and secondly, almost as closely connected with more distant relatives and friends. This picture of informal sociability contrasts starkly with their minimal formal participation, shown in Chapter 4. In line with the Sussman thesis we found young families in Newark building their social lives around family, particularly their siblings and parents, in the period following the birth of their first child, while maintaining at the same time an ongoing relationship with more distant relatives and friends.

This pattern of social life carries past activities into the present, duplicating the intergenerational similarity in social status and family functioning reported above. This finding, namely, the high measure of continuity in social functioning, was in line with our study hypothesis. Some support was also provided for the notion that the maternal rather than the paternal family of origin is the dominant influence, although this finding may represent, above all, the nature of the population selected for study.

NOTES

1. Marvin B. Sussman, "Relationship of Adult Children With Their Parents in the United States," in Shanas and Streib (editors), *Social Structure and the Family*, pp. 62-92; pp. 63-65.

2. Sussman cites as a prime example Murdock's conclusions from a cross-cultural study of some 250 societies, to the effect that kinship structures do not break down, dissolve or radically change as the result of culture contact with even the more technologically advanced societies. George P. Murdock, *Social Structure*, New York: The MacMillan Company, 1960.

3. Sussman, *loc. cit.*, p. 68. See also Bert N. Adams, "Isolation, Function, and Beyond: American Kinship in the 1960's," *Journal of Marriage and the Family*, 1970, 32 (November) pp. 575-597.

4. Jan Stehouwer, "Relations Between Generations and the Three Generation Household in Denmark," in Shanas and Streib (editors), *Social Structure and the Family*, pp. 142-162; p. 160.

5. Marvin B. Sussman and Lee Burchinal, "Kin Family Network: Unheralded Structure in Current Conceptualizations of Family Functioning," *Marriage and Family Living*, 1962, 24 (August) pp. 231-240.

6. *Ibid.*

7. Alvin L. Schorr, "The Family Cycle and Income Development," in Hadden and Borgatta (editors), *Marriage and the Family*, pp. 449-461; p. 461.

8. Research cited in Leonard Reissman, *Class in American Society*, Glencoe, Illinois: The Free Press, 1959, p. 314.

9. *Ibid.*, pp. 319-332.

10. *Ibid.*, pp. 332-339.

11. Herbert Hyman, "The Value System of Different Classes: A Social Psychological Contribution to the Analysis of Stratification," in Reinhard Bendix and Seymour M. Lipset (editors), *Class, Status and Power*, Glencoe, Illinois: The Free Press, 1953, pp. 426-442; p. 441.

12. Reissman, *op. cit.*, p. 366.

13. Geismar, *Preventive Intervention in Social Work*, p. 45.

14. Table 7.1 may well understate the actual intergenerational upward mobility because many of the young families have not, owing to the youth of the family head, attained the status level corresponding to his educational and occupational potential.

15. Reissman, *op. cit.*, pp. 293-319.

16. Bradley Buell and Associates, *Community Planning for Human Services*, New York: Columbia University Press, 1952, p. 620 ff.

17. Clifford Kirkpatrick, "Measuring Marital Adjustment," in Robert Winch (editor), *Selected Studies in Marriage and the Family*, New York: Holt, Reinhart and Winston, 1962, pp. 544-553.

18. Geismar, *Preventive Intervention in Social Work*, pp. 43-46.

19. The decision to use five instead of the customary seven scale points, defined as adequate, marginal plus, marginal, marginal minus and inadequate, represented an attempt to adapt the rating technique to these data which showed a lower degree of differentiation than the information on the young families themselves.

20. The combined index was constituted as follows: category I = adequate ratings in both roles; category II = adequate or marginal plus in one role, marginal plus in the other, or adequate in one and marginal and lower in the other; category III = marginal plus or marginal and lower in one role, and marginal and lower in the other.

21. For the same reason information on paternal family of Negroes was also lacking.

22. Sussman, *loc. cit.*, pp. 68-69.

23. This is contrary to the findings from several studies which show that there is a greater tendency for higher status families to spend more time with friends and for those of lower status to spend more time with kin. See Bert N. Adams, *loc. cit.*, p. 591.

24. This difference is statistically significant ($X^2 = 8.65$, 1 d.f., $p < .01$).

25. This comparison covered only the 175 control group families who remained in the project until the end of the study. The small number of black Class 1-4 families precluded the use of significance tests.

8.

The Unwed Mother

There is rather wide agreement among students of marriage and the family that out-of-wedlock birth is not a "cultural alternative."[1] Goode, after surveying studies and documents dealing with the Caribbean area where, in some instances, illegitimacy rates run as high as 85 percent of live births, reached the conclusion that there is "no special approval of the consensual union, no 'counter norm' in favor of such a union."[2] At the same time his study led him to affirm "that the degree of norm commitment varies from one segment of the population to another... and that the lower strata are less committed than the middle or upper strata to a variety of family norms, in this instance that of legitimacy, and also obey them less."[3] In spite of differences in norm commitment, there is no evidence from illegitimacy research or our present study that either unwed mothers or the social and cultural groups in which illegitimacy is widespread place a higher value on consensual unions or single-parent motherhood than on marriage.[4]

Birth control laws were liberalized during the latter part of the 1960s and early 1970s, and combined with the spread of sex education and family planning centers this may serve to reverse the trend toward a higher illegitimacy rate that began at the start of World War II. Statistics for the United States as a whole reflect a substantial reduction in this annual increase between the years 1958 and 1968.[5] However, this relative rate decrease in national figures does not necessarily reflect the situation in specific areas, such as the Newark and the other United States metropolitan areas (see statistics in Chapter 4).

We do not fully understand why this increase in illegitimacy was larger in metropolitan than nonmetropolitan counties in the early 1960s.[6] On the basis of cross-cultural comparisons, Goode argues that illegitimacy is related to incomplete social and cultural assimilation.[7] That hypothesis was not supported by an analysis carried out by Clague and Ventura relating illegitimacy rates to the proportion of migrants in standard metropolitan areas.[8] Similarly, our own data do not verify the Goode hypothesis, either with regard to length of time since arrival in Newark or to the migration patterns of the families of mothers born outside the city.[9]

There should be no need to stress that the high rate of illegitimacy registered in this study is now a major social problem and will be with us for a considerable time to come. First of all, although norm commitment is much less pronounced in the lower class, where most of the out-of-wedlock births occur, it still affects the unwed mother and her child. Premarital sex and pregnancy in the United States are not condoned at any class level, and there is some evidence that the greater the cultural conservatism the greater the negative effects stemming from norm violations.[10] But beyond the question of acceptance or rejection of the unwed mother's behavior by parents, relatives and peers, there is the problem of the largely middle-class dominated systems of education, welfare, employment and social control. These systems are quite important in the lives of the out-of-wedlock mother and her children. Social and economic upward mobility, perhaps the best hope for improving the lot of the deprived, are likely to be blocked with latent and sometimes open prejudice against these families.

Second, socioeconomic deprivation characterizes out-of-wedlock existence. Some of the deleterious effects of growing up poor have been well documented by Catherine Chilman.[11] The high correlation between mental retardation, particularly in its milder manifestation, and the adverse social, economic and cultural status of various population groups also has been corroborated.[12]

We are better able than many other researchers to supply meaningful information on the social characteristics and functioning of the unmarried mother[13] because our data permit a comparison of ethnically homogeneous groups namely, married and unwed black mothers. The working Ns are 170 for married and 161 for unmarried cases.

A basic difference between black unmarried (OW) and black married mothers, to be referred to for the remainder of the chapter simply as married or in-wedlock mothers, is age. The former are almost two years younger on the average than the latter; over half of the OWs (54 percent) were born after 1946 as compared to 14 percent of the married mothers. Because the research sample was drawn from births occuring in 1964 and the first four months of 1965 the unwed mothers had their first child correspondingly earlier; hence 54 percent of the out-of-wedlock gave birth before their eighteenth birthday in contrast to 14 percent of the married women.[14]

One of the least surprising observations about the families headed by the unmarried mother is their low status classification. Almost three-fourths (74 percent) were classified as belonging to Class 6, 23 percent to Class 5, and only 3 percent had the social characteristics of the higher (1-4) status groups. Families headed by married parents were distributed over the corresponding class groupings in the proportions of 25 percent, 60 percent and 15 percent, respectively (gamma = +.75, X^2 = 77.38, 2 d.f., p<.001). The lower class of the unwed mother reflects less formal education (only 28 percent of the OWs graduated from high school compared to 62 percent of the married women), a lower status employment pattern and/or greater economic dependency on public funds (41 percent of OWs are partly or wholly supported by public assistance in contrast to 2 percent of the married; 11 percent of the former are fully self-supporting versus 92 percent of the latter). Income differences are striking. Ninety-three percent of the families of unmarried mothers have gross incomes under $5,000, 68 percent under $3,000.[15] The corresponding figures for families headed by married parents are 47 percent and 7 percent.

This socioeconomic deprivation, according to our data, has roots in family history. Only 37 percent of the unmarried mothers came from intact families, compared to 60 percent of the married mothers. While the differences between those coming from homes headed by an out-of-wedlock mother are very small (8 percent of the unmarried and 5 percent of the married) as are differences in family breakup due to the death of parent (16 percent for families of origin of unmarried mothers compared to 18 percent for the families of married mothers), there is considerable contrast in the percentages of those coming from homes broken by separation and divorce. Thirty-nine percent of the unwed mothers and 17 percent of the married mothers came from such homes (X^2 for differences between intact and broken homes is 16.89, 1 d.f., p <.001).

The maternal families of married and unmarried women exhibited social class differences which corresponded to those of the families of procreation but at a lower magnitude (Q = +.32, X^2 = 5.27, 1 d.f., p<.05). Mothers of the married women had more formal education than those of the unmarried (30 percent of the first group graduated high school or went beyond compared to 14 percent of the second), but fathers of the wives in the married group had only a very slight edge in formal education over those of the unmarried. Unmarried women by contrast did not come from homes with a larger number of children.[16]

Clearly, the families headed by unmarried mothers are characterized by greater socioeconimic deprivation. The differences in conditions and opportunities largely define the parameter of the problem: the lower incomes, lower educational levels and lower social status of the single-parent households mean that the children will be physically, socially and perhaps psychologically deprived and will have fewer opportunities as they grow older to advance educationally and occupationally. Our comparison of family background with the young families' social situation suggests that out-of-wedlock birth is both a cause and effect of deprived conditions. Unwed black mothers come from more handicapped homes than their married counterparts, but deprivation is much more striking in the young families than in their families of origin. This indicates that the very fact of illegitimate childbirth contributes greatly to the disturbed social situation. The presence of a child without a father to confer legitimacy and provide support and the absence of a father with an occupation places the young family in a low status position and limits the means available for meeting family needs. Despite the family's greater income requirements, the single mother rarely can find a way to join the work force sooner than the married mother (13 percent of the OWs went to work within eight months, 23 percent within a 13-month period after childbirth; the comparable figures for married women were 22 percent and 29 percent).[17] She is much more likely to be dependent on public assistance.

Our findings on socioeconomic differences between families of married and unmarried mothers suggest caution in postulating economic and social conditions as a cause of illegitimacy. Significant differences of a small magnitude registered among families of origin indicate that socioeconomic deprivation is very probably a contributing factor to out-of-wedlock birth, but the very dramatic differences between the two comparison groups are probably a result of the illegitimate pregnancy itself and the arrival of the out-of-wedlock child.

Differences in structural characteristics between families headed by unwed mothers and those headed by two parents suggests corresponding variations in social functioning. Differentials in education, income, social position and financial independence have predictable consequences for the ways in which families carry out such socially assigned tasks as child rearing, maintenance of family well-being and family continuity. Since the family structure, as noted above, delineates the parameter of conditions and opportunities for attaining family goals, functioning which represents activities in pursuit of these is directly affected by the nature of the structure.

SOCIAL FUNCTIONING COMPARISON OF FAMILIES OF MARRIED AND UNMARRIED MOTHERS

Comparing comprehensively the social functioning of families headed by married parents and unmarried mothers, we find striking evidence of greater malfunctioning on the part of the latter. The comparison is based on total scores, factor scores, areas and subcategories. Beginning with the smallest and most concrete units of observation, the subcategories of family functioning, we find that all correlations but two between illegitimacy and social functioning are negative. This means that when we use the foci of specific behavior as delineated in Exhibit 5.5, the families of the unmarried mothers function less well than those headed by married parents. The two exceptions to this are the subcategories of formal associations and church (its use as a community resource) which revealed a very low positive relationship (gammas of +0.02 and 0.03, respectively). This reflects, for the most part, nonparticipation in formal associations and only limited church attendance.[18] Individually not all the correlations were statistically significant, and the six subcategories out of the total of 23 that were analyzed here — where the negative relationship did not reach at least the 5 percent level of statistical significance — were in part sub-areas of functioning revealing very limited problems for the subpopulations under consideration (behavior of the child, health conditions, use of recreational agencies). In another three subcategories, relationship to nonfamily household members, use of money and health conditions (health of mother and child), statistical nonsignificance appeared to indicate that the disturbed functioning of the families of unmarried mothers could be the result of chance factors.

Moving from subcategories of social functioning to higher conceptual units of observation, comparisons in Exhibit 8.1 of the subgroups of research families show consistent and significantly more handicapped performance of families headed by an unwed mother. Of special interest is the juxtaposition of factor scores which constitute the numerical values of the common dimensions underlying the subcategory variables (for details see Chapter 5). It appears that the economic factor differentiates most clearly between the families of married women and OWs, and this is mirrored in area differences as well. However, individual role performance is another variable that sets families of unwed mothers apart from the others. The contrast between the two groups is least pronounced (but still statistically significant) in care and training of children and health conditions and practices, both areas found to be of relatively minor concern for young families with very small children. The care of the child in OW families was shared with another person in about half of the cases and turned over entirely to another in about 4 percent of the families. The corresponding figures for black married mothers were around 16 percent and 1 percent, respectively. In health the practices rather than conditions compared unfavorably with those of families of married mothers.

EXHIBIT 8.1: COMPARISON OF THE SOCIAL FUNCTIONING OF FAMILIES HEADED BY BLACK UNWED MOTHERS AND MARRIED PARENTS

CATEGORY OF COMPARISON	Gamma	x^2	D.F.	P
Total score	-0.53	49.34	3	<.001
Factor Interpersonal-expressive	-0.50	40.02	3	<.001
Factor instrumental	-0.41	33.90	3	<.001
Factor economic	-0.57	53.56	3	<.001
Areas[a]				
Family relationship and unity	-0.41	21.67	2	<.001
Individual behavior and adjustment	-0.71	56.46	2	<.001
Care and training of children	-0.28	9.21	2	.01
Social activities	-0.40	16.88	2	<.001
Economic practices	-0.73	66.22	2	<.001
Home and household practices	-0.43	26.20	2	<.001
Health conditions and practices	-0.20	7.68	2	<.05
Use of community resources	-0.54	27.49	2	<.001

[a]Although this table and the accompanying narrative do not give the absolute ratings of area and subcategory scores, differences between the families of married and OW mothers generally show scores for the former concentrated near the adequate end of the scale continuum while scores for the latter are scattered over the near adequate and above marginal positions, with a more frequent skewing in the marginal and submarginal places.

We studied the relative contribution of the economic situation on married-unmarried differences by comparing the two subgroups while holding class constant. As mentioned earlier, the families of out-of-wedlock mothers were about three times as likely to belong to the lowest status group, Class 6, than families headed by married parents. Controlling for class does not put the two on an identical socioeconomic footing but merely makes them more comparable relative to educational background and occupational level of the head of the household. By equalizing the social class of heads of households of the two groups we are able to determine more clearly to what extent socioeconomic factors are responsible for differences in family functioning.

Comparing cases headed by married and OW mothers for Class 5 and 6 separately (there were not enough Class 1-4 cases to make the comparison), we find that the two groups differ significantly on total score (Class 5 gamma = -0.47, X^2 = 11.72, 3 d.f., p$<$.01; Class 6 gamma = -0.34, X^2 = 12.64, 3 d.f., p$<$.01). Main category differences between the two groups show an almost consistently negative relationship between social functioning and unmarried motherhood[19] which, however, is statistically significant (at the 1 percent level or better) only for individual behavior and adjustment and economic practices in Class 5 and 6 and for four further areas, family relationships and unity, care and training of children, social activities and use of community resources, in Class 5 alone (chi squares are significant at $<$ .05 level).

This latest set of findings means that although the families' socio-economic class accounted to some extent for the differences in social functioning observed earlier, it did not entirely explain them. Equalizing social class (as defined in this study) clearly does not remove all the differences in economic functioning. The reasons for this are not hard to see. Given two heads of households, one a man and the other an unwed mother, with similar educational backgrounds and job skills, the man, unhampered by child-rearing responsibilities, will in all probability be in a position to provide a better income. In addition, the two-parent family can in many instances rely on the supplementary earnings of the wife. (In our study sample a roughly comparable proportion of married [67 percent] as unmarried [60 percent] women went to work sometime after the birth of the first child.[20]) Controlling for social status, furthermore, does not eliminate role behavior differences between the types of families. Unmarried motherhood, it appears, has psychosocial consequences which adversely affect the woman's various familial roles.[21] Most other areas of social functioning were found to yield smaller (in terms of correlation coefficient) and fewer statistically significant differences between families of married and unmarried mothers when class was held constant, which indicates that the families' social status contributes to differences in social functioning.

The above-recorded differences in family functioning between families of married and unwed mothers apply to behavior and task performance at the time of the original research interview several months after the birth of the first child. Thus, the correlations between marital status and specific types of social functioning cannot forecast the long-term consequences of unmarried motherhood, particularly the physical and psychosocial development of the child. Nonetheless, the fact that nearly all aspects of social functioning of the OW family were below that of the two-parent family gives us little reason to believe that conditions

for socializing the illegitimate child or subsequent children will improve
to the point that they are comparable to those prevailing in a legal family.
The disadvantaged material, social and interpersonal positions of the
unwed mother and her child make it unlikely that an OW family will
close the social functioning gap between itself and the two-parent family. This prediction is borne out in findings reported in Chapter 15 which
show that families headed by married partners and out-of-wedlock families show similar change patterns except in care and training of children, an area in which the OW-headed family registers more negative
change over time.

EARLY SEXUAL EXPERIENCES, PREGNANCY
AND PLANS FOR MARRIAGE

In attempting to explore the complex issue of the causation of behavior leading to out-of-wedlock status, we posed some questions concerning the mothers' early sexual experiences and compared the responses according to wed and unwed situations.

Married and unmarried mothers first learned about sex in similar
ways. Thirty-one percent and 38 percent, respectively, indicated that
their mothers were the first to impart sexual information. About one-
fourth in each group cited female friends as the first source of such information. Similar percentages (13 percent and 12 percent) were given
for female relatives and school (9 percent and 10 percent). The greatest
difference, though hardly a striking one, was the percentage of male
friends first giving such knowledge — only 1 percent for the married
but 12 percent for the unmarried mothers. The difference is not a real
one, for the counterpart to this statistic is the 9 percent of married women who cited their husbands as the source of information, and the
interviewers did not ask whether this information was exchanged before
or after he became the spouse. Other sources on which the two groups
scarcely differed and which accounted in the aggregate for no more than
12 percent of the sources of knowledge were books and magazines, male
relatives and the church.

The women in the study first learned about menstruation from their
mothers (55 percent of married and 62 percent of unwed mothers), female relatives (13 percent and 17 percent), female friends (7 percent
each), school (2 percent and 7 percent, respectively), and books and magazines (5 percent and 0 percent, respectively). These patterns of gaining
information about the menstrual cycle are very similar for both groups,
and the only difference that emerges is on the item "received no prior
information," with 18 percent of the married and 7 percent of the un-

married mothers indicating this situation. All in all, then, the patterns of imparting sexual information and knowledge about menstruation were similar in the two groups of mothers,[22] and there is little to indicate — as one would be prone to hypothesize — that the women who eventually gave birth out-of-wedlock were less sophisticated.

There were, however, significant differences between married and unmarried mothers in the timing of their first sexual experiences (X^2 = 33.26, 1 d.f., p <.001). Just over 30 percent of the unmarried mothers had experienced sex by the age of 15, 85 percent by the time they were 18. Few married women had sexual experiences so early in life. Eight percent engaged in sexual relations by age 15, 54 percent by the time they were 18. The earlier exposure of the unwed mothers (see above) may have been a contributing factor to earlier motherhood and also may have increased the chances of out-of-wedlock pregnancy and birth.

Our data do not tell us why the black unwed mothers engaged in sex earlier than their married counterparts. Psychological and biological factors may determine the timing of the first sexual experience, but research has turned up surprisingly little evidence about personality differences between married and unmarried mothers.[23] The sharp contrasts in socioeconomic factors shown above suggest that there were differences in knowledge about birth control,[24] earlier exposure to heterosexual contacts[25] and probably a lesser degree of internalization of sexual mores.

More married (59 percent) than unmarried (49 percent) mothers characterized sex as a positive experience (22 percent and 28 percent, respectively, termed it a negative experience, while the balance viewed it neutrally), but the difference is not statistically significant. The lack of a greater difference in the evaluation of sex is indeed surprising, considering the fact that the unwed mother often feels that since she became pregnant through sexual contact, such contact is undesirable.

Whatever the background variations between the two subsamples that are being compared here, the crucial difference occurred when the women of one group became pregnant and found that marriage was, for whatever reason, undesirable or out of the question. Not only unmarried mothers had out-of-wedlock pregnancies. Over one-third of the married black mothers (36 percent) were carrying children and 10 percent had their first child before the wedding. We don't know how many used the legal ceremony as a last resort or how many were contemplating marriage with or without pregnancy. About three-fourths of the married mothers indicated that at the start of the study (generally well within a year of childbirth) the marriage generally met with their expectations. This leads us to infer that most married women who were pregnant before the ceremony saw marriage as part of a design rather than an emergency measure. The OW mother had no plans for marriage at the time of pregnancy, which created conditions which clearly set off one group from another.

Whereas our research demonstrated sharp differences in social functioning between two-parent families and OW families, another quite sophisticated investigation into personality differences has shown that those differences which could be pinpointed with the aid of psychometric techniques were the result of illegitimate pregnancy rather than its cause.[26]

What were the reasons for the unmarried status of the unwed mothers and how many were thinking about marriage at the time of our first interview? In answer to the first question, eight different reasons were cited, two of them given by nearly half the cases. Twenty-three percent of the mothers said they did not marry the putative father because they and their parents were opposed to marrying so young. Twenty-two percent cited refusal of the father to become involved in marriage. Closely related to the latter reason are the cases where the father denied paternity (6 percent). Eleven percent of the mothers ruled out marriage because they disliked the putative father, and a further 11 percent did not consider marriage because they thought the man would not make a good husband. Marriage was impossible for 8 percent of the mothers because the alleged father of the child was already married. Six percent of the mothers listed a variety of reasons for not getting married at that particular time and 13 percent reported that they were planning to marry the father of the child. Obviously only a minority of the unwed mothers were thinking about marriage at the time of the interview, while for the rest obstacles inherent in the situation (man already married, parents' objections) and in their own attitudes (not ready for marriage, questions about the suitability of the man as husband and father) precluded marriage in the near future.

Although the subject of changes in social functioning during the time of the research project will be dealt with in Chapter 15, the reality of marriage prospects merits consideration at this point. For this inquiry data of the longitudinal study will be used.

The longitudinal or change study confined itself only to 175 control families who remained in the study until its termination. In this there were 54 unmarried women who remained until the end of the project and 53 who answered the questions put to them about not marrying the first child's father. In that group of 53, 13 percent (seven women) indicated that they had plans to marry the putative fathers. Interestingly enough, six did marry, but only three of these were in the group of seven who reported marriage plans. Three women who had not indicated such

plans married the father of the first child and another five married
other men, four of whom were fathers of later children. Thus we find
that during the four years of data collection in the five-year research
project, 11 out of 54, or one-fifth of the unwed mothers, married.[27] Con-
ceding the fact that in the longitudinal study we are dealing with small
figures, the initial responses of the young women on marriage prospects
presented only a rough guideline to their actual behavior in this area.[28]

Only one of the 11 OWs who married and remained in the project until
the end wed within a year of the first child's birth; five married in the
second year, one in the third, two in the fourth and two in the fifth year
after the arrival of the first baby.

At the end of the research program, about one-third (13) of the 43
mothers who remained single during the project period had an ongoing
relationship with the father of the first child, one-fifth (nine mothers)
were in close contact with the father of a second child, 2 percent (one
mother) with the father of a third and 14 percent (six mothers) maintained a close relationship with another male. About one-third (13) of
the unmarried mothers had no ongoing relationship with a member of
the opposite sex. (Information was lacking on one mother in this group.)

Some of the unwed mothers in this group had a second, a third or even
a fourth child out-of-wedlock. Of the 43 mothers who did not marry in
the course of the study, 16 had no further children, 15 had a second, nine
a third and three a fourth child. Some of the 11 mothers who found a
husband while the study was in progress had further children as well.
However, our inability to correlate precise birth and marriage dates
makes it impossible to pinpoint how many of the additional children
were born out-of-wedlock. No matter what these children's status at
birth, their mothers' marriage probably tended to remove some of the
socioeconomic handicaps associated with illegitimacy.

During the course of the study those mothers who were initially unmarried did not have more children than those who were married. The
mean numbers were 2.04 and 2.02, respectively, with more OWs (33
percent versus 28 percent) giving birth to only one child. At the same
time, slightly more of the unmarried (7 percent) compared to the married women (5 percent) bore a fourth child while the study was in progress. For those unwed mothers who did not marry in the course of the
study the mean number of children was 1.98.

CHANGES IN THE ECONOMIC SITUATION
AND IN LIVING ARRANGEMENTS

The unwed mother who remained unmarried did not, for the most
part, receive financial support from the father or fathers of the illegiti-

mate offspring. Only 37 percent of the women received such aid and, of those contributing support, one-half were fathers of the first born.

At the first interview three-fourths of the 54 black OWs who continued in the project lived with the maternal parents, and this proportion is very similar (71 percent) to that for all the 171 unmarried mothers, black and white, who were initially part of the research endeavor. By contrast, only 8 percent of the black OWs lived by themselves with their child. But at the end of the study period only 40 percent of these women still lived with their parents; nearly half (47 percent) had found separate living arrangements for themselves and their children.

The income of the black families headed by unwed mothers who remained single was not only strikingly below that of all two-parent families (see Chapter 4) but also compared unfavorably with the income of two-parent black families. At the beginning of the research program, 42 percent of black OW families who had any income earned under $2,000 a year and 75 percent made less than $4,000 annually. For the families headed by two Negro parents, the corresponding proportions were 5 percent and 26 percent. At the study's end both groups had registered some improvement in income, but for the OW family whose head never married the gain was mostly in terms of fewer chances of being in the extreme poverty category. Only 10 percent now earned under $2,000, but the proportion of those making less than $4,000 had only dropped eight percentage points to 67 percent. The families of black married mothers, on the other hand, had fewer than 2 percent (one family) earning less than $2,000 and 7 percent (four families) earned under $4,000.

The absence of greater income gains for OW families in the below-$4,000 category can be explained by a shift of cases from the completely dependent group, i.e., mothers entirely supported by their own families, to the under-$4,000 rubric. In the course of the project the number of OW mothers who remained single and relied upon their parents for support was reduced from 18 out of 54 (33 percent) to one out of 43 (2 percent). Furthermore, 60 percent of the unmarried Negro women went to work within a four-year period after childbirth, and 33 percent did so within a year and a half. This compares quite favorably with the 32 percent of married Negro mothers who went to work 18 months after giving birth and 67 percent who took a job within a four-year period. All in all, then, there is strong evidence that during the first five years after the birth of their first child, black unwed mothers move noticeably toward greater independence in work, income and living arrangements.

The collective evidence emerging from the analysis of data on the unmarried mother indicates that families headed by OWs start their life cycle with a major handicap, since out-of-wedlock motherhood has an all-pervasive effect on social functioning and puts the single-parent family at a pronounced disadvantage when compared to the two-parent unit. Although changes in family functioning during the study period will be described in a later chapter, it is possible to report here that early patterns of role and task performance are not greatly modified in the family headed by an unwed mother nor, for that matter, in most other types of families in a three- to four-year period.

About four-fifths of the unmarried mothers did not marry in that space of time. As a group they evinced a thrust toward social and economic independence. There were small gains in housing. Ten percent fewer families headed by unwed mothers lived in housekeeping rooms at the end than in the beginning of the study (12 percent to 2 percent). Against this, about 4 percent more families at study termination lived in duplex apartments (33 percent versus 37 percent), 5 percent more in public housing projects (8 percent and 13 percent), and there was a slight increase in the proportion of families in private multiple dwellings (42 percent to 44 percent). [29] These housing patterns were very similar to those of black two-parent families both at the beginning as well as the end of the study, with the main — but not striking — difference being that 9 percent more of the married couples than the OWs had been given apartments in public housing for their families at the termination of the research (the increase in married cases was from 9 percent to 23 percent, among OWs from 8 percent to 13 percent). Social life in both groups showed a slight increase (about 5 percent) in frequent contacts with relatives and friends. However, the relative and absolute financial status of families headed by unmarried mothers did not improve, as we showed above. Living patterns at the end basically reflected, as they did in the beginning, a situation in which a lower-class mother from a particularly deprived home background raised one or more children in an atmosphere characterized by relatively poor social functioning.

IMPLICATIONS OF THE FINDINGS

There is nothing in either the cross-sectional or longitudinal data to suggest that the handicaps associated with early out-of-wedlock functioning will be overcome without far-reaching societal intervention either to help prevent the occurrence of illegitimate births or to give adequate assistance to the family if a child is born. Of the two, prevention is obviously the more economical strategy and, until there is a drastic change in social mores, also the more humane.

Prevention hinges upon knowledge of the causes of illegitimacy which results from the pregnancy, generally unplanned and unwanted, of a single girl who is not prepared for or unable to enter matrimony. Preventing or interrupting the pregnancy depends on the ready availability of inexpensive, harmless and unobtrusive techniques. Whatever the future prospects, the means are not now available. Barriers are both technological (the inexpensive, harmless pill or injection offering long-term protection is not now on the market) and socioeconomic (most states do not permit abortion and those which do, make it an expensive or bureaucratic procedure).

Another way of preventing illegitimate motherhood, though not the pregnancy, is offering the child for adoption once born. This works reasonably well for higher-status white women for whose children there is a ready market. The low representation of families of white OWs in the research sample (see Chapter 4) can be explained by the fact that many white children are undoubtedly placed in adoptive homes. The adoption market is quite limited for blacks, however.[30] Because of differences in economic capabilities as well as a lack of an adoption tradition, relatively fewer black homes are ready to take a child. Moreover, racial prejudice, in many places supported by adoption laws and procedures, precludes widespread interracial adoption. A greater readiness on the part of the Negro woman to keep her child[31] may also account for the disproportionately large number of blacks in the sample.

Once the illegitimate child is born and kept by the mother who remains single, the mother-child dyad becomes a family unit that is not only likely to be burdened by an inferior social heritage (see above) but also tends to generate its own socioeconomic and psychological problems.[32] These are the products of a number of factors: society's non-acceptance of illegitimacy; the fact that nearly all women internalize legitimacy norms despite their differences in norm commitment[33] and their violation of norms; the social and economic difficulties of raising one or more children without male support; discrimination by institutions such as housing authorities and welfare departments who serve the unwed mother.[34]

Intervention to ameliorate the difficulties arising from unwed motherhood must be extensive and multifaceted if the status and family functioning data presented in this chapter are guides. The need for assistance is about equally great in the economic, instrumental and interpersonal-expressive areas of social functioning. The first two call for such measures as: education and/or job training (leading to jobs) matched by day care services for the children or an adequate financial subsidy enabling the mother to stay at home and provide the care; better housing and health care; and, for many of the mothers, information and direction in the use of community services and resources. In the expressive-interpersonal area, guidance in child-rearing is frequently required along with help with the interpersonal relationships of the mother, particularly regarding the father of the child and her family of origin. As suggested here, not all of these types of aid or service apply to every mother. However, if the very significant differences in the social functioning between the families headed by black unwed mothers and two Negro parents can serve as a guide, many of the former can be seen as being in need of effective intervention.

It should be clear from this discussion that in this situation, where unmarried motherhood has gone beyond the biological facts and has taken the form of differential family status and psychosocial and economic functioning, intervention is a far-reaching enterprise. Our data on OW families reveal nothing about the long-range effect on the children. However, knowledge regarding intergenerational continuity in class position and family functioning (Chapter 7) can lead to predict negative, long-term consequences of illegitimacy. That observation ought to provide every incentive to deal with the issue not only through prevention, but also, given the fact of high illegitimacy rates in present-day America, amelioratively through multidimensional programs.

The unmarried mother illustrates the interplay of family structure and function. This statement is not to be taken to mean simplistically that the structure determines the function. The evidence is, in fact, anything but clear regarding the relationship between the one-parent family and such variables as emotional problems of children, peer relations, self-concepts, delinquency and others. [35] But, the structure of the family headed by an OW mother does set certain limits within which the family is able to function and raise offspring. Beyond single parenthood and the absence of the father resides the larger problem of the meaning of illegitimacy, namely, of the family stamped as deviant, particularly by those in control of society's resources and services. The deviancy label affects the opportunity structure of OW families, and almost certainly influences the family's self-concept, the views of peers and neighbors, and, ultimately, the family's total social functioning. Although the present research was unable to tap attitudinal dimensions to the prolem or follow up the families beyond the fourth year, sharp differences in functioning between OW and two-parent families when race and class were controlled make the deviance of the OW family a most cogent problem for future study.

NOTES

1. William J. Goode, "A Deviant Case: Illegitimacy in the Caribbean," in Rose Laub Coser (editor), *The Family: Its Structure and Functions*, New York: St. Martin's Press, 1946, pp. 19-35, p. 29.

2. *Ibid.*, p. 29.

3. *Ibid.*

4. Elizabeth Herzog and Cecelia E. Sudia, "Family Structure and Composition: Research Considerations," in Roger R. Miller (editor), *Race, Research and Reason*, New York: National Association of Social Workers, 1969, pp. 145-164.

5. Abbot L. Ferris, *Indicators of Change in the American Family*, New York: Russell Sage Foundation, 1970, pp. 56-65. Also Clague and Ventura, *loc. cit.*, pp. 541-551. U. S. Department of Commerce, Bureau of the Census, *Pocket Data Book USA 1971*, Washington, D. C., U. S. Government Printing Office, 1971, p. 72.

6. Clague and Ventura, p. 554.

7. William J. Goode, "Illegitimacy, Anomie and Cultural Penetration," *The American Sociological Review*, 1961, 26 (December) pp. 910-925.

8. Clague and Ventura, *loc. cit.*, p. 558.

9. A comparison of black married and unmarried mothers showed a significantly longer residence pattern for unwed mothers (the comparison contrasted those who were either born in Newark or had resided there for more than 15 years with those arriving more recently). That difference is largely explained by the fact that a greater number of OWs were born in Newark, and this raises the interesting question of whether having been born in the city predisposes toward unwed motherhood. The analysis of migration patterns compares rural-urban versus other, and south to north migration versus more limited mobility.

10. Harold T. Christensen, "Cultural Relativism and Premarital Sex Norms," *American Sociological Review*, 1960 (February) pp. 35-39.

11. Chilman, *op. cit.*

12. Randolph P. Hormuth, "A Proposed Program to Combat Mental Retardation," *Children*, 1963, 19 (January-February) pp. 29-31.

13. Ninety-four percent of the unwed mothers in the total sample are black; the balance are white, Puerto Rican and mixed racial background.

14. Two married and five unmarried mothers were under 14 when they had their first child.

15. No annual income could be computed for 33 cases which were being supported entirely by the mother's parents.

16. The mean number of children was 5.51 in the maternal families of married mothers and 4.74 in maternal families of those who were unmarried. The smaller number of the latter group might be the result of a larger number of broken marriages, as was shown above. This difference was not statistically significant.

17. Thirty-three percent of the married and 40 percent of the unmarried mothers did not go to work during the course of the research project. These percentages are based on an

analysis of the 175 control group families who remained in the project until the end and on whom there were consistent work data for the total study period.

18. The following percentages represented the degree of participation which could be coded: formal association—married, 33 percent; unmarried, 8 percent; church—married, 50 percent, unmarried, 34 percent.

19. The exceptions occur in Class 6 in care and training of children and health conditions and practices, both of which show gammas of +0.04.

20. Married mothers went to work sooner than OWs, as was shown earlier in this chapter.

21. In the total sample of black mothers the correlation between being an OW (versus a married woman) and role of mother was —0.70 (X^2 = 51.03, p<.001).

22. Clark Vincent found OWs receive sex information more often from peers than single, nonpregnant females but differences were not statistically significant. Vincent, *op. cit.*, pp. 115-116.

23. Jerome D. Pauker, "Girls Pregnant Out-of-Wedlock: Are They Pregnant Because They Are Different or Are They Different Because They Are Pregnant?" Paper read at the National Conference on Social Welfare, San Francisco, May 1968. Clark Vincent, *op. cit.*, pp. 99-184. Starke R. Hathaway and Elio D. Monachesi, *Adolescent Personality and Behavior: MMPI Patterns of Normal, Delinquent, Dropout, and Other Outcomes*, Minneapolis, Minn.: The University of Minnesota Press, 1963, p. 53.

24. Lee Rainwater, *And the Poor Get Children*, Chicago: Quadrangle Books, 1960. Lee Rainwater, *Family Design*, Chicago: Aldine Publishing Company, 1965, pp. 289-293.

25. Arthur B. Shostak, *Blue Collar Life*, New York: Random House, pp. 170-178. Ira L. Reiss, "Sexual Codes in Teenage Culture," *The Annals*, 1961 (November) p. 55.

26. Pauker, *loc. cit.*

27. Hallowell Pope found that 20 percent of unwed Negro women in a North Carolina sample married within three years of giving birth. Hollowell Pope, "Negro-White Differences in Decisions Regarding Illegitimate Children," *Journal of Marriage and the Family*, 1969, 31 (November) pp. 756-764; p. 757.

28. Of the combined sample of 352 treatment and control families who finished the project, 25 of 161 unmarried mothers, or 15.5 percent, married during the course of the study.

29. The proportion of OW families living in single homes remained close to 5 percent in both periods.

30. Hallowell Pope cites lack of access to adoption channels as an important reason why Negro women keep their children. His data showed that "among Negroes the mothers of girls with illicit pregnancies almost as often suggest that their daughter release the baby to them as they suggest she release it for adoption. Among whites, the latter suggestion is given by the mothers ten times as often as the former one." Pope, *loc. cit.*, p. 760.

31. *Ibid.*, pp. 756-764. Jones, Meyer and Borgatta concluded from a review of the research that subcultural values are particularly useful in interpreting unmarried motherhood and status decisions to keep or place the child, and until subcultural values can be taken into account, it is premature to interpret psychological differences among mothers.

Wyatt C. Jones, Henry J. Meyer, and Edgar F. Borgatta, "Social and Psychological Factors in Status Decisions of Unmarried Mothers," *Marriage and Family Living*, 1962, 24 (August) pp. 224-230.

32. Pauker, *loc. cit.*

33. Hallowell Pope, "Unwed Mothers and Their Sex Partners," *Journal of Marriage and the Family*, 1967, 29 (August) pp. 555-567.

34. Robert Staples' flat assertion that "the illegitimate black child is not stigmatized by the conditions of his birth" may be questioned. He is of course referring to stigma within the black community. Such a statement fails to take into account that few Negro children live in purely black communities and that many blacks working for social service institutions and agencies have internalized the values of the larger American society. Moreover, it appears highly improbable that even blacks who are not associated with the establishment have somehow failed to internalize the attitudes of the surrounding community. Robert Staples, "Towards a Sociology of the Black Family: A Theoretical and Methodological Assessment," *Journal of Marriage and the Family*, 33 (February) pp. 119-138; p. 135.

35. Elizabeth Herzog and Cecelia E. Sudia, *Boys in Fatherless Homes*, Washington, D. C., U. S. Department of Health, Education, and Welfare, Office of Child Development, 1970, pp. 61-71. Also Herzog and Sudia, "Family Structure and Composition: Research Considerations," pp. 145-164. Also Benjamin Schlesinger, *The One-Parent Family*, Toronto: University of Toronto Press, 1969. See Mary Margaret Thomas, "Children with Absent Fathers," *Journal of Marriage and the Family*, 1968, 30 (February) pp. 89-96.

9.

Interpersonal Relations

At the beginning of the longitudinal study the research population was composed, for the main part, of three-person groups — a father, mother and child. Exceptions were the unmarried mothers who, more often than not, lived with their child in the homes of their own families of origin and thus were really part of the extended family. Characteristically, then, the family at the start of the project was a triad, and interaction took place between husband-wife, mother-child and father-child. Two-way verbal interaction, however, was at this point largely confined to communication between husband and wife, since most of the children were in the infant or early toddler stage, still incapable of coherent speech. The small size of the family group and the absence of children who could engage in meaningful verbal communication meant that the husband-wife interaction was the key activity in family life.

The importance of the marital relationship in the family unit leads the researcher to predict that a significant correlation exists between the former and overall family functioning. Stated differently, the character of social functioning in a three-person family where the child is a passive partner is strongly influenced by the ability of the marital partners to agree on means, values and goals and to carry out tasks which are in keeping with mutual expectations. Unlike the extended family, in which subgroups of members may form coalitions that may assume responsibility for directing or influencing family life, the two-parent family with an infant is heavily influenced by marital interaction and decision-making. This prediction is strongly borne out by a correlation (gamma) of $+0.86$ and a chi square of 281.29 (6 d.f., $p < .001$) between ratings of marital relationship and overall family functioning. This compares with a mean correlation of $+0.69$ between all the other subcategories and total family functioning. Nonetheless, the centrality of marital relations is not entirely unique but equalled (correlations between +0.85 and +0.90) by the subdimensions of behavior of the mother, the father, the nature of the physical care of the child and the degree of family solidarity. (In the case of the three-person family the latter is practically coextensive with the marital relationship except that the concept solidarity also takes into account the extent to which a "we-feeling" includes the child.)

The importance of interpersonal relations in the family as well as the marital relationship is pointed out by a set of data first presented in Chapter 5. Of the three main component factors of family functioning used in this study, the interpersonal-expressive was most highly related (gamma of +0.91 as against gammas of +0.85 and +0.77 for the instrumental and economic factors, respectively) to overall social functioning of the project families. The central importance of interpersonal relations to marital happiness was pointed up in the study entitled *Americans View Their Mental Health* by Gurin, Veroff and Feld.[1] The person who is happy with the relationship aspect of his marriage generally tends to be happy with the marriage itself. The reverse was also found to be true.[2] While the study before us did not employ the somewhat ephemeral concept of marital happiness,[3] answers to the question "Does marriage meet with the wife's expectation?" — which could be assumed to be correlated with happiness — were tested for their relationship to family functioning in general and the marital relationship in particular. The wives' responses to this question[4] were highly and significantly related to total family functioning ($Q = +0.82$; $X^2 = 86.70$, 1 d.f., $p < .001$) and marital relationship ($Q = +0.89$, $X^2 = 90.43$, 1 d.f., $p < .001$) as shown in Exhibit 9.1, indicating clearly that the mother's satisfaction is a key element in the family's social functioning and the quality of the marital relationship. More direct evidence of the significance of family relationships in the functioning of families was furnished in a prior study by Geismar in which the social functioning profiles of different groups of client families were compared. The comparison led to the inference that family disorganization tends to start in the intrafamilial relationship areas and over time affects other areas of social functioning as well.[5]

The central role of interpersonal relationships in family development is further demonstrated in an analysis of change in social functioning during the study period, a subject we will deal with in greater detail in Chapter 15. The overall pattern is one of a slight deterioration in total family functioning for the 175 control group families who remained in the study until the end.[6] That pattern of slight deterioration is set by changes in factor 1, interpersonal-expressive functioning, from a beginning score of 62.75 to an end score of 60.69.[7] The other two major factors identified as instrumental and economic showed small rises of .43 and .67, respectively.

As we have already shown in Chapter 6, interpersonal-expressive behavior is related to social class and ethnicity. The higher the class, the greater the relative adequacy in the interpersonal area. Whites are found to function better than blacks in this respect. When allowance is made for class the black-white differences are reduced (see Exhibit 6.10), underlining the point made earlier of the tangible effect of a family's occupational and educational position on the way in which members relate to one another.

In order to get at the more qualitative aspects of interpersonal functioning, it is necessary to examine the components of the interpersonal-expressive factor or dimension, particularly the marital relationship, the relationship to the child and informal social relations with persons other than family members. Some attention will be given under the same heading to the roles of individual family members (subcategories of individual behavior and adjustment) which in the factor analytic process emerged with heaviest loadings in the interpersonal-expressive column, suggesting the predominances of this aspect of functioning in the role performance of family members.

Marital relationships, as stated earlier, hold the key to family functioning — at least in the married population and in the early stages of family life. Before looking at some of the more descriptive components of the marital relationship, we shall consider how several premarital variables tended to affect marital functioning after the birth of the first child.

In our study sample the typical married couple had wed after a formal engagement (56 percent married after an engagement; 44 percent had never been engaged) which generally lasted up to 12 months (only one-fourth were engaged longer). Lower-class and less adequately functioning families were less likely to be headed by couples who had been engaged than those which were higher class and more adequately functioning. Negro couples also were less apt to be married after an engagement than white ones, even when class was controlled. Prior engagement was significantly correlated with a positive rating of the family relationship at the start of the study ($Q = +0.36$; $X^2 = 18.88$, 1 d.f., p<.001), a not unexpected finding. However, engagement per se is probably not a cause of marital compatibility; higher status and white families — which are generally more stable — are simply more likely to become formally engaged than others.

In the same vein, church or synagogue weddings, also more characteristic of the higher status groups, were positively correlated ($Q = +0.43$,

X^2 = 16.70, 1 d.f., p <.001) with the quality of the marital relationship when compared to weddings performed by clergymen in the home or civil ceremonies. Sixty-one percent of the married couples in the sample had chosen the more formal rite as compared to 23 percent who had religious weddings at home and 16 percent who selected civil ceremonies.

Parental approval of marriage was found to be a rather significant variable related to the adequacy of the marital relationship (gamma = +0.52, X^2 = 43.32, 4 d.f., p<.001) as well as total family functioning (Q = 0.41, X^2 = 14.11, 1 d.f., p<.001). Exactly three-quarters of the marriages had the consent of both families of origin, 16 percent were approved by one of the families, and 9 percent of the couples married over the opposition of both paternal and maternal families. Neither social class nor race, however, showed a significant relationship to parental consent of the union. In short, the adequacy of the marital relationship of the young couple was correlated with background factors denoting parental and societal approval (conformity to middle-class conventions) of behavior and actions.

At the time of the first interview our sample of two-parent families exhibited in their division of labor and decision-making a fair measure of egalitarianism, a common phenomenon among married couples near the start of the family life cycle.[8] Forty-one percent of fathers shared household chores and 50 percent cared for the physical needs of the children. Major responsibility for financial management was shared equally in 26 percent of the study families and shared to some extent — with one of the partners having greater responsibility — in another 30 percent of the cases. Fathers assumed exclusive responsibility in 22 percent and mothers in 19 percent of the research population.[9] The disciplining of children was reported as shared in slightly under one-fifth of the families and carried out jointly with one parent — mainly the mother — dominating in nearly one-third of the cases. In only one-fourth of the two-parent families was disciplining and limit setting the exclusive responsibility of the mother.[10] Traditional male tasks, such as making repairs, painting and gardening, were executed by fathers alone in only 23 percent of the research cases, whereas the mother shared such tasks in 39 percent of the cases and did them alone in 3 percent of the families. In other cases (35 percent) such tasks were done by outsiders or not attended to at all.

There are some ethnic differences in the way marital partners share work and make decisions. In a general way the black mother assumes greater responsibility than her white counterpart, but these differences are small and statistically nonsignificant when the comparison is confined to married mothers only and refers to tasks done in the household and caring physically for the children. On the other hand, black married mothers are about twice as likely as white mothers to be the sole child disciplinarian ($X^2 = 8.04$, 1 d.f., p < .01). This is the only one of the above-mentioned tasks on which there are consistent differences by class (the lower the class the more likely that the mother will assume all disciplinarian authority) and ethnicity, with the black mothers more prone to have exclusive responsibility for discipline even when allowance is made for class differences.

It will be recalled that the ratings of the marital relationship are based on the researcher's assessment, encompassing the major dimensions of degree of mutual support, emotional ties and personal satisfaction (which can be termed the welfare dimension), presence or absence of conflict, and the meeting of moral and legal obligations (which can be called the conformity-deviance dimension). How does such an assessment relate to some of the more specific components of personal satisfaction expressed by the main respondent in this study, the mother?

Earlier in this chapter we showed the close association between the marital relationship as evaluated by the research process and the wife's reported satisfaction with the marriage. Over three-fourths (76 percent) of the married women expressed general satisfaction with their marriages, and of those rated adequate in marital relations (55 percent), 95 percent expressed general marriage satisfaction. Of the group rated near adequate and above marginal (6 and 5—36 percent of the sample), 31 percent expressed general satisfaction. In families where marital relationship was rated marginal (4) or lower (9 percent of the sample), only 3 percent of the women responded positively about the marriage.

To what extent did the woman's satisfaction with her husband's economic performance contribute toward a good marital relationship? A survey of recent research on marital happiness and satisfaction indicates that "the instrumental role of the husband is more crucial to marital happiness than social scientists had previously believed.[11] Our data, while not relating the husband's economic role to marital happiness per se, do show a significant link between the quality of the marital relationship and the woman's assessment of the husband's employment and of the adequacy of the income he provides for the family. The wife who generally expresses herself positively about her husband's job (69 percent of the wives) is somewhat more likely to enjoy a good marital relationship ($Q = +0.24$, $X^2 = 4.35$, 1 d.f., p < .05). The wife who believes her husband's income is generally adequate to meet family needs (70 percent of the wives) likewise was more apt to have good marital relations ($Q = +0.36$, $X^2 = 19.83$, 1 d.f., p < .001). Thus, we may conclude that the wife's appraisal of the husband's economic role affects the nature of their mutual life, but the degree of association among the variables does not indicate that we have tapped the key factor in the relationship between the partners. In fact, two other dimensions of marital life, mutual satisfaction in sex and sharing of social and recreational activities, figure more prominently as contributory factors to marital adequacy.

On the question of sexual satisfaction, when "mutual satisfaction" as checked by the woman — versus one-sided or no satisfaction — is correlated with marital relationship, we find the variables reveal a substantial association ($Q = +0.64$; $X^2 = 43.16$, 1 d.f., $p < .001$) with the marital relationship. In the social and recreational sphere, sharing of activities by the marital pair is strongly and significantly correlated ($Q = +0.85$, $X^2 = 124.42$, 1 d.f., $p < .001$) with the marital relationship.

In showing the correlation between the marital relationship and a number of components of the husband-wife interaction, very little attention was given to the actual distribution of the first variable. The scores for the total study sample of 555 families at the beginning of the study is given in Exhibits 9.2 and 9.3.

EXHIBIT 9.1: RELATIONSHIP BETWEEN WIFE'S STATEMENT THAT MARRIAGE GENERALLY MEETS WITH HER EXPECTATIONS AND MARITAL RELATIONSHIP AS WELL AS TOTAL FAMILY FUNCTIONING

TYPE OF SOCIAL FUNCTIONING	Marriage Generally Meets With Wife's Expectations	Marriage Does Not Meet With Wife's Expectations
Marital Relationship[a]		
Adequate	68.8%	11.2%
Less than adequate	31.2	88.8
Total	100.0%	100.0%
N	288	89
Total Family Functioning[b]		
Scores 50-56	82.6%	32.2%
1-49	17.4	67.8
Total	100.0%	100.0%
N	288	90

[a] $X^2 = 90.43$, 1 d.f., $p < .001$.
[b] $X^2 = 86.70$, 1 d.f., $p < .001$.

The research population composed of young families displayed rather adequate patterns of marital relationship at this early point of their life cycle, with fewer than one-third manifesting what might be termed disturbed functioning.

EXHIBIT 9.2: MARITAL RELATIONSHIP SCORES OF STUDY FAMILIES

RATING OF MARITAL RELATIONSHIP	PERCENT OF FAMILIES
Adequate (7)	45.7%
Near adequate (6)	26.4
Above marginal (5)	14.7
Marginal (4)	8.1
Below marginal (3 - 1)	5.1
Total	100.0%
N	455[a]

[a]Excludes 100 unwed mothers with no ongoing relationship to a male.

In the lower status families of Classes 5 and 6, the marital relationship is evaluated as adequate in only 53 percent and 19 percent of the study cases, respectively (compared to 67 percent of Class 1-4), and as marginal or less in 9 percent and 27 percent of the families, respectively (compared to 4 percent of Class 1-4). The husband-wife relations of black families in Class 5 are rated adequate in 40 percent and marginal or less in 14 percent of the families (the percentages for whites are 68 percent and 4 percent). The corresponding proportions for black Class 6 are 11 percent and 27 percent. (The percentages for whites are 39 percent and 18 percent.)

EXHIBIT 9.3: DEGREE OF ADEQUACY OF THE MARITAL RELATIONSHIP AT THE START OF THE STUDY

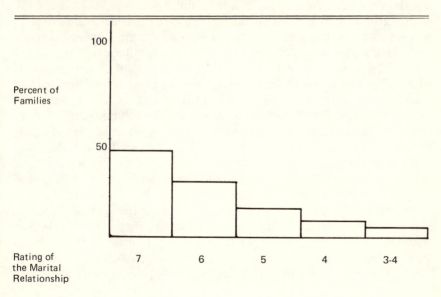

The level of marital relationships is significantly class related (gamma = +0.53, X^2 = 66.69, 4 d.f., p <.001) and also bears a significant negative relationship to being white in Class 5 (gamma = +0.50, X^2 = 18.21, 2 d.f., p <.001) and Class 6 (gamma = +0.44, X^2 = 11.39, 2 d.f., p <.01) but not in Class 1-4 (gamma = +0.32, X^2 = 2.26, N.S.). This observation is consistent with a pattern of black-white differences in social functioning which is most pronounced in Class 5 but not significant on some dimensions in the higher and/or lower status groups. There is a suggestion in these findings that the culture of the middle class with its emphasis on conformity and upward mobility and that of the lowest social status group characterized by poverty and lack of opportunity serve as levelers of ethnic differences in America.

Beyond the marital relationship there are a number of other variables or subcategories that make up the interpersonal-expressive factor in social functioning. One, family solidarity, shows a substantially similar distribution and relationship to the marital relations dimension. There is considerable overlap between the two in that the marital relationship constitutes the nucleus of family solidarity, at least in the three-person family with a very young child. In families headed by unmarried mothers, on the other hand, solidarity pertains to the degree to which the mother sees her life, present and future, tied up with her young child and assumes responsibility for him or her within the limits of economic ability.

In 57 percent of the families, solidarity was rated as adequate, marking the presence of concern for family unity whatever the size of the family group. In 21 percent solidarity was rated as near adequate, in 13 percent as above marginal and in 9 percent as marginal or less. Unmarried black mothers manifested a significantly smaller degree of family solidarity (gamma = −0.39, X^2 = 18.54, 2 d.f., p <.001), a not-unexpected finding which reveals uncertainty and ambivalence on the part of some unwed mothers regarding the future of their children, who were frequently cared for by parents or relatives. The relationship of family solidarity to the class and ethnic variables of the sample was very similar to that of marital relations. Correlations were in the same direction and statistically significant and — as in the case of the marital relationship — Negro-white differences in the highest social status group could be interpreted as being due to chance.

Among adult relationships that were part of the interpersonal-expressive dimension, relationship to other members in the household was found to apply to 235 families, or 42 percent of the cases in the study. In these young families this meant, with few exceptions, that the nuclear family was not living alone but shared quarters, usually with close relatives. This arrangement, as shown in Chapter 8, was characteristic of unwed mothers but not widespread among families headed by married partners. Eighty percent of unwed mothers had another person, someone other than herself and her child, living with her in the household. The same was true for only 24 percent of the two-parent families.

The relationship to other members of the household as a dimension of functioning reveals approximately the same degree of disturbance as other relationship areas. Fifty-five percent of families reporting that there were other members in the household were judged to manifest adequate functioning in their relationship with these members, 22 percent near adequate, 15 percent above marginal and the remaining 8 percent marginal or lower social functioning. In other words, young families in joint living arrangements managed to get along, by and large, with those who shared their household. Friction and antagonisms were kept under control whatever the mutual feeling about one's parents, in-laws or other relations, and in only 8 percent of the cases was there anything resembling a situation where the social and emotional welfare of one of the parties was seriously affected.

Joint living arrangements were clearly class related, with only 16 percent of Class 1-4 but 36 percent of Class 5 and 61 percent of Class 6 making use of them. In part the difference is accounted for by the presence of unwed mothers in the lower status groups; as shown earlier they tend to live with their parents. But even if allowance is made for out-of-wedlock status, we still find shared living arrangements somewhat more common in the lower classes.

Of special interest is the finding that, unlike other variables included in the interpersonal-expressive factor, the relationship to other members of the household is not significantly related to social class, to ethnicity (Negro-white) either by itself or at a class-related level, or to marital status (married versus unmarried). This observation deserves at least a brief comment. Relationship to other household members, because of its selective nature, is not as dependent on the social structure as other forms of family functioning. People resort to joint living arrangements if they are workable and tend to terminate them when they become intolerable. Generally there are options other than living with parents, in-laws or other relatives. It may be the parents who choose another arrangement, for, even in the case of unwed mothers, parents have the choice of not accepting their daughter and her child. The daughter could opt for child placement or support by welfare in separate quarters. Furthermore, the young family of any class level will not continue a living arrangement that is intolerable. The likely explanation for the lack of difference among ethnic and status groups in the relationship to other household members lies in the fact that different social situations make living with persons other than the nuclear family an experience which can be tolerated, regardless of the problems and handicaps encountered, unless they violate certain acceptable standards.

The parent-child relationship on the interpersonal-expressive dimension (factor) is measured by the two variables encompassing the relationship between parents and child, and training methods and emotional care. The former is an assessment of the degree of acceptance, warmth, intimacy, respect, etc., between parents and child; the latter addresses itself to the manner in which parents socialize their offspring.

Because of the tender age of the child, the parent-child relationship — at this stage largely expressed by a one-way verbal communication between parents or mother and child — was judged to be adequate in nearly three-fourths of the families and marginal or less (representing mainly cases of child rejection) in fewer than 3 percent of the families. The training methods variable, by contrast, which takes into account the parents' ways of handling the child, including use of limit setting and consistency in giving directions, showed a somewhat less skewed distribution. Fifty-eight percent of the cases were rated as adequate in this respect, 31 percent as near adequate, 7 percent as above marginal and the remainder, 4 percent, as marginal or lower.

The association between social status and the relationship between parents and children on the one hand and training and emotional care on the other was moderately strong and statistically significant (gamma = +0.46, X^2 = 38.42, 4 d.f., p <.001; gamma = +0.42, X^2 = 41.82, 4 d.f., p <.001). Ethnic differences were significant for both variables in Class 5 (gamma = +0.41, X^2 = 6.73, 2 d.f., p <.05 and gamma = +0.46, X^2 = 12.50, 2 d.f., p <.01), for training and emotional care only in Class 1-4 (gamma = +0.57, X^2 = 8.01, 2 d.f., p <.02), and for neither in Class 6. The earlier comment regarding the possible greater cultural effect in the top and bottom status group resulting in a leveling of ethnic differences may apply here as well.

In the interpersonal relations sphere, the category of informal social activities is the one variable that measures social interaction with persons other than the nuclear family. This is a sub-area of family functioning characterized not so much by problems as by minor shortcomings expressed in such matters as limited social outlets, particularly for the young mother, and dissatisfaction over some aspects of social relations with parents or in-laws. Only 42 percent of the research sample were rated as adequate in their informal social activities, while 36 percent were rated as near adequate, 18 percent as above marginal and the rest, 4 percent, as marginal and below.

Social status was significantly correlated with adequacy in informal relations (gamma = +0.38, X^2 = 32.15, 4 d.f., p < .001) but showed only a weak association with ethnicity (black or white) which reached statistical significance only in Class 1-4 (gamma correlation between being white and a more adequate score in informal social activities = +0.50, X^2 = 6.81, 2 d.f., p < .05). Being black, in other words, set minor limitations as compared to being white in the way families were able to find social outlets and engage in social activities with relatives and friends. Differences between the two racial groups are in the same direction and probably due to chance. The rejection of the null hypothesis by a small margin in the higher social status groups may reflect the limited social outlets of upper status blacks which were discussed in Chapter 7.

Two of the eight variables that make up the interpersonal-expressive factor were individual behavior, and adjustment of the mother and father. These subcategories constitute role sets covering a variety of psychosocial roles, instrumental as well as expressive. Factor analysis, however, demonstrated that the expressive role was predominant in individual behavior (see Chapter 5). In other words, the ratings of the behavior of the parents in the study families were largely determined by the manner in which they related to one another in their marital roles, conducted themselves with their children and got along with other household members, such as relatives, friends and neighbors.

At the start of the study the behavior of the fathers was more likely to be rated as being adequate (53 percent) than that of the mothers (38 percent). This difference does not denote greater interpersonal competence on the part of the father but rather his reduced involvement in family living. Non-involvement also characterizes the unmarried fathers, who were rated (98 out of 171 were omitted) when they maintained a significant relationship with mother and child. Fathers were less likely than mothers to manifest inadequate behavior because their partial and socially sanctioned withdrawal from child rearing precluded a negative assessment.

In spite of the greater apparent degree of adequacy, or absence of data about limitations in interpersonal competence, fathers show overall more low functioning (12 percent) than do mothers (6 percent). The marginal or submarginal functioning of the father generally indicates failure to meet such socially expected role obligations as financially supporting the family—where he was in a position to do so—or failure in meeting the wife's basic needs for companionship, sexual satisfaction, and social and emotional support.

Marital status and social class were highly and significantly related to the roles of the mothers as well as fathers (gammas between +0.50 and

+0.80, chi squares significant beyond the .1 percent level). This is evidence that out-of-wedlock status and membership in the lower social classes represent compelling circumstances affecting the behavior of individuals. This statement carries no implication of a cause and effect relationship. Few people would challenge the notion that being cast in the role of an unwed mother or male head of household with little formal education and few marketable occupational skills due to a particular home atmosphere sets serious limitations upon individual functioning. On the other hand, it is conceivable that poor individual functioning, whatever its cause, can create or contribute to out-of-wedlock status or lower-class existence.

The relationship between race and level of individual role behavior follows a pattern observed in other aspects of family functioning. When social class is held constant there is a significant association between being black or white and the adequacy of the mother's or father's role performance. In Class 6 only the mother's behavior shows a significant relationship to race (gamma = +0.48, X^2 = 13.44, 2 d.f., p<.01), in Class 1-4 neither role sets are significantly related, but in Class 5, both the individual behavior of the mother and the father bear a moderately high, statistically significant relationship to being white (gamma = +0.38, X^2 = 9.48, 2 d.f., p<.01; gamma = +0.49, X^2 = 18.26, 2 d.f., p< .001).

Individual behavior and adjustment, putting the spotlight on interpersonal functioning, also brings together a variety of psychosocial roles, the totality of which reflect racial differences and social status differences in performance level. Overall black-white differences, in part a function of class position (the correlation between being white and individual behavior when class is not controlled is gamma = +0.53, 2 d.f., X^2 = 45.11, p<.001 for the mother and gamma = +0.50, X^2 = 42.58, 2 d.f., p<.001 for the father), are reflected in parental behavior at least at the lower class levels.

The interpersonal relationship, as Chapters 5 and 9 have shown, is a key dimension in the life of the young family. Interpersonal functioning revolves heavily around the relationship among adults, particularly husband and wife, which dominates the family at this life-cycle stage. These relationships, by and large, both within and outside the family, are influenced by the social structure, the one notable exception being relationship to household members other than nuclear family. Attempts at explaining this exception concentrated on the more selective nature of joint living arrangements as compared to other relationship patterns, making relationship to other household members less a function of specific status and social situations. The quality of the marital relationship was strongly correlated with various types of activities and satisfactions reported by the mother, high among which were sharing social and recreational life and mutual sexual enjoyment. All indices of the interpersonal relationship among these young families revealed a pattern of role and task performance which leaned in the direction of adequacy and showed disturbed functioning confined to a minority not exceeding one-eighth of the study population.

NOTES

1. Gurin, Veroff, and Feld, *op. cit.*, pp. 97-98.

2. *Ibid.*

3. Hicks and Platt in a survey of research on marital happiness in the sixties recommend discarding the concept for research purposes. Hicks and Platt, *loc. cit.*, p. 569.

4. Responses were grouped as follows: Family functioning was dichotomized into "highs" and "lows" on the basis of total score. On the question of the marriage meeting with the wife's expectations, the response categories were "generally" versus the combined answers in "somewhat" and "rarely or not at all." N = 378.

5. Geismar, "Family Functioning as an Index of Need for Welfare Services," pp. 99-113.

6. For details see Chapter 15.

7. The computation of factor scores is explained in Chapter 5.

8. Hill, *loc. cit.*, pp. 126-139. Blood and Wolfe, *op. cit.*, pp. 47-74.

9. A residual group of 3 percent had other persons, usually relatives, assume partial or total responsibility for financial management.

10. In roughly one-fourth of the families, mothers did the disciplining jointly with others, generally relatives of the family.

11. Hicks and Platt, *op. cit.*, p. 569.

10.

Child Bearing: Planning and Happenstance

Alice Rossi, who asserts that maternity is to the woman what work is to the man, writes, "On the level of cultural values men have no freedom of choice where work is concerned: they must work to secure their status as adult men. The equivalent for women has been maternity."[1] The fact that half of all married couples have a child during their first year of marriage and 90 percent now produce at least one offspring before the end of their reproductive years[2] lends some support to the Rossi thesis.

There are, of course, fluctuations over time in the intensity of cultural pressures concerning parenthood. During the depression of the 1930s, says Rossi, a widespread awareness of the economic hardships accompanying parenthood served to discourage couples from having children. A different set of pressures operated after World War II, during a period marked by relative affluence.[3] The rise in wages and salaries, the widespread use of labor-saving devices in the home, the greater availability of housing and play space, particularly in suburban areas, and a concomitant societal tendency to seek gratification in the private spheres of home and family were economic and ideological trends sharply reflected in the American birth rate.[4] A drop in the birth rate since the early 1960s, although less readily explainable in purely economic terms, appears to reflect a variety of influences, particularly the emancipation movement of women, concern about the population explosion and the availability of improved methods of birth control.

Among countries furnishing information, the United States outranks many industrially developed countries in what its citizens consider the average size of the ideal family. Preferred family size is larger here than in a number of less-developed countries or areas, such as Jamaica, Puerto Rico and certain urban centers in India.[5] The ideals do not necessarily correspond to the actual number of children families have, and there is a tendency for women in less-developed countries to have more children than they desire. The same discrepancy is found among social status groups within the United States, with lower-class families having more children than they want while the number of children in the upper classes comes reasonably close to the preferred number.[6]

There is evidence that notions about the ideal family, like the number of children actually born, have fluctuated in this country. A Gallup Poll found in 1941 that 27 percent of women thought that four or more children were ideal for the average family. By 1955, Freedman, Whelpton and Campbell found the proportion of women preferring that sized family had risen to 49 percent. Whereas Gallup discovered that 40 percent of women thought the one-or two-child family ideal, Freedman *et al.* noted that only 19 percent expressed such a preference in 1955.[7] The direction of change in the ideal situation corresponds, as far as can be judged by the sparse attitude data, to the direction of change in the actual number of children born in the United States. This would be expected in view of the broad correspondence between the number of children born and the number desired.

NUMBER OF CHILDREN DESIRED BY STUDY FAMILIES

A study by Rainwater in the early 1960s shows that three children is the modal number mentioned as ideal by the middle class and four children by the lower classes.[8] Our own study families expressed a more conservative preference, either because the research was done several years after the Rainwater study at a time when the trend was toward smaller families[9] or because Newark, with its poor housing conditions, imposes special barriers on larger families. A further explanation for the difference may be found in the wording of the studies. The surveys which we have cited sought to find out what the woman or parents consider the ideal family. In our present sample the mothers were questioned more directly on how many children they would like to have. One would assume, of course, that the concept of ideal size is closely linked to what a mother considers appropriate for herself, but it is possible, nonetheless, that working-class and lower-class mothers might answer differently when responding to what they view as an ideal situation as compared to their own condition.

Whatever the reasons, the young mothers in the sample wanted a somewhat smaller family than the ideal cited in the aforementioned studies. For the total sample of 555 families initially part of the research project, the mean number of children desired was 2.37, with a mode of two represented by 37 percent of the responses. Twenty-four percent of the mothers expressed a desire for one child and three children, respectively, and the remainder, 15 percent of the research population, stated that they wanted four or more children.

Social class bears a statistically significant relationship to the number of children mothers desire (gamma = +.27, X^2 = 11.09, 2 d.f., p < .01). There is, then, in our sample a tendency for the mothers of the two higher statuses to want more children than those of lowest status, as is shown in Exhibit 10.1. This finding is not in accord with the observations by Rainwater, who showed the same tendency in the opposite direction.[10] Other studies, however, show relatively little class difference in expected family size.[11] In our sample, differences between Class 1-4 and 5 are minimal as Exhibit 10.1 shows,[12] but mothers in Class 6 are considerably more likely to desire a one-child family than the mothers in the two higher status groups. This difference is largely accounted for by the responses of black OW mothers (most of whom belonged to Class 6), which differed widely from those of the black married mothers. Seventy-four percent of the black unwed mothers compared to only 10 percent of the black married women expressed a preference for a single child.

The unmarried mother, black or white, favors a smaller family (mean number of children desired is 1.43) than the married one (mean number of children desired is 2.67), and the direction though not the magnitude of the difference is maintained when the comparison is extended to black married and unmarried mothers (mean numbers of children desired are 2.33 and 1.43, respectively; the difference is statistically significant: X^2 = 99.08, 1 d.f., p < .001).

White mothers in our sample want more children than do their black counterparts (mean numbers desired are 2.99 and 1.99). Judging by the class differences reported earlier, one is prone to explain the ethnic difference in social status terms. However, a comparison of black and white responses with class held constant shows this supposition to be incorrect. Negro mothers in all three social status groups are more likely than white mothers to prefer a small family. Thus, black motherhood was correlated with a desire for fewer children (Q = +0.75 in Class 1-4, X^2 = 12.57, 1 d.f., p < .001; Q = +0.70 in Class 5, X^2 = 30.57, 1 d.f., p < .001; and Q = +0.69 in Class 6, X^2 = 12.79, 1 d.f., p < .001). The mean number of children desired by black and white mothers respectively were 2.00 and 2.72 in Class 1-4, 2.13 and 3.15 in Class 5, and 1.79 and 3.05 in Class 6. As cross-tabulations in Exhibit 10.1 have already shown, class differences are quite small, and they are overshadowed by ethnic differences which indicate that whites in the two higher classes desired .72 and 1.02 children more on the average than blacks and 1.26 children more than members of Class 6.

What is noteworthy in these data is not so much the lack of difference

in the number of children desired among different status groups — a
finding in line with the conclusions of other studies[13] —but the Negroes'
consistently more conservative preference compared with whites. The
explanation may well lie in the fact that blacks who are more disadvantaged than whites have translated their perception of the socioeconomic
handicaps into differential norms of family size.

EXHIBIT 10.1: RELATIONSHIP OF NUMBER OF CHILDREN MOTHERS
DESIRE AND FAMILIES' SOCIAL CLASS

| SOCIAL CLASS | NUMBER OF CHILDREN DESIRED — PERCENTAGES | | | | | |
| | | | | | Total | |
	4 or More	3	2	1	%	N
1-4	13.2	34.2	38.1	14.5	100	76
5	19.1	24.7	41.2	15.0	100	194
6	12.3	15.4	30.0	42.3	100	130

NUMBER OF CHILDREN BORN
AND EFFORTS TO CONTROL FAMILY SIZE

To what extent is the expression of preference a guide to actual childbearing behavior? Our data, extending roughly only four to five years
beyond the birth of the first child, unfortunately do not cover the total
period of fecundity. It will be recalled that 175 control group families
remained in the project until its termination, and our fertility data are
taken from this group. Status and racial intragroup differences on preferences for family size were similar to the total sample of 555 families
analyzed above. (For details on demographic comparisons see Chapter
15.)

Given the limitation of these data the question can be posed as follows:
Is the expression of preference for family size after the appearance of
the first child any guide to the rate of fertility during the next five
years? The answer is no, as can be seen from the data presented below:
Negro mothers have more children than white mothers, low-status families are more fertile than those of higher status, and black mothers in
every social class give birth to more children than white mothers. The
smallest discrepancy between statuses is in the number of children born
to married and unmarried black mothers. Unmarried black mothers,
who answered more conservatively on family size, had a mean number
of 2.04 children as compared to 2.02 for married black mothers. This
difference is small indeed and accounted for by a 5 percent surplus of
OW mothers who had three and four children (30 percent and 25 percent,

respectively). By contrast, more unmarried than married mothers (33 percent versus 28 percent) had only one child at the end of the study period.

The mean number of children born is 1.80 for Class 1-4, 1.93 for Class 5 and 2.08 for Class 6. The percentages of families having but one child during the study period were 40 percent, 27 percent and 34 percent. Differences for the three classes were statistically significant (gamma = -0.40, X^2_i=6.50, 2 d.f., p<.05). The mean number of children born to black and white mothers in each class grouping were 1.92 and 1.72 in Class 1-4, 2.00 and 1.77 in Class 5, and 2.07 and 1.75 in Class 6. These differences fell short of statistical significance.

One can conjecture that the number of children born during the project period is correlated with the fertility rates of the mothers during their entire childbearing phase. If this is the case the data from the present study would lend some support to the notion that the discrepancy between the desired number of children and the actual number born becomes larger as we go down the social status ladder.[14]

The most immediate explanation for this — as well as for the black-white differential — is the use of birth control. Lower status groups use it significantly less consistently than those of upper status. The percentages for families using birth control regularly at the start of the research were 59 percent in Class 1-4, 50 percent in Class 5 and 22 percent in Class 6, differences which have a high level of statistical significance (X^2 = 47.43, 2 d.f., p<.001, gamma = +0.48). At each status level blacks are less likely to use birth control devices than whites, but the differences are statistically significant only in Class 6 (X^2 = 12.32, 1 d.f., p<.001).

Reasons cited for the more limited use of birth control measures and facilities by the lower classes are a lack of financial means to use better (generally private) health services, lack of education on the subject, lack of information on where to find resources and a widespread failure to plan ahead.

What accounts for the lesser use of birth control devices by Negroes than whites? This is not readily explained except perhaps in terms of the mothers' knowledge of birth control practices or readiness to employ them. Thirty (18 percent) of the 171 black mothers who did not use birth control said they had no information whatsoever on the subject. None of the 72 white mothers who did not use birth control cited ignorance as a reason. In Classes 5 and 6, 13 percent and 19 percent of the black mothers but no white mothers professed ignorance as a reason for nonuse.[15] Reasons given three to five times as often by black women as by whites (but in each case not exceeding 10 percent of the reasons cited) were the beliefs that birth control measures are harmful and too much trouble to use. In each instance Negro mothers rather than white mothers in the two lower-status groups voiced such beliefs during the interview.

Use of birth control services, interestingly enough, does not emerge as a factor favoring the white over the black population. At the start of the project such services were used by fewer than 5 percent of the population, and in each status group Negro families were a little more likely to make use of them than white families. This picture did not change much during the course of the study. Religion as a reason for not employing birth control measures, cited by nearly one-third of the white mothers who did not use it, is given by only 1 percent of the female black respondents. The explanation here lies in the fact that in the study population Catholicism, which takes the most consistent and uncompromising position against birth control, had only 5 percent adherents among the Negroes but 77 percent among the whites.

In brief, the expression of preference for family size is not a good predictor of the number of children the mothers in the major status and racial groups are going to bear during the early stages of the family life cycle. It could be argued, of course, that the limited research period is no test of people's true intentions and that lower-class and Negro families simply have whatever number of children they wish to have in more rapid succession. Our data show that during the early childbearing period covered in this research black mothers and lower-class mothers came much closer to closing the gap between the number of children desired and the number born, as shown in Exhibit 10.2. (Black Class 6 mothers already had slightly more children than originally wanted.) The argument of a relationship between social and racial status, on the one hand, and discrepancy between number of children desired and number born could, therefore, be refuted by showing that the lower-status groups are more likely than the higher ones to have their desired number of children more rapidly.[16] The evidence from our study and others (see below) does not, however, point in this direction.

EXHIBIT 10.2: RATIO BETWEEN NUMBER OF CHILDREN BORN AND DESIRED

SOCIAL CLASS	Black Mothers	White Mothers	Total Sample
1-4	.72	.55	.61
5	.83	.52	.69
6	1.04	.64	1.01
Total sample	.90	.54	—

On an individual basis there is no significant correlation (Q= +0.17) between the number of children a woman desired after she had her first child and the number of children she bore during the period of the study. The lack of consistency can be explained in part by the fact that the child-bearing period studied covers only about one-fifth or one-sixth of a woman's period of fecundity (though perhaps as much as half the period of time when she is likely to have her children) and perhaps because the expressed preference for number of children appears to change somewhat over time.

The issue of change over time was explored by asking mothers "How many children would you like to have?" three times during the course of the project — at the beginning, the middle and the end. These time points were roughly one and a half to two years apart, varying with the total length of time the family stayed with the project. The comparison, confined only to the 175 control group families in the study until the end, showed minor and statistically not significant fluctuation over time. The coefficient of concordance (W) — as a test of similarity among groups in preferred family size — among ranks for mean number of children desired at three points in time for 14 sample groupings (total sample; married and OW; three class groupings; Negro and white; and Negro and white at the three class levels) was +0.20 and not significant at the 5 percent level. The only relatively high measure of regularity observed in this analysis was the low rank or lowest average number of children wanted at the midway point of the study. In seven out of the 14 sample groups, the respondents cited on the average a lower number of children wanted at the midpoint of the study than at its beginning or end. This could be an indication that two to three years after the birth of the first child — a time that frequently coincides with another pregnancy or birth — special problems may encourage greater conservatism on family size. This also coincides with the period of lowest or most problematic family functioning during the course of the study. This latter issue will be dealt with in Chapter 15.

For the research population as a whole the shifts in family size preference from the beginning to the end of the project are very small (mean numbers of children wanted were 2.56 at the beginning and 2.73 at the end), but differ in direction for the subgroups of the sample. Class 1-4 showed a downward shift from a mean of 2.96 to 2.58. Class 6, by contrast, moved up from 2.05 to 2.75, while Class 5 revealed no change in preference, remaining at 2.78. These findings coincide with the results of the research by Rainwater who concluded that "when middle class men and women shift their family size preference as time goes on they do so in the direction of a smaller size; when lower class people shift it is in the direction of a larger size."[17]

Rainwater's explanation for the class differential in shifting preferences for family size is as follows: Middle-class families scale down their earlier desires in the face of the realities of child rearing's great demands upon the energy and resources of family heads. The lower class' upward shift, on the other hand, indicates a passive acceptance of what is considered the inevitable arrival of children.[18]

Blacks, who are predominantly lower class, shifted their preferences upward from a mean of 2.25 to 2.63, while whites, who are more strongly represented in the higher status groups, adjusted it downward from 3.24 to 2.91. Black unmarried mothers, heavily concentrated in Class 6, increased their preference from a mean of 1.58 at the start of the study[19] to a mean of 2.58 at its end. It appears that during the process of rearing a first child, the unmarried mother becomes more accepting of the idea of having a larger family.

We have shown earlier that there is little relationship between family size preference expressed at the start of the project and the number of children actually born during the study's course. But midpoint in the study preference is significantly correlated with the number of children born ($Q = +0.56$, $X^2 = 7.87$, 1 d.f., $p < .01$). The association between number of children and preference stated at the study's termination is even higher (gamma $= +0.77$, $X^2 = 26.72$, 1 d.f., $p < .001$). In effect stated preference and actual behavior come together, probably because the mother's ideals or values are modified by reality. Lower-status families adjust to the reality of already having given birth to about as many children as they had initially desired and to the great likelihood of bearing more before the period of fecundity ends. Higher-status families, impressed by the demands on family resources which accompany children, and confident that birth can be controlled, lose some of their enthusiasm for having a large family (three to four children on the average) and opt for a smaller number instead (two or three).

Aside from differing attitudes towards family size, what other components of family life relate to the number of children born during the early stages of family life? The regular use of birth control, we find, bears little relationship ($Q = 0.28$, $p = N.S.$) to the number of children born during the project. Contraception, it seems, is only one of several factors determining whether a young family will have children born in quick succession or just one child during the early family stages. Other conditions likely to influence the reproduction rate are the woman's fecundity and the frequency of sexual relations. The latter, obviously, is largely dependent upon the partner's absence or presence.

The most commonly used contraceptive device is the condom (35 percent of the families) followed by the oral pill (28 percent), jelly and other chemicals (14 percent), rhythm method (10 percent), diaphragm (7 percent) and miscellaneous techniques including intrauterine devices (IUD),[20] douche, withdrawal and others (6 percent). Differences among status and ethnic groups were relatively minor, rarely exceeding 10 percent. An exception was the rhythm method, which was used by 20 percent of the white population, 77 percent of whom were Catholic, but by fewer than 1 percent of the blacks, who had only a 5 percent Catholic representation.

The 175 study families who remained in the project provided data for a longitudinal analysis of birth control over the project period. Twenty-eight percent of that group used birth control regularly at the beginning of the study,[21] 47 percent at the midpoint and 56 percent at the end. That rise was paralleled in each social class, but it was proportionately most dramatic in Class 6 (from 9 percent to 33 percent to 48 percent) which, nonetheless, did not employ birth control measures as widely (48 percent) as Class 1-4 (70 percent) at the project's end. The other spectacular increase took place among unwed mothers (from 2 percent to 32 percent to 42 percent), representing in large measure a concern over the arrival of more out-of-wedlock children. The most characteristic change in birth control methods in the longitudinal study group was an increase in the use of the oral contraceptive or pills (from 34 percent to 51 percent to 57 percent). This was most pronounced in Class 6 (from 25 percent to 52 percent to 69 percent) and among black unwed mothers (from 0 percent to 70 percent to 63 percent; N = 27), who constituted 61 percent of that status group.

All in all, therefore, study families as a total group as well as in their status subgroupings showed a tendency toward a wider use of birth control measures when the number of children in their families increased and the gap between the desired and the actual number narrowed. Reuben Hill and associates observed in a Puerto Rican study that birth control tends to be used more for terminating a family's growth than for spacing children.[22]

The woman's appraisal of her sexual experience as being positive or not within a year of its inception shows no relationship to the number of children she produced during the five years after she delivered her first child. The age at which she had her first sexual intercourse (13 percent had their first experience at age 15 or less, 58 percent below age 18) is negatively related to the number of children she bore (gamma = -0.31, X^2 = 11.42, 1 d.f., p $<$ .001). In other words, those mothers who experience sex at a younger age bear more children. We cannot explain the behavior mechanisms underlying this relationship. It is possible that earlier sexual experience is related to more impulsive behavior and less family planning early in the life cycle. Or perhaps sexual precocity indicates greater readiness to bear children or at least to have more closely spaced children.

Mutual sexual satisfaction as opposed to unilateral or one-sided satisfaction at the time the research began or ended bears no significant relation to family size. Neither do the wife's satisfactions with marriage, the husband's employment, income, or social and recreational life, either at the beginning or end of the study, show a significant relationship to the number of children born.

The character of family functioning at the start of the research program showed a consistent negative relationship to the number of children born during the course of the study, i.e., the more problem-ridden families had more children. Gammas were moderately low, ranging from -0.13 to -0.35 for the individual areas and not statistically significant. Among the three major components the interpersonal-expressive factor alone correlated significantly with the rate of childbirth during the study period (gamma = -0.22, $X^2 = 13.42$, 6 d.f., p $<$.05).

Although the magnitude of these relationships is low and generally not statistically significant, the high measure of consistency between the variables suggests that we are not dealing with a random relationship. Interpersonal-expressive functioning in particular — comprising family relationships, social and emotional care of children, and informal social activities — appears to be related to the size of the family during the early span of the family life cycle. The direction of this relationship, by the design of the research, makes family functioning the "causal" variable. Social functioning was assessed at the start of the project after the birth of the first child. The total number of children included in this analysis took account of all the offspring, two-thirds of whom were born following that first measurement of social functioning. The number of additional children could, therefore, be related in some degree to the way in which the family managed their interpersonal relations. Families rated in the bottom quartile of cases on the interpersonal dimension were between three and four times as likely to have three or more children (40 percent) than those rated in the top quartile (12 percent). Families in the top quartile were about one-half more likely to have only one child (25 percent) than those in the bottom quartile (16 percent).

Having three or more children — 20 percent of the longitudinal sample had three, 5 percent had four — over the relatively short space of five years could generally be viewed as poor spacing since the mother is forced to proceed directly from one pregnancy to the next. She is unable to recuperate physically and psychologically from pregnancy and child-bearing, and she is presented simultaneously with the double burden of infant care and toddler supervision. In the face of these facts, we assert that the family exhibiting more considerate relationships is also the one that restricts the number of children born during a limited time period.

Although our data are not conclusive, they point in the direction of a nexus between child spacing and early family functioning, particularly in the interpersonal area. Differences are similar for level of family functioning and social class membership, as is shown in Exhibit 10.3. The strong correlation observed in Chapter 6 between social status and the nature of family functioning leads to the conclusion that they interact and, together with other status and attitudinal factors enumerated above, produce distinct differences in fertility rates during the early phase of the family cycle. Given the limitations inherent in the short time-span covered by our research, it appears that the rate at which children are born into the family is both an important dependent variable, i.e., it is affected by numerous behavior and status factors, as well as a potentially significant independent variable. We merely touched upon the latter in showing the connection between the number of children born and changing conceptions of desirable family size. The issue of the arrival of children in the young family as an independent variable will be dealt with further as we consider the subject of family growth and changes in family functioning in Chapter 15.

EXHIBIT 10.3: MEAN NUMBER OF CHILDREN BORN DURING THE PROJECT BY LEVEL OF FUNCTIONING AND SOCIAL CLASS

LEVEL OF FAMILY FUNCTIONING	Mean No. of Children	Social Class	Mean No. of Children
High[a]	1.79[b]	1-4	1.80
Medium-High	1.88	5	1.93
Medium-Low	2.08	6	2.08
Low	2.27		

[a]For an explanation of categories see Chapter 5.
[b]Based on contingency tables the correlations were as follows: for levels of functioning $Q = -0.38$, $x^2 = 4.57$, 1 d.f., $p < .05$; for social class gamma $= -0.40$, $x^2 = 6.50$, 2 d.f., $p < .05$.

NOTES

1. Rossi, *loc. cit.*, p. 366.

2. Gerald R. Leslie, *The Family in Social Context*, New York: Oxford University Press, 1967, p. 512.

3. Rossi, *loc. cit.*, p. 366.

4. Ferris, *op. cit.*, pp. 50-51.

5. Rainwater, *Family Design*, pp. 119-120.

6. *Ibid.*, p. 123.

7. Ronald Freedman, P. K. Whelpton, and Arthur A. Campbell, *Family Planning, Sterility, and Population Growth*, New York: McGraw-Hill Book Company, Inc., 1959, p. 233.

8. Rainwater, *Family Design*, p. 121.

9. Data from Gallup surveys in 1960, 1963 and 1966 show a decline in the number of families considering four children as the ideal number from 45 percent to 42 percent to 35 percent. *New York Times*, February 1971, p. 31.

10. Rainwater, *Family Design*, p. 122.

11. Cavan, *loc. cit.*, p. 558.

12. The mean number of children desired are 2.47 for Class 1-4, 2.54 for Class 5, and 2.02 for Class 6. These means take into account the preferences of a few mothers for five children.

13. Cavan, *loc. cit.*, p. 558.

14. Cavan, *loc. cit.*, pp. 558-559.

15. In Class 1-4, no mother, black or white, cited ignorance as a reason for not wishing to use birth control.

16. Cavan, *loc. cit.*, pp. 558-559.

17. Rainwater, *Family Design*, pp. 124-125.

18. *Ibid.*, pp. 124-131.

19. To avoid confusion, this mean pertains to OWs among the 175 families studied longitudinally while the earlier mean figure of 1.43 applies to unwed mothers in the cross-sectional study sample of 555.

20. The IUD, considered a fairly reliable birth control method, was used by only one woman in the study population. At the time of the survey the local chapter of Planned Parenthood, following reports of high failure rate, was not recommending its use for clients.

21. This is 13 percent less than for the sample as a whole, a larger — and unexplained — deviation from the total sample than was encountered on most other dimensions, demographic as well as behavioral.

22. Reuben Hill, J. Mayone Stycos, and Kurt W. Back, *The Family and Population Control*, Chapel Hill: The University of North Carolina Press, 1959, p. 185.

11.

Child Rearing: Attitudes and Behavior

Family relationships change over time, responding to the fluctuating needs of both parents and children, needs conditioned by intellectual maturity, physical stamina, social interest, size of the family group and so forth. Economic practices also vary in keeping with the changing financial requirements of the family, the wage earner's job experience, the home dependency of the children and other factors. In each instance functions must be modified to meet the needs and wants of family members.

In the case of care and training of children, there are probably fewer continuities in the five-year period following the birth of the first child because of the great changes occurring in the object or objects of such care. The growth of the child from infant to kindergarten pupil requires some drastic adaptations, both in child care and in the approach and methods of those who are basically responsible for him. In the infancy stage physical care predominates, and training and emotional care enter only to a very limited extent. That situation changes radically by the time the child responds meaningfully to commands; and the situation is modified to a greater extent by the time he begins to assume independence in feeding, carrying out toilet functions and dressing himself. The emergence of problems in the care and training of children may not designate a worsening of the situation or reduced competence but may merely indicate difficulty on the part of the inexperienced in performing such new tasks as setting limits or mediating sibling rivalry.

Shifts in the care and training of children denote a change in emphasis — from primarily gratifying physical needs to care patterns shaped by the desire to develop communication, teach values and instill discipline. Young mothers in the study appear more adept at carrying out the earlier functions. The reason for this is undoubtedly the fact that the care of toddlers or preschoolers is inherently more complex. In contrast

to infant care, interaction with young children involves two active partners, bringing a higher probability of disturbed functioning because of
behavior or relationship problems than when the child is capable of
limited response. Thus we find that negative change in the care and
training of children denotes not so much a lessening of competence in
performing the same tasks as lesser competence in handling more complex tasks.

The present chapter does not claim to report in depth on the process of
early child care in young urban families. The social functioning focus of
the research, which constitutes a broader approach to family research —
attempting to cover multiple dimensions of family life — precludes a
detailed study of child-rearing practices. The analysis before us is concerned with three aspects of child rearing: the division of labor in child
care; the attitudes of the mother on a scale which for lack of a better
term could be described as covering the progressive-retrogressive dimension (i.e., parental attitudes placed on a continuum ranging from pro-
gressive to retrogressive as characterized by the popular literature on
education); and the relationship between mothers' attitudes and the
quality of child rearing as measured by the family functioning instrument used in this study.

This choice of focus is designed to permit the study of child rearing
within a basically sociological framework, namely, that of role allocation
and the influence of orientation on practice. Our hypothesis is that status group factors, particularly social class rather than family adequacy,
account for the variations in beliefs and behavior patterns in the care
and training of children. We feel that there are distinct status differences in the practices used to bring up children although no clear-cut
relationship has yet been found between these differences and family
functioning on the one hand and various results of child-rearing on the
other. Perhaps this is because the process of care and socialization is
multifaceted and extremely complex. Wesley Becker has stressed this
point of view, stating that "it is painfully apparent that the social scientists who have set for themselves the task of unraveling the consequences of child rearing practices are faced with a problem with infinite
complexities."[1] The complexity of the whole child-rearing process, covering the interaction of personalities, situations and techniques, makes
it extremely difficult to isolate positive or negative elements. If our
hypothesis is proved correct it does not indicate that research relating
practice to outcome is futile but rather points to the need for sophisticated efforts where the effects of personality, situation, status and
method are carefully controlled. An investigation into the relationship

between certain aspects of child rearing and status is an important link in the chain of such inquiries.

THE DIVISION OF LABOR IN CHILD CARE

To maintain a family unit work must be divided efficiently so that specific tasks are carried out by family members, individually or jointly. In socializing children the functioning of the family depends upon role allocations in which one member, generally the father, assumes major responsibility for support and the other, usually the mother, takes on the duties of homemaker and chief child socializer.

Providing support requires "mediation"[2] between the family and other systems such as business, industry, educational institutions, government and so forth; while child care and homemaking require activities that are concentrated mainly within the family system itself. The dominant norms of role allocation in America assign the major responsibility for child care to the mother while the father is expected to carry out the economic functions and assist the mother as his masculine tasks permit. There is generally a greater tendency to share tasks in the home — including child care — at the beginning of the family life cycle and to increase the specialization in task performance as time goes on.[3] The companionship ideal of sharing is also more closely adhered to by the middle class than working-class couples.[4]

The information supplied by the mothers on the sharing of child care indicated patterns for the group as a whole did not differ very widely from the prevailing norms. Nonetheless, there were considerable intra-group differences which we shall consider in some detail. For the population as a whole, there was relatively little sharing in the physical tasks of child care. Only seven families (or 1.3 percent out of 555 in the study) reported a more or less equal allocation of physical child care functions. These were Class 5, reasonably adequately functioning families where the father had agreed to contribute his full share to the physical care of the child. Otherwise, the mother carried out the physical care alone in 36 percent of the families and received some help from the father in 34 percent. In 19 percent of the cases the mother was assisted by another person, often paid, enabling her to work outside the home. Three-fifths of these cases were unwed mothers. In the remaining families (10 percent) another person, often a relative, assumed the major physical child-care functions.

The disciplining of the children who, at the time covered by the inquiry, were still below school age showed a pattern of task sharing similar to physical care with one exception. Mothers (18 percent) more often stated that disciplining and setting limits for the child or children was carried out to an equal extent by the father and the mother. In 26 percent of the families the mother was the only person who disciplined the child and in 32 percent the mother assumed the major responsibility and the father shared to some extent. In 1 percent of the families the father was the major disciplinarian and the mother played a supporting role. In 14 percent of the families the mother was assisted by another person, and in 7 percent another person was mainly responsible for the discipline of the children. In the residual category of "other caretakers" were eight families (2 percent) — seven headed by unwed mothers — where child care was largely the responsibility of a relative.

The degree to which the parents shared caring for the children was strongly class related.[5] The higher the social class, the greater the degree of sharing in physical care (gamma = +0.52, X^2 = 54.74, 2 d.f., p < .001) and in the disciplining of children (gamma = +0.62, X^2 = 83.83, 2 d.f., p < .001). The percentages for joint care arrangements for Class 1-4, 5 and 6 were 79 percent, 64 percent and 24 percent in the case of disciplining, and for the physical care of children, the percentages were 53 percent, 44 percent and 16 percent, respectively. Ethnic differences were even greater, but the more meaningful comparison of black and white when class was held constant revealed significant differences at all three class levels. The comparisons are shown in Exhibit 11.1.

EXHIBIT 11.1: NEGRO-WHITE DIFFERENCES IN PARENTAL TASK SHARING IN THE CARE OF CHILDREN WITH SOCIAL CLASS HELD CONSTANT

TYPE OF CHILD CARE	Social Class	Q^a	X^2	D.F.	P	N
Physical care	1-4	+0.47	4.75	1	<.05	97
	5	+0.29	4.63	1	<.05	232
	6	+0.65	10.47	1	<.01	186
Discipline	1-4	+0.73	14.64	1	<.001	96
	5	+0.59	19.85	1	<.001	231
	6	+0.66	14.36	1	<.001	185

[a]The comparison is between parental sharing and any other arrangement, such as the mother alone or another person or the mother assuming the task in combination with someone else.

At every social status level, we observe that Negro parents are significantly less likely than white parents to assume a joint arrangement in the care of the child. Differences are particularly pronounced in the disciplining of children, which might indicate either a somewhat greater relative readiness by black fathers to share in physical care than in discipline or a relatively greater withdrawal by the black fathers compared to white fathers as the child grows a little older. We do not have longitudinal data on the husband-wife sharing of child care to determine the reasons for the differences. Nevertheless, Exhibit 11.1 supplies strong evidence that parental egalitarianism in caring for the child is much less prevalent among Negroes than whites, and that this relationship exists independently of class level.[6]

The families' overall level of social functioning was also significantly related to the sharing of child care. The degree of adequacy in social functioning when divided into a high and low group was highly and significantly associated with parental sharing of tasks in the physical care ($Q = +0.63$, $X^2 = 56.78$, 1 d.f., p <.001) and discipline of children ($Q = +0.68$, $X^2 = 82.83$, 1 d.f., p<.001). Better-functioning families were definitely more prone to carry out tasks jointly. For the highest quartile, 82 percent of the families shared the disciplining of the child and 57 percent shared the physical care in one form or another. For the lowest quartile, the corresponding proportions were 22 percent and 13 percent, respectively.

The correlations between level of family functioning and the extent of sharing in child care tasks may reflect an interaction of status and behavioral factors. Families with disturbed patterns of social functioning are much more heavily represented in the lower status groups, as was shown in Chapter 6, and high status was significantly associated with joint care, as noted above. The foregoing correlations lead to the supposition that social class figured prominently in the correlation between adequacy in family functioning and joint parental child care. In order to determine the independent effect of social functioning upon the latter activity, the two factors were correlated with social class held constant. Results of this analysis show that family functioning by itself bears a significant relationship to parental task sharing in the physical care and disciplining of children. The degree of association between the factors is much lower when class is held constant. (The average Q or phi[7] coefficient was +0.44. Chi square values in descending class order and for disciplining and physical care, respectively, were 32.90, 7.27, 10.87; and 8.11, 7.00, 12.08, with one degree of freedom. P values were 3.841 for the 5 percent level, 6.635 for the 1 percent level and 10.827 for the 0.1 percent level.)

The evidence contained in the foregoing set of data indicates that the family's overall level of social functioning has an effect on the manner in which parents allocate child care tasks between themselves. Better-functioning families are more likely to make child care a joint enterprise even though the mother in nearly all instances carries the major share of the work and responsibility. A measure of egalitarianism between husband and wife, it appears, is greatly aided when family members get along reasonably well and the family does not face any major problems.

CHILD REARING: ATTITUDES AND BEHAVIOR

What are attitudes and behavior that help shape patterns of shared parental involvement in child care? To answer this our researchers relied upon a battery of existing tests, ten scales of the Parental Attitude Research Instrument (better known as the PARI[8]), which is designed to tap the woman's attitudes considered relevant to her role as mother. Of the 22 subscales making up the PARI, the present research utilized ten which prior tests had proven to be the most reliable and valid. The criteria for inclusion in this study were as follows: the subscale, according to the Schaefer-Bell survey in 1958 covering two to six reliability tests, must have yielded two or more test-retest coefficients of $+0.70$ or higher, and none below $+0.50$[9]; The subscale must have shown a correlation to family functioning of $\pm.20$ or more.[10] The ten subscales which were included in the present research are given below. Following the name of each subscale is a one-sentence explanation of its contents in brackets.

1. Fostering dependency (children should be sheltered from the hardships of life).
2. Breaking the will (the mean streak must be taken out of children).
3. Martyrdom (children should realize that their mothers make sacrifices on their behalf).
4. Excluding outside influences (the child must be made to feel that the mother is always right).
5. Avoidance of communication (giving too much attention to children's problems is asking for trouble).
6. Inconsiderateness of husband (husbands do not appreciate the contributions of mothers).
7. Suppression of sexuality (young children should be sheltered from sex).
8. Ascendance of mother (for the good of the family mother must take charge of things in the home).
9. Intrusiveness (mother must know what is going on in her children's minds).
10. Acceleration of development (the child should be pushed in his physical and emotional development).

The ten PARI subscales, although a haphazard sampling of issues connected to the socialization of children, do tap some attitudinal aspects of functioning which are important guides to an individual's manifest behavior. The use of PARI scale scores, nonetheless, requires an acceptance of certain assumptions regarding the meaning of response patterns. These assumptions are that low scores on the individual scales represent desirable maternal attitudes and that such expressed feelings, denoting nonauthoritarianism, permissiveness, egalitarianism and flexibility in child care, bear a direct relationship to the mothers' overt child-rearing behavior.

Scale items collected by Schaefer and Bell deal with issues treated in the child development literature, and decisions on the desirable direction of scoring (desirable being low) reflect the findings of studies and the views of experts." Catherine S. Chilman, in an extensive literature survey of child rearing, found it possible to identify a series of child-rearing patterns which authorities agreed were beneficial to children's positive emotional health, social acceptance, educational achievement and good character formation.[12] Becker and Krug, surveying studies using the PARI, found modest agreement between scale scores and related scores obtained by interview and observation.[13] Gerhart and Geismar, relating four PARI subscales to indices of maternal child-rearing behavior, found that the scale has little predictive power, i.e., does not relate significantly to the future behavior of the mother.[14]

Use of the PARI in this study is, therefore, predicated on the contention that low scoring on the ten scales shows at least a predisposition to act in the present in ways which are considered conducive to the positive socialization of children. We are trying to determine whether there is a link between the attitudinal pattern expressed by the mothers in the study and the overall social functioning of the family in general and functioning in the area of care and training of children, in particular.

Exhibit 11.2 presents the correlations and levels of significance of each of the ten PARI subscales employed in the research to the area care and training of children, to the subcategories physical care, and training methods and emotional care, and finally to the overall social functioning of the family. The correlations pertain to attitudes expressed at approximately the same time that an assessment was made of the actual social functioning of the family.

The evidence contained in Exhibit 11.2 strongly supports the supposition that mothers' attitudes on the ten dimensions represented by the PARI are directly associated with the way in which they carry out child-rearing tasks as well as the way in which the family as a whole functions. All gamma correlations are negative, ranging from low (-0.18 to moderately high (-0.44) and statistically significant with a single exception, the correlation of avoidance of communication to training methods and emotional care, which falls barely short of significance at the 5 percent level. Selected attitudes on child rearing, we find, furnish some indication of the family's degree of adequacy in the child-care process, but such attitudes explain only a small amount of the variance and are only one of several factors which account for the quality of their performance. The PARI subscales correlated most closely with physical care (mean gamma = -0.38 compared to mean gammas of -0.27 for care and training of children, -0.24 for training methods and emotional care and -0.31 for total family functioning). The explanation here rests with the fact that attitudes and behavior were studied and correlated at a time when child rearing in most families centered on meeting the needs of infants or toddlers.

The correlations in Exhibit 11.2 carry the implicit assumption that parents put present beliefs about child raising into action. There is more inherent logic in accepting such a premise than in assuming the opposite, namely that practice has shaped beliefs, at least with regard to the care and training of children. At the time of the first research contact, the families had barely started their child-raising careers, although they may have had ideas on the subject for some time. This is not to deny the possibility that first experiences in child care may have also helped shape their values and ideas on the subject. Nonetheless, a safe assumption regarding the interpretation of this analysis puts the direction of casual interaction mainly from beliefs to practices, rather than in the opposite direction.

This thesis should be considered valid only with regard to the relationship between PARI scores and child care; it does not refer to the PARI scores and total family functioning. Although the concept of a two-way relationship between the variables may have some validity here, it would seem more logical to postulate the family's overall functioning as a factor influencing child care beliefs rather than the reverse. In other words, the significant correlations between attitudes expressed on the ten PARI scales are being interpreted to mean that a family's general level of getting along together, looking after members' well-being, and conforming to laws and mores exerts a measure of influence on the formulation of child-rearing beliefs. Satisfactory functioning, it appears, discourages authoritarian and punitive attitudes. The question of whether such a relationship is largely the result of class differences will be examined below.

The survey by Becker and Krug of studies using the PARI showed that the scores produced by the instrument are affected by the educational level of the mother and, to a lesser extent, by the occupational level of the father as well.[15] A direct association between these factors indicates that more formal education and/or a life style associated with higher status occupations means exposure to a child-rearing philosophy

EXHIBIT 11.2: TEN PARI SCALES AND THEIR RELATIONSHIP TO CHILD CARE AND TOTAL FAMILY FUNCTIONING[a]

PARI SUBSCALE	Care and Training of Children				Physical Care				Training Methods and Emotional Care				Total Family Functioning			
	Gamma	X^2	D.F.	P	Gamma	X^2	D.F.	P	Gamma	X^2	D.F.	P	Gamma	X^2	D.F.	P
Fostering dependency	-0.20	14.36	4	<.01	-0.35	27.92	4	<.001	-0.18	10.74	4	<.05	-0.28	30.54	6	<.001
Breaking the will	-0.27	18.38	4	<.01	-0.39	29.51	4	<.001	-0.24	13.60	4	<.01	-0.27	29.59	6	<.001
Martyrdom	-0.30	25.37	4	<.001	-0.44	43.16	4	<.001	-0.27	18.43	4	<.01	-0.37	56.37	6	<.001
Excluding outside influences	-0.20	14.44	4	<.01	-0.26	16.09	4	<.01	-0.20	10.98	4	<.05	-0.23	27.92	6	<.001
Avoidance of communication	-0.22	13.71	4	<.01	-0.33	22.71	4	<.001	-0.18	8.98	4	N.S.	-0.25	28.60	6	<.001
Inconsiderateness of husband	-0.34	20.44	4	<.001	-0.42	28.80	4	<.001	-0.29	15.88	4	<.01	-0.42	53.48	6	<.001
Suppression of sexuality	-0.34	28.20	4	<.001	-0.44	37.16	4	<.001	-0.29	19.91	4	<.001	-0.34	50.25	6	<.001
Ascendance of mother	-0.31	23.37	4	<.001	-0.42	43.29	4	<.001	-0.29	19.08	4	<.001	-0.36	54.76	6	<.001
Intrusiveness	-0.23	14.86	4	<.01	-0.38	31.85	4	<.01	-0.19	13.43	4	<.01	-0.25	31.62	6	<.01
Acceleration of development	-0.26	17.23	4	<.01	-0.33	23.69	4	<.01	-0.26	15.57	4	<.01	-0.32	43.44	6	<.001
Mean gammas	-0.27				-0.38				-0.24				-0.31			

[a]The potential Ns for the tables are the 555 families who made up the initial study population. The actual Ns are reduced by ten to twenty cases because of missing information except for inconsiderateness of husband where, because of fathers' absences, only 428 responses were recorded.

characterized by less authoritarianism, repressiveness, mother dominance and punitive behavior than is found in the lower classes. Finding a strong association between PARI attitudes and class does not diminish the value of the earlier results, which demonstrated a significant connection between child-care ideas and practices. Differences in attitudes and behavior which are connected with status do, however, have great significance for the development of policy. If child-rearing behavior is tied to attitudes on that subject, and if such attitudes are part of a larger complex of beliefs that are endemic to social position, efforts at modifying such behavior must take into account the total constellation of attitudes and social situation. Such an awareness will help to discourage attempts to change one without paying attention to the other.

We inquired into the class relatedness of child-rearing attitudes by correlating PARI scores with the social status classification used throughout this project. The striking effect of status factors is indicated by the fact that social status and ethnic group membership were significantly and negatively correlated with the responses on all the PARI subscales. Higher social status was associated significantly (all chi squares were significant beyond the 0.1 percent level) with answers representing behavior considered to be conducive to positive child rearing. The mean (gamma) coefficient of correlation is -0.41 with a range for the ten subscales of -0.29 to -0.49. Being a white mother was likewise correlated with higher PARI scores at a highly significant level (all chi squares were significant at the 0.1 percent level), and the degree of association is represented by a mean (gamma) coefficient of -0.46 with a range from -0.32 to -0.63.

The lack of independence of the ethnic factor from the status variable is shown by the fact that race is no longer consistently correlated to scoring on the PARI when allowance is made for social class. Out of 30 correlations between the two variables, only 15 are statistically significant. Statistical significance or nonsignificance is not equally distributed. In the top social status group, Class 1-4, only the subscale acceleration of development differentiates significantly between the responses of Negroes and whites (p<.01). In Class 5, six correlations are significant at the 5 percent level or beyond, and in Class 6, eight correlations attain that level of statistical significance. Acceleration of development is the sole PARI subscale which correlates significantly with being white in every status grouping at the 1 percent level or better. (Gamma coefficients are -0.56 in Class 1-4, -0.54 in Class 5 and -0.65 in Class 6.)

The distribution of correlations can be interpreted to mean that social position indeed affects the beliefs of blacks and whites on the subject of child rearing. Racial differences in beliefs are mitigated by social position. The higher a black mother's social status, the less likely she is to differ from her white counterpart on the subject of authoritarianism, restrictiveness, domination, etc., in child rearing. Acceleration of development is the only attitudinal dimension on which black mothers of every class are stronger advocates than white mothers. A possible and rather plausible explanation, applicable especially to the higher status mothers, may be that blacks as a minority group are more anxious to gain a headstart for their children, making up for past deficiencies.

An unmarried mother is likely to perform less than adequately in the care and training of children (see Exhibit 8.1), but this does not necessarily mean she has a less favorable set of attitudes toward the process of child rearing. When a comparison is made — as was done throughout most of this volume on PARI scores between black married and black unmarried mothers — only three subscales discriminated significantly in favor of the married women at the 5 percent level or better. The scales were fostering dependency (gamma = -0.30), martyrdom (gamma = -0.31) and excluding outside influences (gamma = -0.16). Black mothers who find themselves illegitimately pregnant do not seem to differ greatly in degree of ideological sophistication, perhaps because they are exposed to fundamentally the same media and social influences. By contrast, the discrepancy between married and unmarried mothers is substantial in their actual performance of child-care tasks. Task performance is more heavily dependent than beliefs or orientation on the social and economic conditions facing the young mothers.

Given the finding that differences in the mothers' notions about child care appear to have some influence on the quality of their performance, and adding to this the observation that differences in beliefs are to a large extent a function of status differences, does the set of attitudes covered by the PARI correlate with child care practices within each major class status? To obtain an answer to this question the ten subscales were correlated with the main category care and training of children for each of the three social strata.

The results, in the form of 30 correlations, 10 for each status level, indicate a lack of evidence that the ideas of mothers about child rearing are associated with their actual practices independently of their class membership. Only two of the correlations reached statistical significance at the 5 percent level. The exceptions were the association between care and training of children and the subscales inconsiderateness of husband (gamma = -0.65, X = 12.31, 2 d.f., p < .01) and acceleration of development (gamma = -0.43, X = 8.91, 2 d.f., P < .02). These two significant correlations were found in Class 1-4, the top social status group, only. Why the 7 percent of statistically significant associations between child-care beliefs and practice should be concentrated in Class 1-4 is not clear. The predominant relationship pattern is, nonetheless, one of nonassociation between attitudes and practices when allowance is made for the effects of class.

Given this lack of evidence of a relationship between attitudes and behavior when social status is the intervening variable, do we find that the class factor also tends to mitigate the relationship between these variables when the causal flow is assumed to move in the opposite direction? Earlier in this chaper we showed a significant relationship between total family functioning and the ten PARI scales which was interpreted to mean that the family's level of social functioning has some influence on child-rearing attitudes (Exhibit 11.2). Does this relationship indeed constitute a genuine association between functioning and beliefs or does it reflect mainly the substantial attitudinal differences that were shown to exist among the social strata of the research population?

The foregoing question was tested by examining the relationship between overall social functioning and PARI scores within the three social class levels employed in the study. The results show that there is a much more limited association between family functioning and child-rearing beliefs when class is held constant than when it is not. Cross-tabulations between the variables were significant in the following status groups and for the following PARI scales: Class 1-4: inconsiderateness of husband ($Q = -0.75$, $X^2 = 7.69$, 1 d.f., $p < .01$); Class 5: martyrdom (gamma $= -.30$, $X^2 = 9.46$, 2 d.f.,[16] $p < .01$); inconsiderateness of husband (gamma $= -0.36$, $X^2 = 9.08$, $p < .02$); suppression of sexuality (gamma $= -0.27$, $X^2 = 6.58$, $p < .05$); ascendance of mother (gamma $= -0.22$, $X^2 = 6.01$, $p < .05$); Class 6: ascendance of mother (gamma $= -0.30$, $X^2 = 6.30$, $p < .05$). As the above data are juxtaposed with the previously shown higher and consistently significant correlations between PARI scores and total family functioning without class being controlled and with the separate correlations of the PARI with class and social functioning, the conclusion emerges that social class is a more decisive influence in the formulation of child-care attitudes than is the family's overall social functioning. In other words, whether the presumed direction of influence is from beliefs to practices or in the reverse direction, social class emerges as a major mediating factor between the two variables.

Do these findings lead to the conclusion that beliefs are not significant factors for social functioning because differences are determined by social class? There has been a general tendency in the social sciences in recent years to view behavior patterns of different status and culture groups in relativistic and nonevaluative terms. The approach represents a defensive stance against another position — held by some leading behavior scientists during the earlier part of this century — in which social and cultural deviations are equated with the innate inferiority of one group or another.

The danger in a value-free approach to behavioral differences lies in the possibility that the dysfunctional consequences of differences could very well be disregarded. Granted that sociocultural variations frequently represent viable alternatives to which people have adapted and for which they may have developed an affinity, the existence of dysfunctional behavior patterns and beliefs in the realm of family living has been documented. [17] Therefore, even though striking intraclass relationships between ideological sophistication and the nature of practices are absent the relationship between these variables can still be considered without limiting the investigation to any one specific social or cultural context. The knowledge of intergroup differences has greatest relevance for the development of a strategy of intervention rather than for decision-making on whether change is needed.

The final aspect of this investigation into the relationship between beliefs and behavior in the area of child socialization deals with the possible connections between attitudes expressed and future behavior. We seek to determine whether the battery of opinions expressed through the ten PARI subscales can serve as an index of the direction in which child-care practices change over time.

Past efforts to establish the predictive power of the PARI have not been particularly successful. [18] Here we attempted to correlate PARI scores for the 175 study families who remained in the project until termination to changes in four types of functioning: care and training of children; physical care and training methods, and emotional care; and total family functioning. The analysis comprises 40 cross-tabulations between attitudes expressed at the start of the research and changes occurring during the course of the study.

The results furnish only limited evidence of the predictive power of the PARI scales when prediction is defined as an ability to forecast future behavior. Eight cross-tabulations showed significant associations between high scores on a subscale and positive change in functioning during the study period; these correlations, however, were quite low, ranging from -0.17 to -0.27. Changes in physical care of the child was significantly associated with fostering dependency (gamma = -0.20, X^2 = 17.33,[19] p <.01), martyrdom (gamma = -0.24, X^2 = 18.16, p <.01), avoidance of communication (gamma = -0.17, X^2 = 13.74, p <.01), inconsiderateness of husband (gamma = -0.27, X^2 = 15.37, p <.01), ascendance of mother (gamma = -0.21, X^2 = 17.12, p < .01) and acceleration of development (gamma = -0.15, X^2 = 13.29, p < .01). Beyond these the area care and training of children and the subcategory training methods and emotional care also related significantly to breaking the will (gammas are -0.20 and -0.24, X^2's are 9.63 and 10.70, both significant with 4 d.f. at the .05 level). The greater prevalence of physical care among factors whose change correlated with selected child-rearing attitudes suggests that behavior changes in that area represented a more sensitive index of modification in child-care competence because it permitted, considering the young age of the child, a more meaningful assessment of actual parental performance than did training methods and emotional care. According to this line of reasoning, difficulties in disciplining children occurred in more families as the study progressed, largely as a function of the children's development rather than the parents' orientation or degree of adequacy.[20] Physical care, it can be assumed, was measured from a more precise baseline because it could be evaluated more accurately at the beginning of the study. We must stress, nonetheless, that none of the attitudinal positions registered at the beginning of the research supplied a sensitive index of future changes in overall family functioning, and only one attitudinal dimension had a bearing on closely related child-rearing behavior.

The present chapter has furnished evidence of the influence of social and, to a lesser extent, ethnic factors upon the role allocations and beliefs in the area of child care and socialization. The assignment of roles in the family, contrary to our research hypothesis, was equally or even more strongly influenced by the family's level of functioning, and a statistically significant association between role sharing and level of social functioning was maintained when the class factor was held constant. Child-care practices, like many other forms of family behavior, are firmly rooted not only in a family's status conditions but also in its competence in meeting the health-welfare needs of members and its adherence to or deviance from social norms.

The situation is different with regard to beliefs. Attitudes on child rearing, in line with our hypothesis, appear much more strongly related to status factors than level of functioning, although the latter does exhibit a degree of association. Opinions held by mothers, it seems, are particularly influenced by a family's position in the status hierarchy, while the adequacy of overall family functioning appears to play a secondary role in the formulation of beliefs.

The association between social class and attitudes as well as practices has been rather well documented in the child-rearing literature.[21] A less common form of inquiry, which was also undertaken here, sought to establish the nexus between beliefs and practices in general, and in their class-specific context in particular. A finding of significant relationships between selected beliefs and child-care patterns across class lines but not — allowing for some exceptions — within status boundaries poses this question of importance for the student and practitioner of child-care. If the research continues to show that certain class-related beliefs are clearly dysfunctional for child-rearing behavior, what are the implications of a strategy aimed at improving functioning in this area?

The issue is complex and goes beyond the data furnished here. Basically, the answer needs to be given in terms of whether the cost of dysfunctionality, arising out of class-related behavior, exceeds the cost of changing familiar and perhaps convenient practices. Clearly, however, those seeking an answer to this question are not likely to accept either one of two widespread and doctrinaire positions, namely, that the behavior patterns of the culturally more sophisticated are naturally superior or that the practices of the lower classes are invariably most functional to their way of life.

NOTES

1. Wesley C. Becker, "Consequences of Different Kinds of Parental Discipline," in Martin L. Hoffman and Lois Wladis Hoffman (editors), *Review of Child Development Research, Volume I*, New York: Russell Sage Foundation, 1964, pp. 169-208, p. 201.

2. John A. Clausen, "Family Structure, Socialization, and Personality," in Lois Wladis Hoffman and Martin L. Hoffman (editors), *Review of Child Development Research, Volume II*, New York: Russell Sage Foundation, 1966, pp. 1-53, p. 35.

3. Blood and Wolfe, *op. cit.*, pp. 47-74. Clausen, *loc. cit.*, p. 37.

4. Cavan, *loc. cit.*, p. 550; p. 564 ff.

5. Walters and Stinnett in a survey of the literature on the parent-child relationship conclude that "basic differences exist in parent child relationships according to social class which reflect different living conditions." James Walters and Nick Stinnett, "Parent-Child Relationships: A Decade Review of Research," *Journal of Marriage and the Family*, 1971, 33 (February) pp. 70-111; p. 95.

6. The analysis made no allowance for the presence of unwed mothers, most of whom were not living with the father of the child. However, there were so few cases of joint child care in black families of Class 6 (where more OWs were concentrated) that removing unwed mothers from the analysis would not have fundamentally changed the results. On the other hand, the above described relationship held true in Classes 1-4 and 5 in which only 6 percent and 15 percent of the families were headed by OWs.

7. The phi coefficient was used to measure degree of association in two instances where the Q gave a distorted picture of the relationship because of very low cell frequencies.

8. Earl S. Schaefer and Richard Q. Bell, *loc. cit.*, pp. 339-361.

9. *Ibid.*, p. 350.

10. Unpublished research with a sample of 216 young families in New Jersey. A high score on the PARI denotes a disapproved child-rearing attitude.

11. Schaefer and Bell, *loc. cit.*, pp. 341-348.

12. Catherine S. Chilman, *op. cit.*

13. Wesley C. Becker and Ronald S. Krug, "The Parent Attitude Research Instrument — A Research Review," *Child Development*, 1965, 36 (June) pp. 329-365.

14. Ursula Gerhart and Ludwig L. Geismar, "The PARI as a Predictor of Parental Behavior," *Child Welfare*, 1969, 58 (December) pp. 602-605.

15. Becker and Krug, *loc. cit.*, pp. 338-343.

16. All the remaining chi square tests have two degrees of freedom.

17. Catherine S. Chilman, "Child-Rearing and Family Relationship Patterns of the Very Poor," *Welfare in Review*, 1965, 3 (January) pp. 9-19; also Chilman, *Growing Up Poor*.

18. Becker and Krug, *loc. cit.*, Gerhart and Geismar, "The PARI as a Predictor of Parental Behavior," *loc. cit.*

19. All tables have four degrees of freedom.

20. The average negative movement was .79 of a scale point in training methods and emotional care but only .13 in physical care.

21. For a survey of research see Cavan, *loc. cit.*, pp. 559-567, and Bettye M. Caldwell, "The Effects of Infant Care," in Martin L. Hoffman and Lois Wladis Hoffman (editors), *Review of Child Development Research, Vol. I*, New York: Russell Sage Foundation, 1964, pp. 9-87; pp. 67-75.

12.

Economic Practices

"Throughout human history," Ralph Linton has written, "the family has been an economic unit....Romantic love, or even congeniality between partners, is even now less important in most societies than economic need to keep the family clothed, fed, and sheltered."[1] In a 1955 study by Blood and Wolfe, a sample of Michigan wives listed the economic goals of decent standard of living, including house, clothes, car and so forth, as the least valuable part of marriage when given a chance to choose among five aspects including companionship, a chance to have children, the husband's understanding of the wife's problems and feelings, and his expression to her of love and affection.[2] The researchers interpreted the findings to mean that most wives did not rate economic goals very high because "Michigan families in 1955 took it for granted that a good income would come their way."[3] To support this contention, Blood and Wolfe showed that "wives who mention the standard of living first are largely those who can't take it for granted,"[4] namely, those married to men with low incomes or downward mobility, i.e., those who have failed to reach the occupational level of their fathers.

Although we did not collect data on personal goals, an earlier study of a representative sample of 216 urban families, most of them Newark residents, showed that young mothers rated better housing, a good education for the children and financial security above other goals including a happy home life.[5] The low rating of the latter goal was interpreted to mean — and this is a reversal of the explanation given by Blood and Wolfe — that young mothers tend to take a happy home life more for granted than good housing and economic security. The difference in the responses of the two populations probably reflects dissimilarities in the economic situation of the families. The Michigan group in 1955 had larger incomes than the Eastern study families ten years later (no income data were available for the 1963 study that used a comparable sample) even though the intervening decade brought an annual rise in the cost of living. Ten percent of the Michigan families as compared to 20 percent of the New Jersey families earned under $3,000 yearly. Forty-one percent of the former as compared to 47 percent of the latter were making less than $5,000 per annum. The proportion earning over $5,000 was 59 percent in the Michigan research and 53 percent in the New Jersey study population. Although the younger age of the Newark families may account to some extent for the lower income and may also reflect more limited financial need (Michigan families had a mean number of 2.1 children while New Jersey families had one child each), we must remember that the Michigan study included 20 percent farm families whose real income probably was larger than reported.

The above comparison suggests that the importance families assigned to material goals bears a relationship to their economic situation, and that people order their priorities according to where they feel the pinch. Older, somewhat more affluent families in Michigan were more keenly aware of those aspects of life that may have eluded them after many years of marriage — love and companionship. Young families, recently married but for the most part members of deprived minorities living under conditions of urban blight, are mostly concerned about improving their economic situation.

DIMENSIONS OF ECONOMIC FUNCTIONING

The economic function of the young families in the present study — according to factor analysis of subcategories of social functioning (see Chapter 5) — is represented by four sets of activities which are subcategories of family functioning, three of which belong under the main category economic practices and one under use of community resources. The former three are source and amount of income, job situation and use of money; the latter is use of social agencies. Factor analysis shows that those families using social agencies have found them primarily an economic resource. This may be a particular characteristic of young and predominantly lower-status families; and it may not be true for older families, who make more extensive use of resources offering other (non-economic) forms of service. Mainly the 555 sample families made use of public assistance agencies (between 18 percent and 28 percent turned to them during the project period), public housing (9 percent to 16 percent) and the local branches of the Office of Economic Opportunity (5 percent to 16 percent). In the aggregate only about 40 percent of the population used social agencies during the initial stage of the study. For them, use of social agencies represented an activity which parallels social functioning, summarized under source and amount of income. This would be especially true for those families (15 percent at the start of the project) who derived their income wholly or partly from public assistance.

The economic factor or dimension in social functioning serves in this study as the most comprehensive index indicating how the family manages in the establishment and maintenance of the material base sustaining family life. Since social status as measured in this study by way of education and occupation constitutes the main potential for economic adequacy, the high correlation between a family's class position and its economic functioning (see Chapter 6 for details) was practically a foregone conclusion. Put differently, the family whose head has more education and a higher status occupation is likely to have a better income, more job satisfaction, less difficulty in managing money and less trouble in dealing with social agencies if they are used at all. If the higher status family does use a public resource providing a service that has economic value, it will weigh its utility against the alternative of doing without or purchasing the service from a private source.[6] For that reason the higher status family is less likely than one of lower status to make poor use of a social agency. However, the very limited instances of turning to social agencies by the higher status group (4 percent of Class 1-4 used social agencies) did not provide a satisfactory test of this thesis. Adequacy of social agency use is defined in the St. Paul Scale of Family Functioning. Essentially, it means cooperating with agency personnel, following through on recommendations, not dropping out of treatment, etc. Adequacy of social agency use was positively but not significantly correlated with class (gamma = +0.24).

The three other components of the economic factor are more closely tied to the social status of a family as indicated by the following gamma correlations: source and amount of income +0.68 (X^2 = 125.79, 4 d.f., p<.001); job situation +0.54 (X^2 = 50.63, 4 d.f., p<.001); and use of money +0.47 (X^2 = 44.62, 4 d.f., p<.001). The last of these four is the only subdimension which deals mostly with the internal aspects of economic behavior, namely, with the way money is managed.

In relating adequacy of the families' economic performance to the social characteristics, it is helpful to make a distinction between those functions which involve dependence and interaction with other systems and those which are more or less independent of them. We hypothesize that class and ethnic factors are clearly correlated with economic functions involving other systems. In American society social and racial characteristics reflect above all the nature of those forms of social functioning where the individual is in contact with and dependent on the larger society, which has put a premium on these distinctions in the first place.

For purposes of this analysis we shall focus only on the three subcategories in the area of economic practices excluding the subcategory use of social agencies since it is inapplicable to over half the sample and to all but a tiny minority of higher status families.

Source and amount of income represents the subdimension of family functioning where the family's dependence on the surrounding society is by far the greatest. The possibilities of obtaining a satisfying job are heavily dependent upon one's education, job training and experience, and to no small extent — as has been documented frequently in recent years — upon one's skin color. For that reason we should expect source and amount of income to be most closely related to the status variables used in this research.

The subcategory job situation represents a type of functioning involving a high degree of interaction with the economic system but a somewhat lesser dependence upon the business and industrial community or other employers than does source and amount of income. We make this distinction because the economic system, when it selects and discriminates, does so most readily by offering or refusing jobs. Once a person is employed the condition of his employment is, of course, also greatly influenced by his social and ethnic characteristics, but the transaction between employer and employee no longer wholly occurs at the acceptance-rejection level.

Use of money as a variable of analysis is obviously not completely independent of the social systems surrounding the family, for the adequacy with which a family manages money is in no small measure a function of the amount available for meeting family needs. Beyond this aspect of interdependence, budgeting and monetary decision-making becomes an internal matter to be decided upon by the family members themselves.

The measurement of source and amount of income combines under one heading several subdimensions of economic functioning. These are: specific source of income, i.e., employment versus support from relatives, insurance, public assistance or a combination of these; the amount of the family's annual gross income; work patterns of the main wage earner; type of occupation of the chief wage earner; employment of the mother; and the degree of satisfaction with the amount as well as the source of income. Each one of these factors will be considered from the perspectives of total group and subgroup characteristics.

Only two-thirds of the project families[7] (66 percent) were fully self-supporting, and 7 percent had their employment income supplemented by financial aid from relatives. At the other end of this continuum were the 9 percent of families — almost all unwed mothers — where the source of support was the extended family and 8 percent (82 percent of whom were unmarried mothers) whose sole support was public assistance. The remaining 10 percent of families supported themselves from income representing various combinations of the above sources and insurance, particularly unemployment insurance.

STATUS AND ETHNIC DIFFERENCES IN INCOME

The most dramatic differences between subgroups in the proportions of self-supporting families (aside from the married-unmarried differences which were 92 percent and 11 percent for black mothers) were those between black and white families (52 percent of black and 88 percent of white families were self-supporting) and the three social class groupings (1-4 — 91 percent, 5 — 82 percent and 6 — 35 percent). Self-support was, furthermore, highly and significantly correlated (X^2 = 117.21, 1 d.f., p< .001) with the families' overall social functioning as categorized in Chapter 5 (93 percent — High, 76 percent — Medium-High, 52 percent — Medium-Low and 32 percent — Low). Negro-white differences in the extent of self-support versus other forms of support were small and not statistically significant in the top social status group (92 percent of black and 87 percent of white families) but increased sharply at each of the next two lower status levels. Ninety-three percent of the whites as compared to 73 percent of the Negroes were fully self-supporting in Class 5 and 66 percent of the Negroes and 27 percent of the whites in Class 6, respectively. Both differences were clearly statistically significant (X^2's are 14.03 and 14.69, respectively, at 1 d.f., p< .001). Thus, the better educated and more highly skilled black head of a young family is able to furnish the full economic support for his family at about the same rate as his white counterpart. The less educated and less skilled Negro fares badly in this comparison, at least in part because the family head is more likely to be a woman (especially in Class 6, where about three-fifths of the families are headed by unmarried mothers). Unequal job opportunities, particularly pronounced in many skilled and semi-skilled occupations, may account for a good portion of the differences between self-support rates among black and white families.

The amount of gross annual family income reveals a distribution that is positively skewed as shown below:

The distinction between the two residual categories which were not included in the percentage base is as follows: thirty-seven families, 34 of whom were headed by unwed mothers living with relatives, could not

EXHIBIT 12.1: FAMILY INCOME OF STUDY FAMILIES

INCOME	Percent of Families	N
Annual income below $2,000	14.0%	66
Income between $2,000 and $2,999	7.0	33
Income between 3,000 and 3,999	14.9	70
Income between 4,000 and 4,999	15.1	71
Income between 5,000 and 5,999	18.7	88
Income between 6,000 and 6,999	10.4	49
Income between 7,000 and 7,999	8.5	40
Income between 8,000 and 8,999	4.7	22
Income between 9,000 and 9,999	1.0	5
Income of $10,000 and over	5.7	27
Total	100.0%	471
Amount of income could not be determined because of joint living arrangement with other family		37
No information given on income		47
Total N		555

produce a separate budget. Additionally, 47 cases were either unwilling or unable to furnish data on income.

We have already commented in Chapter 4 on the economic deprivation revealed in these data on family earnings. The internal income distribution — by research subgroups — reveals a picture that is essentially similar to that supplied by self-support data. Thirty-one percent of the blacks in contrast to 3 percent of the whites earn less than $3,000 per year. For the three social class groupings, 3 percent of Class 1-4, 9 percent of Class 5 and 49 percent of Class 6 earn less than $3,000 annually. In each of these class strata Negro families have a larger percentage of cases in the poverty-income category. In Class 1-4 no white families, contrasted with 11 percent of black families, earned less than $3,000 a year. In Class 5 the proportions were 1 percent and 14 percent, and in Class 6 they were 21 percent and 54 percent, respectively.

From these figures, based as they are on intraclass comparisons, income discrimination — in contrast with job discrimination between black and white families — shows up particularly strongly in the highest status group, especially when we take into account that the rate of self-support through employment is not significantly different (see above). The figures, though based on small Ns (60 white, 27 black Class 1-4 families), are consistent and even more striking as the comparison is expanded to other income brackets. Forty-one percent of blacks compared to 13 percent of whites in Class 1-4 earn less than $5,000 a year. Fifty-five percent of white families in that class have an income over $7,000 and 35 percent over $8,000. The parallel percentages for black families are 33 percent and 19 percent.

Income, like other indices of social status, is clearly correlated with the way in which a family functions. The general level of family functioning is inversely associated with low income, with 50 percent of the Low, 29 percent of the Medium-Low, 15 percent of the Medium-High and 3 percent of the High groups in social functioning earning less than $3,000 per year. Correlatively, the percentages of those earning over $7,000 yearly are 4 percent, 12 percent, 17 percent and 37 percent.

OCCUPATIONAL PATTERNS

Full-time work at one job is the predominant work pattern for male heads of the project families. This is equally true for black and white, different social classes and differing levels of family functioning. In two segments of the study population a substantially smaller proportion of men are employed full time, namely, in the group with the most problematic functioning and in white Class 6 families. Only 60 percent and 65 percent of the males in the two groups work full time in one position compared to roughly 80 percent in the other groups. The next most frequent occupational pattern for the group lowest in social functioning is unemployment (19 percent) and a full-time plus a part-time job (9 percent). The latter arrangement is second in frequency (10 percent to 15 percent) for the other social and ethnic status groups with the exception of Class 6 blacks, whose second most frequent pattern (9 percent) is unemployment.

Occupational data available for the heads of the families who were in the labor market[8] show 33 percent in the clerical, sales, technical and skilled blue-collar category. The next heaviest concentration is in the semiskilled group, comprising 24 percent of the heads of households. Seventeen percent can be classified as in unskilled and service jobs and 18 percent are unemployed, without occupation and, for the most part, dependent on public assistance. Finally, 8 percent of the family heads can be categorized in the broad category covering professional, semi-professional, managerial occupations and proprietors of businesses.

As expected, there is an exceedingly close relationship between occupational stratification and social class (gamma = +0.90, X^2 = 449.16, 8 d.f., p<.001) simply because occupation constitutes one of two indices (the other is education) in the system of status classification used here (Hollingshead). Income, by contrast, is not quite so closely associated with occupational level (gamma = +0.66, X^2 = 310.91, 12 d.f., p <.001) seemingly because the economic reward system in American society tends to favor certain skilled occupations over higher status professions and also because the latter tend to bestow deferred rather than immediate financial rewards. Not surprisingly, racial characteristics bear a close relationship to occupational stratification (gamma = +0.57, X^2 = 85.25, 4 d.f., p< .001). The contrasts are striking in the top and bottom occupational groups. Seventeen percent of whites as compared to 2 percent of blacks are classified as holding professional and managerial positions. By contrast, 3 percent of the whites but 27 percent of the Negroes are unemployed and have no occupation. The contrast is also substantial in the second highest occupational group, the clerical-sales, technical and skilled blue-collar category, where 44 percent of white and 26 percent of black heads of families are concentrated.

A comparison of occupational position of family heads by race with social class held constant reveals significant differences in two out of three status groups as shown in Exhibit 12.2.

EXHIBIT 12.2: RELATIONSHIP BETWEEN OCCUPATION OF FAMILY AND RACE WITH SOCIAL CLASS HELD CONSTANT

OCCUPATION	Class 1-4		Class 5		Class 6	
	White	Black	White	Black	White	Black
Professional, semiprofessional, managerial, proprietors	47.0	23.3	1.1	0.0	0.0	0.0
Clerical and kindred work, sales, technical skilled blue collar	50.0	66.7	50.0	38.2	10.7	3.8
Semiskilled operatives	0.0	10.0	39.3	42.7	10.7	12.8
Unskilled, service occupations	1.5	0.0	9.6	13.0	64.3	30.0
Unemployed, no occupation	1.5	0.0	0.0	6.1	14.3	53.4
Total percent	100.0	100.0	100.0	100.0	100.0	100.0
N	66	30	94	131	28	133
Gammas	+0.49		+0.26		+0.50	
X^2	4.81		3.70		14.08	
p with 1 d.f.[a]	< .05		N.S.		< .001	

[a]Chi squares were computed from 2 x 2 tables because the larger tables did not meet the requirements of the test.

The percentage distribution reveals that in each status group proportionately more whites are found in higher status occupations than blacks, which appears to be a contradiction in view of the fact that controlling the class factor should have eliminated most of the occupational differences between the two groups. The apparent contradiction hinges around the word "most." The three class groupings which combine education and occupation are broader than the five occupational categories and leave room for the emergence of differences, particularly at the two ends of the occupational scale. Thus, in the top status group over twice as many whites as blacks hold professional-managerial positions in spite of the fact that the combined educational and occupational background of the two is similar. In Class 5 no whites but 6 percent of the black heads of families have no employment, even though the overall educational and occupational status of the two groups is comparable.[9] In Class 6 the picture is somewhat blurred by the fact that many Negro heads of families are unwed mothers who, although potentially able to work, may have been held back because they preferred taking care of their child or had no recourse. In Class 1-4 a possible explanation for the occupational difference may be the relatively greater concentration of whites than blacks in the first two classes, 1 and 2 (of 66 whites in Class 1-4, only 30 or 45 percent were in Class 4; of 31 blacks in Class 1-4, 24 or 77 percent were in Class 4, and none in Class 1 and 2). That still leaves substantial occupational differences in favor of whites in Class 5 and proportionately more high-status blacks working in semiskilled occupations and more lower-class whites employed in white-collar and sales jobs.

Educational data available on the families in Exhibit 12.3 made it possible for us to test the notion (see footnote 9) that the inferior occupational status of the Negro heads of families was counterbalanced by their superior educational status. The test involves black-white comparison of mean levels of education for comparable occupational groups.

Exhibit 12.3 supports the suppositions that status similarity means in effect a higher educational level for Negro heads of families counterbalancing a lower occupational level, and that black heads of families, in spite of comparable or superior formal education, hold lower-status jobs.[10] The difference in mean educational level is especially pronounced for semiskilled workers in Classes 5 and 6. Only in the professional-managerial category of Class 1-4 do we find a reverse situation with whites having more formal education than blacks. The probable reasons for that were discussed above. On the basis of these data it is hard to escape the conclusion that black-white differences in occupational status

EXHIBIT 12.3: MEAN EDUCATIONAL LEVELS FOR WHITE AND NEGRO HEADS OF FAMILIES BY OCCUPATIONAL GROUPINGS AND SOCIAL CLASS

OCCUPATIONAL GROUPING	MEAN EDUCATION BY SOCIAL CLASS[a]					
	1-4		5		6	
	Whites	Negroes	Whites	Negroes	Whites	Negroes
Professional, semiprofessional, managerial, proprietors[b]	7.64	6.17				
Clerical and kindred workers, sales, technical skilled blue collar	6.13	6.28	5.52	5.64		
Semiskilled, operatives			5.31	5.68	3.67	5.25
Unskilled, service occupations			4.75	5.50	4.65	5.25
Unemployed, no occupation					4.33	5.19

[a]Means do not represent years of education but have approximately the following values:
4 = completed ninth grade; 6 = graduated high school; 8 = graduated college.

[b]No educational mean figures are given where there are fewer than three cases in one of the cell pairs. For Ns see Table 12.1.

in the various class strata reflect a difference in job opportunities.

Slightly over half (52 percent) of the women in the study went to work sometime during the tenure of the project[11] and thereby contributed to the family income. The intragroup variations were substantial but did not follow entirely the patterns of differences which emerged in earlier analysis. Thus, 40 percent of the women in the most adequately functioning families (High group) went to work either part time or full time in the course of the study. For the lower functioning groups the percentages were 64 percent (Medium-High), 48 percent (Medium-Low) and 57 percent (Low). In short, level of family functioning *per se* is not correlated with mothers going to work. Sixty-seven percent of black married mothers went to work but fewer than half that amount (29 percent) of white married mothers.[12] For the three social class groupings the percentage of women working was 30 percent (Class 1-4), 52 percent (Class 5) and 61 percent (Class 6). Negro-white comparisons in each one of these status groupings showed two to three times as many black mothers as white mothers employed.

It may be seen that a number of factors interplay here. More Negro mothers than white mothers go to work during the early years of marriage. The former are much more in need of the money because their family's gross income, which includes all earnings, is substantially below that of whites. For the same reason lower-class mothers are more prone to seek employment than those of the higher classes. But in each class grouping black women are much more likely to take a job than white ones (Class 1-4, 56 percent and 17 percent; Class 5, 65 percent and 37 percent; Class 6, 64 percent and 25 percent). The class differences for black mothers who work are not substantial; for neither group is there a consistent relationship to class (Class 5 has the largest proportion of black and white working mothers), but in combination, because of the increasing proportion of Negroes in each successively lower-class category, we find that the number of project mothers who go to work is inversely related with social class.

The higher proportion of working Negro mothers stands in contrast to the lower proportion of black fathers — as compared with white fathers — who are employed full time. This undoubtedly reflects a differential in the relative employment situation for black men and women. Low-paid, unskilled jobs, particularly in the service occupations, do not present the same barrier to black women as they do to black men.[13] Some of them have, in fact, traditionally been reserved for blacks. Furthermore, a black married woman, searching for additional family income, may be less reluctant to turn down such a job than a Negro male head of a household who requires a living wage to support the whole family. Additionally, the Negro subculture may have a more favorable attitude toward working women than white society.

SOURCE AND AMOUNT OF INCOME

Rating of the subcategory source and amount of income (adequate in 40 percent, near adequate in 31 percent, above marginal in 18 percent and marginal or less in 11 percent of the families) constitutes an overall evaluation of adequacy in this dimension of economic functioning. Its relationship to the major independent variables in the study is shown in Exhibit 12.4.

Exhibit 12.4 summarizes the close interrelationship between family income and the class factor as well as overall social functioning.[14] Even when we control for class, statistical differences in adequacy of income still exist between black and white families (except in Class 6), leaving blacks at a substantial economic disadvantage.

How does the actual income situation compare with the wife's assessment of the adequacy of her husband's income? Seventy-five percent of the white wives compared to 64 percent of the black wives thought their husbands' income adequate ($X^2 = 5.31$, 1 d.f., p < .05). The level of fam-

EXHIBIT 12.4: RELATIONSHIP OF SOURCE AND AMOUNT OF INCOME TO SOCIAL CLASS, ETHNICITY, ETHNICITY WITH CLASS CONTROLLED AND TOTAL FAMILY FUNCTIONING

STATUS VARIABLES	Gamma	x^2	D.F.	P	N
Social class	+0.68	125.79	4	<.001	536
White versus black	+0.62	68.85	2	<.001	523
White versus black Class 1-4	+0.58	6.27	1	<.02	97
White versus black Class 5	+0.44	12.15	1	<.001	231
White versus black Class 6	+0.35	0.98	1	N.S.	183
Total family functioning	+0.75	233.54	6	<.001	548

ily functioning was significantly correlated with the wives' satisfaction (X^2 = 70.10, 1 d.f., p<.001) and so was the social status of the husband (X^2 = 10.72, 2 d.f., p<.01). However, the women's satisfaction bore no significant relationship to racial characteristics when comparisons were made within the three class strata. Satisfaction with financial resources is not a completely relative matter but bears a relationship to the objective situation. However, it appears that attitudes don't differentiate as sharply on the race variable as actual conditions, suggesting that certain concessions to reality have been made in the expression of attitudes of satisfaction or dissatisfaction.

JOB SITUATION

The second dimension of economic functioning, job situation, is more personal and subjective than source and amount of income. Job situation signifies the way in which a person gets along at his job, i.e., enjoys his work, relates to his boss and fellow employees. Slightly under two-thirds (65 percent) of employed family heads reported conditions which could be rated as adequate, 31 percent were given ratings of below adequate and above marginal, and 4 percent were rated marginal or less, representing rather troubled work situations. Class and ethnic differences on job situation were statistically significant, but correlations were of a smaller magnitude than on the dimension source and amount of income (gamma r ated to class +0.54, X^2 = 50.63, 4 d.f., p<.001, gamma related to race or being white +0.22, X^2 = 9.22, 2 d.f., p<.01). There are no significant differences between Negroes and whites when class is controlled, which means that Negroes are about as well adjusted to their jobs as whites. Job satisfaction is mainly related to a worker's social class. Those in the higher socioeconomic brackets are more satisfied with their work for many reasons. The work may be more interesting, may pay better and may be more secure. Total family functioning, reflecting the interplay of psychological, social and economic factors in family life, is highly correlated with job situation (gamma +0.60, X^2 = 110.93, 6 d.f., p<.001).

The wife's satisfaction with her husband's job was taken into account in the rating of job situation, but data concerning whether the husband's employment meets with her expectations were tabulated separately. Sixty-eight percent of the wives state that they are basically satisfied with the work their husbands are doing. There is no significant relationship between that factor and the racial status of the family or its level of functioning, but the social status of the family is significantly related to it (gamma +0.46, X^2 = 20.57, 2 d.f., p<.001). The absence of a correlation between total family functioning and the wife's appraisal of the spouse's job may mean that wives, in contrast to the research coders, are able to view the husband's job outside the context of family life. Moreover, a wife may be willing to accentuate the positive as a tribute to her mate even though she is aware of the problems and limitations of her husband's employment.

USE OF MONEY

The third dimension or subcategory of economic functioning to be dealt with in the present analysis is use of money, or the manner in which the family makes decisions about spending. As stated earlier, there is probably a close connection between the amount of financial resources available to the family and the ability to budget. Decisions on financial management, as we learned in Chapter 9, are made in a fairly egalitarian manner in the young families, with the father as the sole decision-maker in only a minority (10 percent to 20 percent) of the cases.[15]

Use of money as an economic activity (subcategory) was rated as adequate for 64 percent of the families, near adequate or above marginal for 30 percent and marginal or lower for 6 percent of the cases. The degree of troubled functioning was similar to that for job situation, but less than source and amount of income. In contrast to the latter, use of money constitutes a form of social functioning in which individual psychosocial modes of adaptation (willingness to make do, accept limitations, etc.) mediate between the functions of the family and the social structure. The extent of interdependence between use of money and social and ethnic status is also more similar to the relationship of status and job situation than of status and source and amount of income. Thus, social class is associated significantly (gamma +0.47, X^2 = 44.62, 4 d.f., p<.001) with use of money as is race when class has not been controlled (gamma $+0.43$, X^2 = 22.24, 2 d.f., p<.001). However, when class is held constant, ethnicity is not significantly associated with use of money. On the other hand, the correlation between the latter and the family's overall level of social functioning is high and very significant (gamma $+0.78$, X^2 = 188.55, 6 d.f., p<.001), suggesting that a combination of interpersonal and social class characteristics tends to influence the ability of the families to manage money.

The foregoing data support the hypothesis that the dimension of economic functioning that is the most directly dependent on the economy or the community, source and amount of income, is most closely related to ethnic status and class position. Overall family functioning, on the other hand, showed a uniformly high statistical correlation to all three economic subcategories. These variables are neither conceptually nor statistically independent of family functioning. They are three of the four components (the fourth is use of social agencies and has application to only 39 percent of the research sample) making up the economic factor in family functioning. The relationship between economic and overall family functioning is, of course, a reciprocal one. Performance in the economic area affects the way the family functions as a psychosocial unit; this functioning, in turn, influences and sets limits to the performance of family members in the economic realm. The family's socioeconomic status, as we have learned, circumscribes their economic performance and interacts with the more personal, biopsychological characteristics of family members to generate diverse levels of functioning adequacy.

CHANGE IN ECONOMIC FUNCTIONING

The question of change in the families' social functioning will be dealt with in the final chapter. Nevertheless, we will address ourselves to it here briefly because it casts light on the internal dynamics of economic functioning. Comparisons will be confined to the 175 control families which remained in the study until the end.[16] The mean factor score for this group of families at the launching of the study was 62.94, and it had increased slightly to 63.61 when the project ended. [17] The small change indicates that the family did not experience a major change in its economic functioning during the project but was performing in a slightly more positive manner some four to five years after the birth of the first child than it did about one year after the baby's arrival. By itself this change in factor scores does not reveal the nature of any modifications in the components of economic functioning. However, a comparison of changes in the subcategories will uncover such modifications.

Change in the three main components of the economic factor works in opposite directions. In source and amount of income there is a very slight improvement in the situation as assessed by the researchers (the mean score is 7.08, with a value of 7 indicating no change). One of the components of such change is a rise in family income during the study period of roughly 27 percent (from a sample mean of $5,200 to $6,600),[18] which is considerably more than the rise in consumer prices during the study period.[19] This increase denotes improvements in wages and salaries that generally coincide with the early stages of a man's working career. Changes for this group were especially marked for families earning under $5,000 a year; the proportion of such families in the study group was reduced from 50 percent to 26 percent.

There was no change in the mean rating of job situation (mean change score is 7), but there was some decrease in the adequacy of social functioning on the dimension use of money. Quite obviously, the increase in financial resources did not match the greater needs resulting from the presence of more children in the family (the mean number increased from one to 1.97), better housing (59 percent lived in a residential neighborhood at the study's start compared to 73 percent at the end; the proportion living in single homes increased from 4 percent to 13 percent) and other improvements in standard of living.

The only dimension of more substantive change in the economic factor is that of use of social agencies, where measurement was confined to the largely lower-status families (40 percent) who had been using this resource. A change, represented by a mean movement score of 7.25, denotes greater improvement in social functioning than in any other specific dimension covered in this study. This positive change, incidentally, parallels change in the main category use of community resources,[20] clearly the area of greatest improvement in social functioning for the 175 study families.

During the tenure of the project, lower-class families and those with social problems showed greater gains in economic functioning than their counterparts. In the absence of good theory on the subject, one would have been inclined to hypothesize that low status and functioning problems at an early stage in the family life cycle would tend to predispose families toward negative change because initial handicaps might reduce the chances of successful coping in the economic realm. Such, however, was not the case. The data shown below reveal that low functioning families showed more positive than negative or zero movement. The reverse is true on a more extreme scale for families who functioned more adequately in an all-around way at the beginning of the study.

EXHIBIT 12.5:   RELATIONSHIP BETWEEN BEGINNING FAMILY
FUNCTIONING AND CHANGE IN ECONOMIC FUNCTIONING

CHANGE IN ECONOMIC FUNCTIONING (FACTOR)	OVERALL FAMILY FUNCTIONING AT THE BEGINNING OF THE STUDY	
	Low	High
Negative change	28%	35%
Zero change	19	36
Positive change	53	29
Total	100%	100%
N	72	103

Gamma = -0.30, x^2 = 10.69, 2 d.f., p $<$.01.

Greatest positive movement, as inspection of the detailed work table
(not shown here) reveals, was experienced by 17 (52 percent) of the 33
families in the most problem-ridden group. These 17 cases also constituted one-half of all the families who registered positive change. Other
more qualitative data in support of more positive movement on the part
of the more handicapped families emerges on the subject of self-support.
The data on self-support indicate a greater proportional increase for
families functioning at the lower half than for those at the upper half of
the continuum. The percentage increase for the former group was from
39 percent to 47 percent. For the latter it was from 82 percent to 85 percent. Correlatively, there was also a greater relative gain in self-support
for Class 6 families than for those of Class 5 and Class 1-4. The former
had 11 percent more family heads in the self-supporting group (a rise
from 34 percent to 45 percent), while there was only a 4 percent gain
(from 81 percent to 85 percent) in Class 5 families and a 3 percent decrease (from 93 percent to 90 percent) in the number of families in Class
1-4 who were entirely self-supporting. The data do not reveal whether
the greater positive change in economic functioning among the more
deprived families is the result of greater need, pressure toward social
conformity, better opportunities or a combination of these.

Whatever the multiple factors accounting for these assocations among
variables, it is very clear that the gains in economic functioning among
lower-class families are a relative matter. The socially disadvantaged
and more handicapped young families, responding both to need as well
as pressures to conform to societal norms of family life, are just a little
less likely than the more adequate families to show a deterioration and
considerably more likely to register positive change in economic functioning. But the relative gain does not go far toward closing the economic
gap. At the end of the study only 47 percent out of the low-functioning

group, compared to 39 percent at the start, were fully self-supporting. The comparative figures for the high-functioning group are 82 percent and 84 percent. The mean annual incomes for the two groups, though they rose about $150 more for the lower than the higher group, are still about $2,000 apart.

Economic change, of course, represents only one dimension, albeit an important one, in the change patterns in the social functioning of young families. Are economic changes characteristic of the more general modifications in family life, and do they correspond to changes in other dimensions of family functioning? These and related questions will be examined in Chapter 15.

NOTES

1. Ralph Linton, "Women in the Family," in J. E. Fairchild (editor), *Women, Society, and Sex*, New York: Sheridan House, 1952, pp. 67-82.

2. Blood and Wolfe, *op. cit.*, p. 81.

3. *Ibid.*, p. 80.

4. *Ibid.*, p. 81.

5. Geismar, *Preventive Intervention in Social Work*, p. 35.

6. This would apply particularly to housing, job training and employment services.

7. The N on these percentages is 554, which means information was available on all but one case.

8. This excludes unmarried mothers who are not in a position to take a job.

9. By the very nature of the modified Hollingshead Index of Social Position used here, it must be assumed that the amount of education of blacks is the equal of or superior to that of whites in most cells of Exhibit 12.2, for placement in one of the class strata (except for Class 1-4 which combines several educational and occupational groups — see p. 150) involves a reciprocal balancing of the educational and occupational factors.

10. This corresponds to the findings of Blau and Duncan which reveal that black males fall far behind white males in occupational attainment at every educational level. Peter M. Blau and Otis Dudley Duncan, *The American Occupational Structure*, New York: John Wiley and Sons, Inc., 1967, p. 208.

11. This analysis is based on the 175 cases who remained in the study.

12. Sixty percent of unwed black mothers were employed sometime during the project (see Chapter 8).

13. Some support of this thesis is contained in Newark and national statistics on the employment of black men and women by major occupational groups. See Chernick, Indik, and Sternlieb, *op. cit.*, p. 23.

14. Income has been identified as the class variable most closely associated with marital stability. See Phillips Cutright, "Income and Family Events: Marital Stability," *Journal of Marriage and the Family*, 1971, 33 (May) pp. 291-306.

15. See also Mirra Komarovsky, "Class Differences in Family Decision-Making on Expenditures," in Marvin B. Sussman (editor) *Sourcebook in Marriage and the Family*, Boston: Houghton Mifflin Company, 1963, pp. 261-266.

16. Small discrepancies in percentages for beginning situation reported here and earlier can be explained by the fact that present figures pertain only to cases remaining in the study.

17. This is in contrast to a slight negative change in the area economic practices which, unlike the economic factor, does not include the subcategory use of social agencies. More positive movement was registered on this dimension than on the three others (see p. 196).

18. Because of the open-endedness of top and bottom categories, the exact amount could not be determined.

19. The rise in consumer prices between 1965 and the first half of 1969 was 16 percent. Encyclopaedia Britannica, Inc., *Book of the Year 1970*, p. 25.

20. Use of social agencies is one of the subcategories of the conceptual area use of community resources, although in the factor analysis this subcategory appeared most heavily loaded under the economic factor. For details see Chapter 5.

13.

Relationships with the Community

George P. Murdock has stated that the community and the nuclear family are the only social groups that are genuinely universal,[1] and to this we might add that in any society these two groups or systems exist in close interdependence and influence each other's development. "Nowhere on earth," Murdock points out, "do people live regularly in isolated families. Everywhere territorial propinquity, supported by divers other bonds, unites at least a few neighboring families into a larger social group all of whose members maintain face-to-face relationships with one another."[2]

Although the family as an institution exists in a variety of forms which can be subsumed under one or another of a few satisfactory classification systems, the concept of community encompasses a seemingly infinite variety of forms which defy ready classification.[3] Families are almost invariably associated with communities of one kind or another, although these may be as dissimilar as a compact village based on patrilineal bonds in Northern Nigeria and the city of Tokyo. Communities, on the other hand, are not inevitably made up of families, for there are many instances of settlements composed of religious or occupational groups such as, for example, monasteries, military posts or mining camps.

The theoretical framework used in this research takes into consideration the interdependence of family and community in a twofold manner. Half the areas or main categories of functioning, namely social activities, economic practices, health conditions and practices, and use of community resources, comprise at least some role and task performances that bring individuals into contact with social systems beyond the boundaries of their immediate families. Use of community resources, in particular, designates family functioning in which the two systems interact.

The family-community relationship is not a one-way street in which the family as the dependent partner receives services, resources and other benefits from the dispensing community. Family-community relations are very much a two-way passage, and inputs, far from being a community monopoly, are probably more sustained and concentrated when coming from the family. Being the basic social unit of most societies, the family pays taxes, votes, takes part in many other aspects of the political process, runs voluntary organizations and shares in the governing of various public bodies. The community, in turn, furnishes services and resources that include provisions for educating children, for basic utilities, for the safety of citizens, for meeting the needs of socially and economically dependent persons, for regulating the political process, etc.

The scope and nature of services supplied by a community ranges widely, depending on the type of settlement, its size, economic resources, demographic composition, etc. Similarly, the services families require vary according to their social class, family structure, life-cycle stage, ethnicity and other factors. Mogey calls the American city an open community where members have selective attachments to a variety of associations — in contradistinction to the closed community where members share reciprocal roles in kinship networks, work and recreation groups, and, as a consequence, have developed a common culture.[4] To this might be added that in the open community different spheres of activity are likely to be quite detached, and with each situation the individual is confronted with new and disparate social contacts.

Without becoming too deeply involved in definitions, we can accept Roland L. Warren's formulation that a community is "that combination of social units and systems which performs the major social functions having locality relevance."[5] Elaborating, he writes that the community represents "the organization of social activities to afford people daily local access to those broad areas of activity which are necessary in day-to-day living."[6] There are essentially three dimensions underlying this definition: (1) territoriality, meaning the area called community must be spatially limited though its size may vary; (2) interaction among people and subsystems that are part of the community; (3) reciprocal expectation between the community or those responsible for its governance and its constituent elements, such as individuals, families, businesses, voluntary associations, etc., so that each has certain duties and responsibilities and, in turn, is entitled to certain kinds of resources or services.

Warren enumerates five basic functions of community activities, namely, production-distribution-consumption, socialization, social control, social participation and mutual support.[7] In a city such as Newark, and perhaps in most large American cities, families relate to the community most strongly in terms of the second and third factors mentioned above. Community in the United States stands, above all, for education, and this is particularly true in New Jersey, where the school districts generally coincide with municipal boundaries. Social control, covering the means through which groups seek to influence their members toward law and norm conformity, is at the roots of local government and involves the police, the courts and the administrative machinery for regulating the political process. The other activities, though crucially important to some citizens (public assistance or mutual support to the economically disadvantaged is an example), are yet less universal in nature either because many citizens are independent — as would be the case of individuals and families who do not need welfare — or because residents are in a position to use resources available elsewhere. Thus, for some members of a city the main locus of production-distribution-consumption is beyond the municipal limits, perhaps in the suburbs or in another larger city. (For many Newark residents this is New York, which is within easy commuting distance from them.) Likewise, social participation may be centered in another place because it may follow kinship or ethnic or interest group lines which often are not confined to municipal boundaries.

During the course of the project the families in the study population were at a stage of development where dependency upon the community was more restricted than it is for older families. They were not yet dependent upon agencies of child socialization, for they had as yet no children of school age. (A few had children who had reached kindergarten age at the end of the study.) Because of their youth the families were generally in good health and not dependent on community health services except for well-baby clinics. Participation in formal associations was minimal, as is generally the case with families in the child-rearing stage.[8] As we learned in Chapter 7, social participation was mainly informal and built around close kin and friends.

The family-community relationship of these young Newark families comprises three aspects: (1) the actual relationships which comprise the types of resources used by the study families and the sample subgroups; (2) the attitudes of study families toward community services and resources and towards ways of bringing about desired changes; and (3) an evaluation of the study families' use of these resources.

RESOURCES USED

Evidence has already been presented in Chapter 4 that the only resource used by over half the study population was public health, namely well-baby clinics, city clinics, hospital in- and outpatient departments. Sixty-two percent of all the study families used these resources at the time of the inception of the research project. There was about a 9 percent reduction in their use during the project's tenure — from 62 percent to 53 percent — because parents used the facilities of well-baby clinics more infrequently as their first child grew older. We feel that the mother's increasing experience in handling the health problems of children rather than a switch to private services accounts for this reduction, for it occurs about equally among blacks and whites and in all social classes. The degree to which the different social status groups used community health resources at the start of the study suggests, nonetheless, that the financially more affluent availed themselves of private medical services. Twenty-seven percent of Class 1-4, 55 percent of Class 5 and 86 percent of Class 6 made use of the Newark health services. More noteworthy, however, is a striking difference in the way the two ethnic groups at every class level turned to the services, as shown by the following percentages for blacks and whites, respectively: Class 1-4, 47 percent and 17 percent; Class 5, 79 percent and 22 percent; and Class 6, 91 percent and 52 percent. Since there is no reason to suspect that there are substantial disparities in the health needs of black and white young families, the conclusion emerges that Negroes are more ready to use community facilities, and that the whites choose to use private services to a much larger extent even in instances where the family has only limited financial means.

Is the sharp difference in usage between the groups a case of attitudes toward health services only or toward public services and resources in general? Omitting from such a comparison public assistance agencies (their use is heavily determined by economic need, and they are the most frequently used community resource after health resources), we discover a picture of greater black participation. Public legal services, utilized by only 2 percent of the sample, were used slightly more often by Negroes than by whites. (There was a 1 to 3 percent difference in each status group.) Community family-planning services, in which about 4 percent of the total sample participated, were used to a somewhat greater extent by Negroes than whites (Class 1-4, 7 percent and 2 percent; Class 5, 5 percent and 0 percent; Class 6, 5 percent and 3 percent). Not surprising is the fact that Negro participation exceeded that of whites in civil and welfare rights groups (Class 1-4, 3 percent and 0 percent; Class 5, 3 percent and 0 percent; and Class 6, 1 percent and 0 percent) and also in Office of Economic Opportunity projects such as Youth Opportunity Center, Job Training and Neighborhood Youth Corps (Class 1-4, 3 percent and 0 percent; Class 5, 7 percent and 0 percent; and Class 6, 10 percent

and 3 percent). The latter two types of organizations, however, are closely associated with the quest to improve the lot of the Negro population.
Other services used more extensively by black than white families were
day nurseries (Class 1-4, 25 percent and 11 percent; Class 5, 5 percent and
3 percent; Class 6, 10 percent and 0 percent), preschool programs (Class
1-4, 10 percent and 11 percent; Class 5, 8 percent and 3 percent; Class 6,
7 percent and 4 percent), and recreational services such as YMCAs and
YMHAs, neighborhood houses for the lower classes (Class 5, 3 percent
and 2 percent; Class 6, 5 percent and 0 percent), but not for Class 1-4,
where Negroes made less extensive use of services than whites (3 percent
and 8 percent). The use of other types of community services was too
restricted in scope to merit making black-white comparisons.

Negro families reported a somewhat greater use of public parks and
playgrounds than did whites (Class 1-4, 50 percent and 40 percent; Class
5, 37 percent and 29 percent; Class 6, 39 percent and 35 percent), fitting
into the general pattern of greater use of community resources by black
rather than by white families and probably reflecting inferior housing
and play facilities for blacks.

Granted that we are dealing here with small numbers, since young
families have more limited need for social resources than those who are
older and in other ways restrict their social participation, the data do
indicate that Negro families are more extensive users of community
services and resources, and that the very large differences observed in
the use of health services by blacks and whites were unique only in their
magnitude not in their direction. The explanation for these differences
would appear to lie in the fact that whites, now and since the mid-sixties
a minority in Newark, may well view community services in a city that
has experienced racial conflict as black institutions. If this is indeed the
case, their alternative would be private medical services or, in the case
of children's day care or family recreation, ignoring services completely,
relying solely upon family resources. However, we are reluctant to dis-
miss the explanation of subcultural differences in the form of differential attitudes by blacks and whites toward public services, in view of the
fact that national statistics also show that Negroes make more extensive
use of public health services than do whites in comparable income
groups.[9]

Three services that were used with greater frequency than all others
save community health services were public assistance (18 percent),
public housing (13 percent) and public employment agencies (12 percent).
This use is probably less a matter of choice than of necessity, although
within given need categories there are differences in the extent to which
individuals will use or refrain from using services. For instance, it has

been estimated that only one-third to one-half of the persons and families in financial need who are eligible for public assistance will actually apply for aid. The same may be true for public housing and employment aid. In citing much greater use by Negroes than whites of local and county public assistance (Class 1-4, 7 percent and 0 percent; Class 5, 10 percent and 2 percent; Class 6, 45 percent and 14 percent), we are not certain whether the difference reflects the greater economic need of blacks documented in Chapter 12 or a greater readiness to apply for assistance. The same question arises in relation to public housing, which was used more extensively by Negroes than whites (Class 1-4, 10 percent and 2 percent; Class 5, 15 percent and 1 percent; Class 6, 13 percent and 7 percent).

This predominant pattern of black families using community resources to a greater extent did not extend to public employment services, where differences in Class 5 were very small (13 percent and 11 percent), while in Classes 1-4 and 6 they favored whites (Class 1-4, 4 percent and 8 percent and Class 6, 13 percent and 19 percent). It is possible that the greater use by blacks of OEO-sponsored training and employment programs (see above) meant a channeling of black job seekers away from the private employment services.

Interestingly, the more extensive use of community services by black residents of the city is not linked to a generally more favorable attitude on their part toward these resources. Of 36 pairs of responses to questions about attitudes towards services and resources, black mothers expressed themselves as more pleased than their white counterparts in 18 pairs of responses, the reverse was true in 15, and in three cases black and white mothers were equally affirmative.[10] This would again lend support to the above-mentioned thesis that greater use of community resources by Negro families, aside from being rooted in greater material need, results because facilities are viewed as serving a predominantly black community.

Class differences in the use of community resources were most pronounced in the case of the health services (see above) and those meeting economic, housing and financial needs. Beyond these, the various status groups differed little and in no consistent manner in the extent to which they used community services. Comparisons, it must be repeated, were handicapped by the limited use of most of these services, and knowledge of such limited use is actually the most salient finding emerging from the analysis so far.

ATTITUDES TOWARD RESOURCES AND SOCIAL ACTION

Does nonuse of services signify a lack of dependence upon them or does it indicate rather a reluctance to use them in spite of need? We have no accurate way of gauging need, let alone balancing it against willingness to use an existing resource. However, some indication of a family's readiness to use a service is provided by its attitude, and these attitudes were explored independently of use by asking the mother whether her feelings about a given service, resource or facility were basically favorable or positive, neutral (indifferent) or negative. Values of responses were scored as follows: 1 = positive, 2 = neutral, 3 = negative, and the group scores represent means with a theoretical range from 1 (most positive) to 3 (most negative). The actual range was from 1.08 on preschool programs (where 92 percent expressed themselves positively, none negatively) to 2.15 on correctional penal institutions and services (where 26 percent showed a positive attitude, 33 percent a neutral one and 41 percent a negative attitude). The lowest ratings were given to services that carry a stigma because they serve the deviant or poor (correctional-penal institutions, 2.15; parole and probation, 1.82; public assistance, 1.95; public low-cost housing, 1.97). Services for children and recreational programs and facilities were rated most highly (preschool programs, 1.08; day nurseries, 1.16; recreational services, 1.16; parks and playgrounds, 1.31). Attitudes toward the remaining community resources reflected various degrees of satisfaction, with the positive responses falling within the one-half to two-thirds range and negative responses ranging from 8 percent to 22 percent. Most of the services in the latter group could be considered optional in the sense that families have alternatives they could turn to instead of using them. The relatively low degree of affirmative expression toward these services may, therefore, also account in part for the fact that the services were not extensively used.

The most generalized indicator of a person's attitude toward the community is his feeling of relatedness in the very broadest sense, meaning people and institutions with which an individual experiences a degree of belonging and interdependence.[11] This attitude is tapped by a simple five-item instrument known as the Srole Anomia or Anomie Scale.[12] The eunomia-anomia dimension, as conceived by Srole, refers to the individual's generalized, pervasive sense of "self-to-others belongingness" at one end compared to "self-to-others distance" and "self-to-others alienation" at the other end of the continuum.[13] A large series of studies have applied the anomie scale to social and psychological variables.[14] The score range is from 5 to 20, and the higher the score the greater the degree of anomie manifested by the respondent.

The mean anomie score for the sample of 555 families who completed at least one interview (only 540 filled out the questionnaire for the anomie scale) was 12.82, with a standard deviation of 3.26. For purposes of correlating the scale to other variables, it was divided into units of approximate thirds of the population tested.

Not surprisingly, anomie as measured by the Srole Scale was found to be highly and significantly related to being Negro (gamma = +0.58, X^2 = 68.64, 2 d.f., p<.001) and lower class (gamma = +0.46, X^2 = 66.50, 4 d.f., p<.001). With social class controlled, differences between black and white respondents were only statistically significant for Classes 5 (gamma = +0.44, X^2 = 19.15, 2 d.f., p<.001) and 6 (gamma = +0.63, X^2 = 18.69, 2 d.f., p<.001), an indication of the fact that middle-class culture tends to mitigate to some extent — at least in the case of the mothers who were the respondents in this study — the feeling of alienation so prevalent among American Negroes. Unwed motherhood — involving a comparison of black mothers only — was also significantly related to anomie (gamma = +0.35, X^2 = 15.59, 2 d.f., p<.001), an indication above all that the unmarried mother feels more alienated from her environment than the married one.[15]

The family's overall social functioning bore a strong and significant negative relationship to the mother's feelings of anomie (gamma = -0.45, X^2 = 78.58, 6 d.f., p<.001), and here again we are observing a situation where social deprivation in the form of inadequacy in role and task performance is related to a feeling of alienation. Because we have learned that social status and family functioning are interwoven (see Chapter 6), the question arises whether anomie is correlated with troubled social functioning independently of social status. The answer is a reserved yes. With class held constant, anomie and family functioning are correlated at a low to moderate but significant level at each class stratum (Class 1-4, gamma = -0.39, X^2 = 14.15, 6 d.f., p<.05; Class 5, gamma = -0.29, X^2 = 14.78, 6 d.f., p<.05; Class 6, gamma = -0.34, X^2 = 17.26, 6 d.f., p<.02), although the strength of the association between the variables has been greatly reduced. We conclude from this that a feeling of alienation from the social environment not only reflects status deprivation but also a socially handicapping condition rooted in family life. The data do not reveal the causal flow of the relationship, and it seems reasonable to hypothesize that an anomic attitude represents cause as well as effect, perhaps much more of the latter vis-à-vis a disturbed family situation.

If anomie scores are an index of an individual's general feeling toward the social environment, then attitudes on that dimension should be related to the way in which he or she uses community resources. This indeed turns out to be the case. The families' use of community resources, as measured by this scale area, is significantly and negatively correlated (gamma = -0.41, X^2 = 31.26, 2 d.f., p<.001) with the mothers' anomie score. This relationship holds up when the variables are correlated for both Negro (gamma = -0.36, X^2 = 14.95, 2 d.f., p<.001) and white (gamma = -0.33, X^2 = 7.13, 2 d.f., p<.05) families separately.

The attitudes of project families toward community services, facilities and resources were explored in greater depth with the aid of a substudy which assessed the mothers' opinions regarding the adequacy of existing community services. The N for this substudy is 225, and the study sample differs somewhat from the samples used in the book as a whole, since the investigation was carried out during the final phase of the project when many control group families had already completed their final interview. Out of the 175 control cases who completed the study, only 70 are included in this inquiry. The remainder are 155 or 88 percent of the 177 treatment families who were seen regularly until the end of the project and could be motivated to participate without much difficulty.

Treatment cases were included in this substudy to enlarge the sample and on the basis of the contention that the service program does not represent a significant variable affecting mothers' attitudes toward the resources of the community. While control group families manifested slightly more positive (but not statistically significant) change in the use of community resources,[16] there is no evidence that their attitudes differ significantly from those of project families who received services.[17]

The instrument employed in this substudy is an early version of a scale for the indirect measurement of community functioning[18] by having a sample of community respondents express their views on the extent to which existing provisions for serving the local population were adequate or in need of improvement. The rationale for this procedure is the contention that the most significant aspect of a community's rendering of services is the degree to which the needs of the population are met. According to this, community functioning is not an absolute state of performance but rather the relationship between what people believe they require and what they are being given. In line with this conception, a community offering minimal provisions to an affluent population may be said to function quite well. By contrast, another, putting forth a major effort which falls far short of its mark on behalf of a very deprived population, may be said to function poorly. Granted the existence of substantial differences in need, it must be said that all communities in urban societies face certain universal tasks such as furnishing educational facilities, roads, utilities, police protection, welfare assistance and others. All communities, even those serving the economically privileged, will have to put forth some effort to satisfy the needs of their residents, and the quality of the community's social functioning is at least partly reflected in the magnitude of that effort.

Conceptually this substudy differentiates between two levels of provisions for meeting the needs of the local population: primary provisions for meeting basic survival needs and maintaining a minimum level of social functioning and basic socialization; and secondary provisions to effect social control, promote social participation, recreation and culture, and meet various less urgent instrumental needs. Primary provisions are: services, resources and facilities in the areas of income, employment, social security; housing; basic socialization; health and social adjustment. Secondary provisions cover areas of social control, social participation and recreation, secondary socialization (such as adult education), and provisions for derived instrumental needs.[19] A total of 34 items grouped under the nine areas are listed in Appendix 8.

The primary provisions mentioned above can be viewed as making up the more essential services which society is expected to extend but which, in a situation rarely found to exist in technologically advanced societies, have not been given to meet the basic material needs of the population. Characteristically, services classified under primary provisions are thought to be of greater importance for lower-class populations, heavily dependent upon the community for meeting basic survival needs and minimally adequate functioning. Any one service, however, becomes less significant to a population when society has already made adequate provisions in a given area of functioning. Thus, job training and job finding, a crucial service for those who have difficulty finding employment, becomes a nonessential service in time of full employment and labor shortages.

Three hypotheses guide the present investigation: (1) that primary provisions for services and resources will be considered less adequate and more in need of improvement than secondary provisions; (2) that the lower the social status of the respondent the more he is likely to endorse change in service patterns, particularly in services which are termed primary; (3) that Negro respondents are more in favor of change than white respondents. The last is based on the belief that, as more extensive consumers of community services, blacks have a greater stake in their improvement. The greater inclination of lower-class respondents to favor change would be based on the fact that they exhibit more need even if clear-cut evidence of greater use by these groups is absent. Primary services are viewed as meeting a more urgent need than secondary ones for a predominantly lower-class population such as we are studying.

For purposes of this inquiry, the respondents, who were all mothers of the families included in the substudy,[20] were asked whether existing services were adequate as they stood or whether there was need for more, for better, or more and better services. The present analysis combines the three categories calling for qualitative and quantitative improvement into a single expression of belief that change is needed. Thus, the data presented here show the percentage of mothers for each group who indicated that improvement in services is needed. The balance were respondents who felt that services were adequate.

Exhibit 13.1 shows endorsement of change by respondents (expression of need for improved services) by total sample as well as by social class for areas of community functioning, primary and secondary provisions, and overall mean scores. The data in this table permit several salient observations. A decisive majority of respondents believe that services, resources and facilities need improvement. Two-thirds or more of the respondents favor upgrading in practically every area of community functioning; that is to say, the degree of their satisfaction with existing

EXHIBIT 13.1: PERCENTAGE OF MOTHERS EXPRESSING NEED FOR CHANGE IN COMMUNITY SERVICES BY SOCIAL CLASS OF FAMILY

AREA OF SERVICE	Class 1-4	Class 5	Class 6	Total Sample
Primary provisions	82.4	86.5	89.7	87.4
Income, employment and social security	81.4	85.5	86.6	85.4
Housing	81.9	88.3	90.7	88.4
Basic socialization	87.5	90.2	93.5	91.3
Health	70.7	81.0	85.8	81.8
Social adjustment	90.3	87.7	92.1	90.0
Secondary provisions	75.7	78.7	80.8	79.3[a]
Social control	84.1	84.1	83.8	84.1
Social participation and recreation	93.9	91.3	91.2	91.7
Secondary socialization	65.5	75.0	71.6	72.3
Derived instrumental needs	59.1	64.5	76.7	68.9
Total mean score	79.4	83.1	85.8	83.8
N	34	95	95[b]	225

[a]Difference between primary and secondary provisions is statistically significant beyond the 1 percent level.

[b]No information on class was available for one family.

arrangements is rather low. In keeping with the first hypothesis there is a significantly more extensive endorsement (Z = 2.38, p = .009) [21] of change for services and resources falling under the primary provisions category than under the secondary. The relationship between lower status position and an expression of need for change was not statistically significant. Class differences on primary services follow an almost consistent class-related regression pattern (except for social adjustment). In areas under secondary provisions, patterns of differences are more erratic and follow class lines in a clear-cut manner only on derived instrumental needs (arrangements for clean streets, garbage collection, shopping and transportation).

The second hypothesis postulating class differences on endorsement of change was not supported by the data even though most score differences were in the predicted direction. The class data suggest, nonetheless, that the young, lower-class mother has more of a stake in some improved services, resources and facilities than does one with a higher status. The differences are particularly pronounced and statistically significant when Classes 1-4 and 6 are compared in two areas: derived instrumental needs, mentioned above (Z = 1.96, p = .03), and health services (Z = 1.97, p = .02). The former involves conditions and situations that confront the lower-class family with particular harshness, since they live more often than not in rundown areas of the city. Well-lit streets, good public transportation and easily reached shopping are of particular importance to inner-city families who reside where the streets are often unsafe at night, fewer people own cars and parking is likely to be a problem. Health services, because of high cost and the shortage of skilled manpower, constitute a problem for most Americans, but they particularly affect the lower class, who frequently lack medical insurance and are forced either to go into debt to pay their bills or to accept free care which is often accompanied by interminable waiting and discourteous treatment.

Score differences between black and white respondents are very substantial (75.7 percent of whites express need for improved services compared to 87.7 percent of the Negroes), but this disparity is likely to be at least partly a function of class differences. When social status is controlled we find, nevertheless, that at every class level more blacks than whites favor improved services, as is shown below:

The differences in attitudes between Negro and white mothers is consistent though, because of the small Ns, they reach statistical significance only for Class 5, thus giving only partial support to the hypothesis on black-white differences. The high degree of consistency in differences extends to the individual services and is reversed on only three items

EXHIBIT 13.2: BLACK-WHITE DIFFERENCES ON NEED FOR CHANGE
WITH CLASS CONTROLLED

| | PERCENT EXPRESSING NEED FOR CHANGE | | | | | |
| | Class 1-4 | | Class 5 | | Class 6 | |
	Whites	Blacks[a]	Whites	Blacks	Whites	Blacks
Primary provisions	79.0	89.5	79.7	91.6[b]	83.0	90.1
Secondary provisions	71.4	85.4	66.0	86.0[c]	78.9	81.6
Total of services and resources	75.6	87.7	73.6	89.5[d]	81.2	86.3
N	23	11	35	57	9	79

[a]Puerto Ricans are omitted from this comparison.
[b]Difference is statistically significant at 5 percent level.
[c]Difference is statistically significant at 1 percent level.
[d]Difference is statistically significant at 2 percent level.

(out of 27), two involving .4 and 2.5 percentage points, respectively, and the third, which is secondary socialization as endorsed by Class 6 respondents, involves 7.6 percentage points (80 percent of whites and 72.4 percent of Negroes expressed the need for improved services). It can be stated that, by and large, Negro mothers were less satisfied with existing community services and resources, and it seems clear that black families, as greater consumers, show more concern for the quality and quantity of services than white families. Furthermore, differences in the views expressed may also be a function of a generally greater dissatisfaction — rooted in reality — with the status quo in American society.

The greatest dissimilarity in responses toward local services was found in a comparison of families living in the city of Newark with those who had moved to a nearby suburb. Of the 225 families in this sample, 186 were still living in the city, 38 had moved to suburbia and one, not included in this comparison, had moved to another nearby city. The mean proportion of Newark respondents expressing the desirability of improved primary services was 89.2 percent, secondary provisions, 81.9 percent and all services 85.9 percent. For suburbanites, 77.6 percent desired improved primary services, 66.4 percent wanted better secondary services and 76.2 percent felt that all services should be improved. These differences are all significant at the 5 percent level or beyond.

It is scarcely surprising that residents of Newark have a significantly greater commitment to a change of city services than those who have moved away. Although the question was posed in relation to the situation in Newark, it is highly probable that responses were colored by the overall experiences of the families at the time of the interview, wherever they happened to have occurred. A 20 percent difference that characterized the responses on education indicate that the more satisfactory situation of those who had moved to the suburbs influenced the degree to which they favored better educational facilities in Newark.

Unfortunately, the city-suburban comparison does not allow us to examine pure groups because of the small number of suburban families, which precludes holding race and class constant. An ethnic breakdown shows that 75 percent of those remaining in the city but only 18 percent of those who moved to the suburbs were black. Therefore, the foregoing juxtaposition of percentages also includes differences due to race as well as social class. Still, the greater contrasts on the city-suburbia than on the black-white or social class comparison justifies the assumption that place of residence influences the response patterns on satisfaction with community services and resources. This is further borne out by a rank order comparison (Spearman rho) of the proportion of respondents who favored change in each of the nine areas.

EXHIBIT 13.3: RANK-ORDER CORRELATIONS BETWEEN SETS OF STUDY SUB-GROUPS ON NEED FOR CHANGE

GROUPS COMPARED	SPEARMAN RHOS
White-black	+0.83
Class 1-4 to 5	+0.88
Class 1-4 to 6	+0.82
Class 5 to 6	+0.88
Class 1-4, white-black	+0.85
Class 5, white-black	+0.86
Class 6, white-black	+0.84
City residents-suburbanites	+0.47

There is a high measure of similarity in the way racial and status groups express a desire for change in the various areas. It is, in fact, the similarity of response patterns rather than the dissimilarity which is the characteristic feature of these comparisons. All correlations are significant beyond the 5 percent level, save the coefficient relating Newark residents to suburbanites. Hence, we may conclude that type of residence affects to a measurable degree attitudes of young mothers toward community services and resources.

Given the respondents' rather high degree of dissatisfaction with services as they are, what do they see as the means for bringing about a more satisfactory situation? The subjects in the study were presented with a list of 11 alternatives for action to bring about desired changes. The questionnaire items appeared in the order shown here:

1. Letters to legislators.
2. Phone calls to legislators.
3. Visits to officials and legislators.
4. Legal help.
5. Organizing new groups.
6. Action through existing groups.
7. Newspaper and other publicity.
8. Nonviolent demonstrations.
9. Violent demonstrations.
10. Using influential people with "pull."
11. Voting.

Each respondent was asked whether she believed that the type of action listed is or is not likely to bring about results.

These 11 means of attaining desired goals can be categorized into two groups: collaborative strategies based most on persuasion, and contest strategies which rely on activities expressing opposition.[22] The former approach assumes that there are shared values and interests which create a common base through which agreement on the desirability of a given goal and ways to attain it can be reached. The latter strategy recognizes dissension and accepts the assertion that a given goal can only be attained by activities which oppose the groups now determining policy.[23] According to this categorization, items 1 to 3 and 10 could be termed collaborative, the remainder contest strategies. Beyond this, one might also postulate that some types of strategy are more acceptable to the prevailing ethic than others. This is a much more tricky issue than the collaborative versus contest categorization of strategies. One might rightly ask, "acceptable by whom," and one can also raise the question of whether what is unacceptable at one time may not become acceptable at another. For example, demonstrations against the war in Vietnam, much frowned upon by a wide segment of the American public in the early 1960s, are commonplace and widely accepted in 1971. In view of the shifting standards in American society, only two types of strategy could be termed clearly less acceptable than the rest: using influential people with "pull" (collaborative strategy) and engaging in violent demonstration (contest strategy).

Exhibit 13.4 shows the percentage of responsents who believe that each type of social action, grouped by type of strategy, was likely to yield results.

As is evident from Exhibit 13.4, the responding mothers expressed, by and large, more confidence in the acceptable contest strategies than in acceptable collaborative ones. They were, on the whole, skeptical that violent demonstrations could get results, but thought that using influ-

EXHIBIT 13.4: PERCENT OF RESPONDENTS WHO BELIEVED THAT VARIOUS KINDS OF SOCIAL ACTION, GROUPED BY TYPES OF STRATEGY, WERE LIKELY TO PRODUCE RESULTS

COLLABORATIVE STRATEGIES

Most Acceptable		Least Acceptable	
Letters to legislators	53.0	Using influential	
Phone calls to legislators	38.1	people with "pull"	86.0
Visits to officials and			
legislators	79.4		

CONTEST STRATEGIES

Most Acceptable		Least Acceptable	
Voting	88.5	Violent demonstration	25.5
Action through existing			
groups	93.0		
Newspaper publicity	67.3		
Organizing new groups	91.2		
Legal help	85.6		
Nonviolent demonstrations	67.9		

ential people holds promise of attaining desired goals. Newarkers have had bitter experiences with violent demonstrations. The riots of 1967 and the inconsequential results of that upheaval may be reflected in the respondents' low endorsement of violence as a means of getting results. The small number of affirmative responses which letters and phone calls to legislators drew on the list may indicate a belief that these approaches tend to be largely ignored by those to whom they are addressed.

The experience of Negroes as a disadvantaged minority leads us to hypothesize that they would tend to take a position more strongly in favor of contest measures than whites. That hypothesis is tested in Exhibit 13.5.

Comparing the responses by black and white mothers, only one statistically significant difference, on the item nonviolent demonstrations, was noted. On both forms of social action blacks were more hopeful of results than were whites. Proportionately larger numbers of Negroes were confident that positive results could be attained through more kinds of social action (eight out of 11). Where the reverse occurred, percentage differences were small.

There is not much evidence that black mothers are more prone to believe in the efficacy of contest strategies than white mothers,[24] except for the use of nonviolent demonstrations where the belief may be part of a commitment to the civil rights struggle, which used peaceful mass demonstrations as the main instrument for attaining its goals.

Overshadowing the differences pointed out between black and white

EXHIBIT 13.5: PERCENT OF BLACK AND WHITE RESPONDENTS WHO BELIEVED THAT VARIOUS KINDS OF SOCIAL ACTION WERE LIKELY TO GET RESULTS

COLLABORATIVE STRATEGIES	Most Acceptable			Least Acceptable	
	Blacks	Whites		Blacks	Whites
Letters to legislators	54.6	51.6	Using influential	89.4	81.0
Phone calls to legislators	41.1	34.4	persons with		
Visits to officials and			"pull"		
legislators	79.4	79.4			
CONTEST STRATEGIES					
Voting	88.2	89.1	Violent demon-	29.1	18.5
Action through existing groups	94.4	93.7	strations		
Newspaper publicity	65.7	71.9			
Organizing new groups	93.7	87.5			
Legal help	88.1	82.3			
Nonviolent demonstrations	76.4	55.6[a]			
Ns	147	68		147	68

[a]Difference is statistically significant beyond the .01 level. $X^2 = 8.86$ with 1 d.f.

respondents — as well as between different social classes which are generally small and not statistically significant — on the confidence expressed in the 11 measures listed, are the similarities between the groups. The rank order correlation on the black-white comparison (Spearman rho) is $+0.90$ which is statistically significant beyond the .01 level. Similarity of response patterns also marks the comparison of social classes and Newark versus suburban residents. Only one of 44 comparisons showed differences in the percentages of responses to the various items of social action to be statistically significant,[25] and the degree of similarity in response patterns is indicated by the high rank order correlations (Spearman rhos) shown below.

EXHIBIT 13.6: RANK ORDER CORRELATIONS AMONG SOCIAL CLASSES AND TYPES OF RESIDENCE ON BELIEF IN THE EFFICACY OF KINDS OF SOCIAL ACTION

GROUPS COMPARED	SPEARMAN RHOS[a]
Class 1-4 and 5	+0.89
Class 5 and 6	+0.94
Class 1-4 and 6	+0.89
Newark residents and suburbanites	+0.90

[a]All the correlations are significant beyond the .01 level

An inspection of the actual response percentages per item (not shown here because differences are small) reveals a limited tendency on the part of the higher social classes to express greater confidence in most forms of social action, particularly voting (endorsed as likely to bring results by 97.0 percent of Class 1-4, 87.0 percent of Class 5 and 86.0 percent of Class 6) and legal help (endorsed by 93.3 percent of Class 1-4, 87.0 percent of Class 5 and 81.5 percent of Class 6). Only on the item violent demonstration did fewer Class 1-4 respondents (21.9 percent) than lower-class respondents indicate that the tactic might achieve desired results (Class 5, 26.1 percent; Class 6, 25.3 percent). All in all, however, in this research on services and resources the subgroup analysis revealed an amazing uniformity of response on the question of the means which respondents felt could bring about the kind of changes they viewed as desirable.

One might wish to speculate on this phenomenon and ask why there was not more class discrepancy in the answers to action remedies for unsatisfactory conditions. One explanation may be that young urban Americans are neither action-oriented nor experienced, and that they tend to react to proposals for bringing about change in terms of cultural stereotypes regardless of class or ethnic membership or residency pattern. The fact that all the respondents were women may also have contributed to the lack of greater group differences, for women, especially young mothers, may be preoccupied with affairs of the home and less involved than men in the problems of social change. Beyond this the high degree of similarity between racial and status groups on attitudes toward services as well as toward ways of effecting change can be interpreted to mean that the gross inadequacy of the service structure has a levelling influence on the attitudinal patterns of these groups.

Whereas the use of community resources category was found to be significantly related to the anomic attitudes of the mother, the 11 social action alternatives bore no significant relationship to the eunomia-anomia dimension. All gamma correlations were close to zero and none of the chi squares came near the 5 percent level of statistical significance. This observation seems to furnish further evidence that we are dealing here with generalized, culturally rooted response patterns which do not vary much either by status group or by individual feelings of social integration in the larger society.

A general observation that can be made about the responses to action alternatives is that they favored the least controversial of contest strategies, voting and the organization of groups, and viewed skeptically the one which would be most widely held unacceptable, violent demonstrations. This held true even for lower-class blacks who have ample reason to question whether the conventional means for bringing about change were ever of benefit to them.

EVALUATING THE USE OF COMMUNITY RESOURCES

The present chapter on the relationship of the families to the community has given considerable attention to the subject of attitudes. Such an emphasis is justified in part because the study families are generally potential rather than actual consumers of community services at this early life-cycle stage. Data presented at the beginning of this chapter revealed their limited use of such services. An evaluation of their use of community resources also has to rely heavily on their attitudes toward the five types of agencies and institutions (school, church, health agencies, social agencies, recreational services and facilities) because, with the exception of health, fewer than half of the study families actually use them.

From an evaluative point of view, use of community resources is the least problem-ridden of the eight areas or main categories of social functioning. Adequacy is defined as using services when needed and following through on recommendations. Sixty-eight percent of the total study population, the 555 families who started the research project together, were rated as adequate at the outset of the study, 24 percent as near adequate, 6 percent as near marginal, and only 2 percent were judged to function at the marginal level or below. The social class factor was positively and significantly related to the use of community resources category (gamma = +0.53, X^2 = 51.66, 4 d.f., p <.001) and so was ethnicity, with whites showing more adequate functioning (gamma = +0.31, X^2 = 11.08, 2 d.f., p <.001). The latter difference, however, is almost entirely a function of social status, for when class was held constant all significant differences between black and white families completely disappeared. Black married mothers in Class 5 also made somewhat better use of community services than unwed mothers (gamma = +0.50, X^2 = 6.88, 1 d.f., p <.01), but in Class 6 no such differences were noted. In short, the relationship between the study population and community agencies, institutions and facilities is modified mainly by the family's social class position. Eighty-nine percent of Class 1-4 families were rated as using community resources adequately. The percentages for Classes 5 and 6 were 74 percent and 52 percent, respectively. The other variable that is highly and significantly related to use of community resources is a family's overall social functioning (gamma = +0.81, X^2 = 206.31, 6 d.f., p <.001). Here the reader should recall that the area correlated is one of the eight components of overall social functioning, hence related by definition. The close correlation observed in Chapter 6 between class and level of social functioning suggests an interaction of the structural and functional factors in the present analysis. Nonetheless, it is clear that families that function inadequately make poorer use of local community resources than families whose total functioning is characterized as adequate.

The pattern of use of agency services during the course of the project — determined by comparing the extent of utilization by the 175 control group families at the beginning and then at the end of the study — revealed a general slight increase, the exception being community health services for reasons discussed above. Although the proportional increases often meant a doubling and a tripling of service use, the actual percentage rise was inconsiderable because it started from a small base. Increased use appeared to be largely a response to the developmental needs of the families. Thus, there was an 8 percent increase in the use of day nurseries (from 1 percent to 9 percent of the families), an 8 percent rise in the use of family planning services (from 3 percent to 11 percent) following the birth of two children on the average, and an expanded use of parks and playgrounds (from 41 percent to 69 percent). The only other resource registering an increase of 8 percent or more was the Office of Economic Opportunity, whose expansion in Newark coincided with the research period. More extensive use may reflect greater accessibility and availability of the services rather than more extensive need for them.

What are the evaluative changes paralleling these increases, however slight, in community services? Use of community resources is the only main category of family functioning in which the 175 control group families who remained in the research project registered improved social functioning during the study. That improvement mainly reflected a slightly more extensive use of social services based on need. It was not statistically significant; the research group basically remained a population of nonusers.

It is quite possible that restricted use of community resources is not purely a function of limited need at this early life-cycle stage; it may also indicate skepticism regarding the efficiency of those services which are available.[26] The high proportion of substudy responses expressing the belief that there should be improvement in services seems to indicate that the families lacked the motivation to use the community's resources. Additional evidence which supports this thesis comes from the fact that the treatment group families (N = 177), who were the focus of a concerted effort toward better use of community services, showed less positive change in use of community resources during the research period than did the control group.[27] This is quite a contrast to similar experimental control studies where this area was the one in which significantly greater change was measured in the service group.[28] Finally, a Rutgers University study carried out at the time of the present project revealed that in Newark there were very extensive gaps between social needs and the resources of the community. [29]

While none of the data supply irrefutable evidence of the fact that the restricted use of community services by the young study families is due to the nature of the services themselves (comparative data from other communities could provide a more rigorous test of this thesis), the cumulative evidence of the attitude study reported earlier and available data on the services and agencies of the city point to a link between people's attitudes and their collective use. [30]

NOTES

1. George P. Murdock, "Statistical Relations Among Community Characteristics," in Paul F. Lazarsfeld and Morris Rosenberg (editors) *The Language of Social Research*, New York: The Free Press, 1955, pp. 305-311; p. 306.

2. *Ibid.*

3. John Mogey reports that well over 100 different definitions of community have been reported, and a search of the literature could add new ones to the list. John Mogey, *loc. cit.*, pp. 501-534; p. 512.

4. *Ibid.*, p. 517.

5. Roland L. Warren, *The Community in America*, Chicago: Rand McNally and Company, 1963, p. 9.

6. *Ibid.*, p. 9.

7. *Ibid.*, pp. 9-11.

8. John Mogey, *loc. cit.*, p. 518.

9. U. S. Bureau of Census, *The Social and Economic Status of Negroes in the United States*, 1970, Publication P-23, No. 38, Washington, D. C.: Government Printing Office, 1971. Regarding the more extensive use by blacks than whites of multiservice neighborhood centers, see Edward J. O'Donnel and Otto M. Reid, "The Multiservice Neighborhood Center," *Welfare in Review*, 1971, 9 (May-June) pp. 1-8; p. 3.

10. For details on how these data were procured, see p. 166.

11. In its more narrow and accurate usage the concept of community is applied to a territorially limited area.

12. Srole, *loc. cit.*

13. Charles M. Bonjean, Richard J. Hill and S. Dale McLemore, *Sociological Measurement*, San Francisco, California: Chandler Publishing Company, 1967, p. 34.

14. *Ibid.*, pp. 35-38.

15. For comparable findings see Leo G. Reeder and Sharon J. Reeder, "Social Isolation and Illegitimacy," *Journal of Marriage and the Family*, 1969, 31 (August) pp. 451-461.

16. Geismar, Lagay, Wolock, Gerhart and Fink, *op. cit.*, p. 70.

17. The mean difference in responses between the two groups was 4.1 percent (not statistically significant), with the treatment families being in favor of change to a greater extent on 11 items and control families on 23 items. The rank order correlation on extent of endorsement of change desired in services for nine areas of community functioning is +0.98.

18. See Chapter 5 of Ludwig L. Geismar, *Family and Community Functioning*, Metuchen, N. J.: The Scarecrow Press, 1971, pp. 152-195.

19. This conceptual framework is an adaptation of Warren's five category scheme of community functions. The present approach, in contrast to Warren's schematization, details mutual support by substantive areas of service and breaks up production-distribution-consumption into two categories (income, employment, social security; and derived instrumental needs) which highlight the consumer aspect while covering the production-distribution side only to the extent that it represents a direct service to community residents. Such an emphasis is in line with the health-welfare focus of the present study. See Warren, *op. cit.*, pp. 9-11.

20. Ten fathers who had answered the questionnaire were dropped from the analysis in order to retain comparability.

21. Test of significance of percentage difference. John H. Mueller and Karl F. Schuessler, *Statistical Reasoning in Sociology*, Boston: Houghton Mifflin Company, 1961, pp. 399-401.

22. Concepts borrowed from Roland Warren, *Truth, Love and Social Change*, Chicago: Rand McNally and Company, 1971, pp. 15-25.

23. *Ibid.*, pp. 16-22.

24. This is in line with Scanzoni's observation that blacks appear to value dominant society patterns. John H. Scanzoni, *The Black Family in Modern Society*, Boston: Allyn and Bacon, Inc., 1971, p. 147.

25. This occurred on "newspapers and other forms of publicity" which was significant beyond the 1 percent level for the difference between Class 1-4 and 6. The respective percentages are 81.8 percent and 59.8 percent.

26. See Chapter 1 for a discussion of the problems besetting the community at the time the research was undertaken.

27. Geismar, Lagay, Wolock, Gerhart and Fink, *Early Supports of Family Life*, pp. 69-72.

28. *Ibid.*, pp. 169-190.

29. George Sternlieb with Mildred Barry, *Social Needs and Social Resources — Newark 1967*, Newark, N. J.: Graduate School of Business Administration, Rutgers University, 1967.

30. Evidence of the effects of the community value structure on the use of services is furnished by Kenneth C. W. Kammeyer and Charles D. Bolton, "Community and Family Factors Related to the Use of a Family Service Agency," *Journal of Marriage and the Family*, 1968, 3 (August) pp. 488-498.

14.

Family Deviance

The title of the present chapter is likely to strike an unfamiliar chord in the ear of the sociologically oriented reader. Although the term *deviance* is thoroughly familiar, being one of the central sociological concepts, it is infrequently used in the study of the family. Where the term is employed it may refer to families that are different in structure and status from the statistical average, such as those headed by an unmarried mother, widow or widower, one in which the main wage earner is unemployed or where one of the parents is institutionalized. Family deviance may also denote that society considers the unit a "problem,"[1] meaning it departs from the desirable or acceptable. The community then becomes the authority that defines what is acceptable. Deviance under this heading may comprise such phenomena as criminality, delinquency, alcoholism or drug addiction of one or more family members, long-term economic dependence, extensive use of public and private welfare agencies (sometimes incorrectly referred to as "multiproblemicity"), out-of-wedlock births by either mother or daughter, neglect or cruelty toward children, conflict among family members that has come to the attention of neighbors or simply unconventional behavior which violates community mores.

The researchers wished to separate out one of the two distinct variables of family functioning, which, as was shown in Chapter 2, were (adequate versus inadequate) health-welfare and conformity-deviance. The original decision to combine the two into an overall index of evaluation sprang from a recognition — the result of testing alternate evaluative schemes — that in assessing family roles and functions the two dimensions overlap considerably, often making it difficult to decide whether a given type of functioning should be termed inadequate because of its deviant character or because of its negative consequences upon a family member's physical or mental health. Employing a composite index of evaluation satisfied the requirement for a reliable tool of measurement to identify families that are of concern to the community and possibly in need of professional intervention. The question of whether a judgment of inadequacy represented a case of deviant behavior rather than a situation harmful to the person involved was subordinated to the need for accurately identifying handicapped families.

Deviant behavior can be viewed as behavior that violates rules[2] and, more specifically, it may be defined as "action taken by individuals or groups that violates the cultural standards that regulate life and give life meaning within a society."[3] The concept of deviance helps in the understanding of social organization and disorganization, for adherence to and violation of rules and standards are important criteria, albeit not the only ones, of the stability of organization. Albert Cohen reminds us that while deviance is not synonymous with disorganization, its existence, if not contained, is always a threat to organization. Much remains to be done, he states, to specify the conditions under which various types of deviance have certain consequences.[4]

This chapter attempts an initial identification of family deviance and to submit a framework for applying the deviance concept to the family. In its broadest sense, *family deviance* denotes the violation of norms by action or inaction as well as the expression of unacceptable attitudes. A more conservative definition of deviance would confine the measurement of committing or expressing a potential readiness to commit clearly illegal acts. But rule-violating behavior that constitutes true illegality is not characteristic of young families and does not represent a dimension of sensitive measurement in the context of our research. At the same time, this writer believes that family deviance is not most meaningfully expressed by confining the definition to illegal acts. Deviance is defined here as encompassing attitudes and behavior which are at variance with the prevailing mores and laws, producing strain or conflict within the family system.

The question of defining family deviance as contrasted with individual deviance requires comment. "In the literature of deviant behavior," writes Albert Cohen, "it is usually taken for granted that deviant acts are always the acts of individuals. This probably reflects an underlying assumption that super-individual entities or 'collectivities' are fictitious or illusions; as such they can not 'do' things, and only individuals really commit acts."[5] Challenging this view, Cohen points out that collectivities such as corporations, fraternities, trade unions, armies, etc., are real, and many engage in deviant acts. This collective deviance, Cohen holds, has the same claim to our consideration as individual deviance has, but its explanation requires an analysis of the interaction processes that culminate in those events which are socially defined as the deviant acts of collectivities. He concedes that this process is very complex as is the problem of relating collective deviance to that of the individual.[6]

Our framework for the analysis of family deviance bypasses, as it were, the issue raised by Cohen and seeks to identify norm-violating behavior occurring in the basic family roles played by adults. When the deviance study was carried out at the start of the research project, the children were infants or young toddlers, and the deviance concept could not be meaningfully applied to them.

In contrast to examining family functioning, the process of assessing deviance does not make social task or function a unit of analysis. If this were to be done we would be faced with a problem similar to that described by Cohen, namely, the need to explain task deviance by analyzing the interaction process of individuals who participate in carrying out a task. Defining task or function deviance is very difficult; while not impossible, it requires data we have not attempted to collect in the present study.

We feel that an analysis of family deviance, based on the relatively simple index of adult roles related to family functioning, leads to the identification of most norm-violating behavior occurring in family life, for the roles are defined broadly enough to comprehend a variety of specific kinds of relevant family behavior. By separating the roles of husband and wife, the analysis supplies information on how family deviance ties in with the functioning of the group's key individuals. The roles used in the analysis before us are husband, wife, father, mother, homemaker, breadwinner (male and/or female), money manager (male and female), employee (male and/or female), member of the community (male and female) and member of the extended family (male and female).

A distinction is made among four types of deviance — legal deviance, social deviance, role insufficiency and role conflict. Legal deviance constitutes law-violating behavior which, when brought to the attention of the authorities, might lead to prosecution. Social deviance is an act or a series of acts violating accepted norms or laws which are not generally enforced (adultery would be an example of the latter). Social deviance is generally punished through criticism, scorn, ridicule, gossip or ostracism. Role insufficiency denotes a person's failure to carry out familial obligations, particularly when this is actually or potentially harmful to the health and welfare of family members. Role conflict, which may be said to represent more of a case of nonconformity than outright deviance (though it may be that, too), is defined as "a situation in which the incumbent of a position perceives that he is confronted with incompatible expectations."[7] A person who becomes subject to role conflict is one who has avoided conforming with the most "appropriate" norms in favor of struggling for another solution. A mother who reluctantly stays home to care for her child though she would much rather go to work has a role conflict. This type of conflict is likely to arise out of contradictory demands within the same role relationship, stemming from incompatible values and expectations which the individual has internalized, or from opposing requests coming from the environment, or a combination of these. Role conflict is the least manifest of the four types of deviance, but before a decision to characterize behavior as such could be made it had to be based on a clear-cut expression of dissatisfaction or concern by the role incumbent.

All the families (N = 555) starting the longitudinal research together constituted the sample for the deviance study. The profile of family functioning that was used for coding social functioning also served as the source of data for the deviance analysis.

A point made in Chapter 3 regarding data validity must be repeated here. Deviance data pertaining to the time when the study was launched were collected from the first profile of family functioning which, in turn, was based on the initial research interview. It would also seem, however, that the probability of being able to obtain information on deviance in the initial contact is less than it is in later interviews when a relationship has been established with the family. In our analysis we were able to transfer later information on deviance which pertained to the beginning situation. But even with this built in safeguard there is no doubt that some sensitive information was not picked up in this study.

The process of coding the profile information for content on the four types of deviant behavior took the following form. A coder read the total family protocol, then examined closely the several family roles identified above. The coder then decided whether any of the roles could be characterized as representing any one form of deviance. He then chose, if appropriate, which of the deviance categories applied to each case. The four types of categorization are not mutually exclusive. For example, the role relationship "mother" may be characterized by both role conflict as well as by social deviance. Legal deviance, however, was never double coded.[8] The coding scheme was subjected to reliability testing on a sample of 33 cases. The overall proportion of agreement was exceedingly high (97 percent), but this applied to a combined judgment on whether a role could be coded as deviant as well as the type of deviance. When those role relationships which were identified as showing deviance (16 out of the 33 did) were set aside and coded for types of deviance, errors occurred in approximately one out of five ratings. A single coder rated the total research sample.

Deviance, as indicated earlier, represents a basic dimension of family functioning and, as such, a close correlation between the two is anticipated. Of the four types of deviance, we see role conflict as least closely associated with overall malfunctioning, for it is the most universal and is found in many segments of the American social structure. Unlike legal and social deviance and role insufficiency, it does not take the form of overt acting-out, except verbally, and therefore it is quite compatible with otherwise adequate functioning, which by definition is characterized by a fair measure of conformity. When role conflict becomes acute it is likely to turn into social-legal deviance or role insufficiency, chiefly marked by failure to carry out well-prescribed family roles. We feel that these forms of deviance are more characteristic of disturbed than non-disturbed family life. What was said about the relationship of role conflict to total family functioning can be applied hypothetically to social class because this least-blatant form of deviant behavior is more compatible with higher social status than more extreme forms of deviance.

Role conflict occurs most frequently being present in one form or another in 54 percent of the study families. Role conflict is concentrated mainly in the following role relationships: wife (32 percent of families),[9] husband (24 percent), mother (16 percent), employee — male (14 percent), member of extended family — male (12 percent) and member of extended family — female (25 percent). Role conflict in other role relationships affects fewer than 10 percent of the families in each category, and the only two that came close to the percentage were the roles of homemaker (9 percent) and employee — female (8 percent). Thus, perhaps surprisingly, we find that in one-quarter to one-third of the marriages the spouses experience a measure of contradiction that affects role demands or the meshing of their desires with their obligations. In the relationship of spouses the role conflict is, of course, not synonymous with disturbed marital functioning (only 13 percent of the marriages are rated as marginal [4] or below), but it does indicate an underlying dissatisfaction with one or more of the roles in which the young couples have been cast. Equally surprising is the finding that only 17 percent of the women experience a conflict in their role as mother. That proportion was 27 percent for unwed mothers and 10 percent for those who are married. It is quite possible that in their verbal account — as contrasted with their emotions — the women tend to displace maternal conflict to the marital arena or the girlfriend-boyfriend relationship. As shown above, one-third of the married women report role conflict in the wife-girlfriend role. This role of girlfriend or spouse, only coded for those unwed mothers (N = 41) who are in constant touch with the father of the child, indicates conflict in 51 percent of this subgroup. A greater measure of conflict in the woman's role as member of the extended family reflects her greater involvement with relatives. Nonetheless, men are not unaffected, as indicated by the fact that 12 percent of the fathers experience clashing demands in this area. Conflict in the male employee role, affecting about one-seventh of the fathers, generally indicates that the employee's wishes are sharply at odds with the demands of the job or that contradicting demands are made by various segments of the employment system.

Social deviance is the second most frequent type of deviance, and it affects 35 percent of the families. The only roles in which this form of deviance occur with any statistical frequency, beyond 2 percent of the families, are mother (31 percent of the families); father (28 percent); husband, excluding unmarried fathers (4 percent); and wife, excluding unwed mothers (2 percent). The first two, by definition, constitute cases of unmarried individuals.[10] The rationale here is that the unwed state is an example of behavior that society does not condone and is not even approved—allowing for some exceptions—by relatives and peers. The percentage discrepancy between the mother and father roles is due to the fact that some putative fathers (1.3 percent), having failed to provide the financial support ordered by the courts, were rated as legally deviant, while a number of others (2 percent) could not be identified. Social deviance in the husband and wife roles represents instances of gross failure in the spouse role such as cruelty, emotional neglect and adultery.

The third most common form of deviance, role insufficiency, which denotes failure to carry out socially expected familial roles, is noted in 22 percent of the study families. Though for our analysis its significant characteristic is the violation of behavioral norms, the criteria for determining whether norms have been violated rest on a judgment of whether family standards of health and welfare have been contravened. Role insufficiency illustrates how the two dimensions of social functioning, deviance and health-welfare, intertwine, even though at the level of observed behavior a distinction between the two can often be drawn. The only social role frequently registered insufficient (affecting 18 percent of the families) is that of the father, and it signifies, by and large, a lack of interest in the child-rearing process and the failure to assume some responsibility in it. Other forms of role insufficiency are scattered as isolated cases of behavior over nearly all the familial roles. Concentrations exceeding 2 percent (11 cases) are found only in the roles of homemaker (3.7 percent), husband (3.4 percent), male breadwinner (2.7 percent) and money manager — male (2.2 percent). Three of these involve the father (unmarried fathers are not included) and denote failure to meet psychosocial and economic role obligations. The only female role in which a handful of individuals manifest behavior that clearly falls short of social expectations is that of housekeeping-homemaking. Poor housekeeping to the point where it could be labeled role insufficiency is, in fact, remarkably uncommon, and this holds true for higher and lower status households, black as well as white families (all of the subgroups have under 10 percent of the women rated as insufficient in the homemaker role).

Legal deviance is by far the least common, occurring in one form or another in only 9 percent of the study families. Its manifestation is very low (from 0 to 1 percent) in most roles with the exception of member of the community — male (7 percent of the families), member of the community — female (2 percent), husband (1.4 percent), father (1.3 percent). For the most part the last category represents unmarried fathers' cases of nonsupport where a court order has been issued. Legal deviance in the husband role makes up behavior that has become subject to legal action, marked by neglect and cruelty. Legal deviance in the role of member of the community covers a variety of delinquent acts, both adjudicated and nonadjudicated, including fraudulent use of welfare funds.

If deviance is conceptually a major dimension of family functioning, there ought to be a close statistical relationship between the two factors. In Exhibit 14.1 the interrelationship between total functioning and the four components of deviance is drawn.

EXHIBIT 14.1:   RELATIONSHIP BETWEEN TOTAL FAMILY FUNCTIONING[a] AND FOUR DIMENSIONS OF DEVIANCE

TYPE OF DEVIANCE	Gamma	x^2	D.F.	P
Role conflict	-0.45[b]	55.36	3	$<.001$
Social deviance	-0.73	147.27	3	$<.001$
Role insufficiency	-0.68	99.27	3	$<.001$
Legal deviance	-0.69	54.17	3	$<.001$

[a]Deviance is dichotomized as being either present or absent. Total family functioning is broken down into four score groupings. For details see Chapter 5.

[b]A negative gamma means that lower family functioning is associated with more deviance.

As predicted, all four types of deviance are significantly correlated with overall family social functioning. In line with the previously stated hypothesis, role conflict shows a lower degree of association than the other types of deviance. In addition to the reason cited earlier, that role conflict is the most latent form of deviancy and more compatible with adequate functioning, it also represents a struggle in coming to terms with acceptable norms. Contrast this to legal and social deviance, which indicate the abandonment of such norms. The fact that role conflict is, nonetheless, correlated with poor functioning seems to indicate that it is likely to have an adverse effect upon many different areas of family functioning.

The arguments cited regarding the differential relationships between the four types of deviance and social functioning can also be applied to their relationships to social status (see Exhibit 14.2). Role conflict, constituting the lowest degree of nonconformity, shows a statistically significant measure of association with the class factor. Social deviance is, in both instances, most highly correlated. The lower coefficients denoting the relationships to legal deviance can be explained largely by the low frequency of illegal behavior. Clearly, higher-class membership imposes a decided restraint upon family deviance, particularly its extreme manifestations.

EXHIBIT 14.2: RELATIONSHIP BETWEEN SOCIAL CLASS AND FOUR DIMENSIONS OF DEVIANCE

TYPE OF DEVIANCE	Gamma	x^2	D.F.	P
Role conflict	-0.23	10.91	2	$<.01$
Social deviance	-0.78	141.13	2	$<.001$
Role insufficiency	-0.66	74.51	2	$<.001$
Legal deviance	-0.51	14.17	2	$<.001$

An attempt to explore ethnic (black-white) differences in deviant behavior associated with family functioning might address itself usefully to this question: Do we have a theoretical basis for predicting substantial differences on the deviance dimensions similar to those found on social functioning? (See Chapter 6.) As has become evident from earlier chapters, family functioning has a strong socioeconomic underpinning, and these differences are sharply reflected in a comparison of black and white families. As mentioned earlier, when ethnic groups were compared on social functioning but class was held constant, differences became greatly attenuated but were not reduced below the level of statistical significance, at least in relation to total functioning scores. Although the thesis of subcultural differences furnishes perhaps an all-too-ready explanation of ethnic differences, this study also has provided some cogent evidence (see especially Chapter 12) of intraclass economic inequalities between black and white families. Deviance, as we showed above, is also significantly class related, and one would anticipate a carryover of status differences into black-white comparisons. One would expect, furthermore, that intraclass differences will be found to exist not only because controlling for class leaves residual economic differ-

ences (see Chapter 12) which are likely to have behavioral consequences
but also because blacks, as the more deprived social group, would be
more likely than whites to exhibit deviant reactions to low socioeconomic status. If this is true, then black-white differences in deviant
behavior should be more pronounced in Class 5 and 6 than Class 1-4.

EXHIBIT 14.3: RELATIONSHIP BETWEEN WHITE VERSUS NEGRO
STATUS AND FOUR DIMENSIONS OF DEVIANCE

TYPE OF DEVIANCE	Q	x^2	D.F.	P
Role conflict	-0.14[a]	2.51	1	N.S.
Social deviance	-0.89	114.51	1	<.001
Role insufficiency	-0.65	32.54	1	<.001
Legal deviance	-0.27	2.58	1	N.S.

[a] A negative gamma means that being white is related to less deviance.

Exhibit 14.3 presents the relationship between ethnic characteristics
of the project families and their degree of deviance on the four dimensions of that variable. This comparison, which disregards intraethnic
class differences, reveals high and statistically very significant differences in social deviance and role insufficiency. Nonsignificance in legal
deviance is mainly the result of the small number of such instances. The
lack of a difference on role conflict, indicated by both a low Q and a low
chi square, is essentially in line with the previous findings which related
that dimension of family functioning to social status. Role conflict is
experienced by a considerable number of heads of families — especially
mothers — in the various social classes and ethnic groups. Figures in
Exhibit 14.3 suggest that whatever the consequences of heading a Negro
family, being significantly more subject to role conflict is not one of
them. We can assume that the low negative correlation reflects the influence of class on racial status, for when black and white families are
compared on role conflict separately for each one of the status groups
both gamma and chi square coefficients are close to zero.

The lack of statistical significance in the relationship between black
and white cases on legal deviance carries over to the cross-tabulations
when class is held constant. The near absence of illegal acts in Class 1-4
families (one case among the whites) precludes a meaningful comparison.
In Classes 5 and 6, showing 17 and 26 instances of legal deviance respectively (more blacks are deviant), Q coefficients are -0.27 and -0.28, and
not statistically significant.

The hypothesis of significant differences was borne out by our data,
as shown in Exhibit 14.3, on the variables social deviance and role insuf-

ficiency. Social deviance, as was explained earlier, is a violation of mores or laws which are not rigorously enforced. Unwed motherhood, the most frequent kind of social deviance in our young population, was almost completely confined to black families (94 percent of all cases).[11] This phenomenon of unmarried father- and motherhood explains to a large extent the striking differences not only in a total comparison of black and white families but also in one where social class was held constant. The correlations (Q) between being white and socially deviant were -0.32 (X^2 = 10.03, 1 d.f., p < .01) for Class 1-4, -0.86 (X^2 = 26.42, 1 d.f., p<.001) for Class 5 and -0.80 (X^2 = 27.93, 1 d.f., p<.001 for Class 6. The high prevalence of unmarried parenthood in the social deviance category, however, puts a clear limitation on the findings regarding the black-white comparison. More white than black illegitimate babies are placed for adoption (see Chapter 4). This means that our ethnic comparison on deviance, necessarily restricted to mothers who kept their children, does not cover a representative group of those who give birth out of wedlock.[12] In that sense, black-white differences are mainly a function of the framework of analysis which does not attempt to measure the act of unwed parenthood *per se* but only unmarried parenthood where the mother has decided or is forced to keep the child. In other familial roles blacks also show a larger degree of social deviance, but the frequencies are too small for a meaningful statistical comparison.

Role insufficiency is the other deviance dimension which shows a high and statistically significant relationship to ethnic status. The relationships for the three class groupings were only moderately high (Qs -0.39, -0.53 and -0.44) and significant only for Class 5 (X_2 = 5.80, 1 d.f., p <.02) and Class 6 (X^2 = 4.47, 1 d.f., p <.05). The small incidence (eight cases) of role insufficiency in Class 1-4 restricted the probability of obtaining significant differences. These findings, given the limitations due to small Ns, lend some support to the hypothesis postulating black-white differences in deviant behavior paralleling those found in social functioning and to that of greater differences in the two lower social classes than in the top status group. Clearly not in line with the hypotheses are the findings relating to role conflict, the variable with the highest prevalence in the population studied. Role conflict, which Albert Cohen has stated is inherent in the structure and rules of the system,[13] is apparently as prevalent in the social situations faced by white families as in those faced by black families. One is led to hypothesize that the difference between these groups is not in the number of role conflicts they face but in the alternatives at their disposal, which permit them a nondeviant resolution of such conflicts.

NOTES

1. Hadden and Borgatta, *op. cit.*, p. 10.

2. Albert K. Cohen, *Deviance and Control,* Englewood Cliffs, N. J.: Prentice-Hall, Inc., 1966, p. 12.

3. Robert A. Dentler, *Major American Social Problems,* Chicago: Rand McNally and Company, 1967, p. 8.

4. Albert K. Cohen, *op. cit.*, p. 11.

5. *Ibid.*, p. 21.

6. *Ibid.*, pp. 21-22.

7. Neal Gross, Alexander W. McEachern and Ward S. Mason, "Role Conflict and its Resolution," in Bruce J. Biddle and Edwin J. Thomas (editors), *Role Theory,* New York: John Wiley and Sons, Inc., 1966, pp. 287-296; p. 288. The objection may be raised, of course, that the incompatible expectations may be legitimate and do not constitute a form of deviance. However, it is in the nature of most role conflict that demands for behavior which are in line with the most widely accepted norms clash with demands, desires or expectations which deviate from such norms. The person who becomes involved in such a conflict is the one who exhibits a degree of nonconformity or deviance by virtue of such involvement.

8. It could be argued that most forms of legal deviance are also social deviance. In this respect legal deviance — which occurred with a low frequency — could simply be counted as additional cases of social deviance. We decided against automatic coding because in some instances involving court adjudication the exact nature of the law violation was not known to us.

9. The computations omit from the percentage base cases that are not applicable such as unmarried mothers, fathers who are not part of the family, women who are not employed outside the home, etc.

10. Only one married father and two married mothers were rated as socially deviant.

11. This percentage is not representative of the total population. The reasons for the elimination of white OW cases were given in Chapter 4. The ratio of nonwhite to white illegitimate first births in the United States was 5.8 to 1 in 1964. Clague and Ventura, *loc. cit.*, p. 555.

12. While 94 percent of the out-of-wedlock families in the sample were black, the percentage of nonwhite (nearly all black) primiparae with illegitimate children in Newark was only 70.

13. Albert Cohen, *op. cit.*, p. 16.

15.

Family Growth and Changes in Social Functioning

In the present chapter we will view the family as a changing system whose career can be likened to the life cycle of an individual. To be sure, the Family Life Improvement Project covered only a small span of the family life cycle, stages 2 and 3 according to the Duvall scheme,[1] and yet, these periods, when the first-born is under 30 months old and between two and one-half to six years old, are considered formative stages in the life of a family.

The sample for this analysis, the 175 control group families of the Family Life Improvement Project (177 experimental group cases who received services are excluded), is demographically similar to the original starting group of 555 families. The proportion of Negroes in the longitudinal sample is 66 percent, compared to 61 percent in the total sample. Thirty percent are white and 4 percent Puerto Rican compared to 35 percent white and 4 percent Puerto Rican in the total research group. Sixty-seven percent are married both in the smaller sample and the larger one.

In the longitudinal study group there were 28 percent Catholics, 62 percent Protestants and 4 percent Jews. The original research population was composed of 34 percent Catholics, 58 percent Protestants and 3 percent Jews. The remainder were mixed marriages. In the longitudinal study group, 17 percent belonged to Class 1-4, 42 percent to Class 5 and 41 percent to Class 6, while the original research population had a distribution of 18 percent — Class 1-4, 45 percent — Class 5 and 37 percent — Class 6. At the beginning level of family functioning, likewise, there is a fair measure of comparability. For the 175 control group families, 30 percent rated High, 29 percent Medium-High, 22 percent Medium-Low and 19 percent Low. The original 555 families were rated 30 percent High, 26 percent Medium-High, 20 percent Medium-Low and 24 percent Low.

CHANGES IN DEMOGRAPHIC STATUS

Although the research project covered a five-year period (September 1964 to August 1969), the span of observation of control families was necessarily shorter. It took almost a year to locate and interview the original group of 555 cases, and the final research interview of the 175 control families was scheduled five months before termination. As a result, the mean research period for the 175 families studies longitudinally was 38 months with a standard deviation of four months and a range of from 28 to 49 months. During this time children born when the project was new grew into preschoolers and just over two-thirds of the study families (68 percent) who remained added to their families. Forty-three percent had a second child, 20 percent had two more children, and 5 percent had three more.

During the research period families were on the move, searching for more adequate quarters. Eighty percent moved after the birth of their first child and, of that group, nearly half moved two or more times. For 14 percent of families this meant moving from a commercial or mixed commercial-residential neighborhood to one which was largely residential. (The proportion living in residential neighborhoods increased from 59 percent to 73 percent.) The percentage living in single homes went up 9 percent (from 4 percent to 13 percent), and there was also a 6 percent rise from 8 percent to 14 percent in the number of families residing in public housing projects. The proportion living in multiple dwellings (apartments and duplexes) dropped 12 percent from 84 percent to 72 percent, and there was furthermore a 3 percent decline from 4 percent to 1 percent in the number of families who lived in single rooms or had other arrangements that fell short of the requirements of a self-contained dwelling unit.

All in all, then, the housing status of the young families did not change radically during the research period, and the lack of a more decided change can be ascribed, at least in part, to a housing shortage in the metropolitan Newark[2] area. Likewise, the families' economic status did not register any dramatic change during the project's tenure (see Chapter 12), and the changes in the families' legal status were inconsiderable. The percentage of the 175 control families who were legally married when the study ended was identical with that at the study's beginning. The percentage of separated couples rose from 1.1 percent to 6.9 percent, and divorced parents added one case, making a total of two (0.6 percent to 1.1 percent). Against this, the proportion of unwed mothers decreased from 31.4 percent to 25.1 percent.[3]

Along with the relatively minor changes involved in income and type of housing, two-thirds of the young families added children, as explained above, and the first-born, who had been infants when the study started, grew into youngsters ready to enter school. Although we have no data on the budgets of the families, we can assume that their expenses rose not only because there were more mouths to feed and bodies to clothe but also as a result of the moves (involving four-fifths of the families) to new and presumably more spacious quarters which required higher rental payments. More than added financial responsibility is required in the larger family, of course. The network of meaningful social interaction is extended from two members to three or four. Children must be taken into account when planning for such matters as housing (living space, play areas, availability of schools, etc., must be considered), family recreation, vacations, etc. The larger family also frequently requires reorganization of parental priorities.

The question to be discussed here is: What are the changes in the family's social functioning that correspond to the structural changes described here? Do the shifts in the social role networks and relationships from an essentially two-person group to one which is larger, along with added social and financial responsibilities, substantially affect the ways in which family members carry out their socially expected roles and tasks?

The family development literature that deals with issues related to family functioning (see Chapter 2) considers changes from a long-range perspective, usually a decade or more. The present inquiry takes a shorter view of change, covering the more limited period described above, although it seems reasonable to view change during this shorter time span as part of the larger developmental period to which it belongs. Thus we hypothesize, on the basis of the predominant evidence from the research literature, plus our own arguments, that family functioning tends to decline during the period of this study.

We shall endeavor to deal with this question in two stages: first, we will look at the changes in social functioning occurring among all 175 control group families; second, we shall relate change in family functioning occurring during the time of the project to some of the basic family characteristics which have constituted the chief independent variables of this study.

PATTERNS OF CHANGE IN FAMILY FUNCTIONING
AMONG THE STUDY FAMILIES

Basic indices used in this study for measuring family functioning are the total scores and the factor scores (for details see Chapter 5). Changes in total scores are represented by positive numbers on a continuum whose midpoint corresponding to zero change is 30. The mean change for the 175 families who remained in the study is 28.98 with a standard deviation of 6.34,[4] a change which is not statistically significantly different from zero change.[5] In other words, by the first criterion selected for studying the movement in our families' social functioning, the basic research hypothesis, which postulated negative movement for the population, is not supported in spite of the fact that change was in the predicted direction.

Factor scores stand for family functioning on a number of dimensions identified by the factor analysis of subcategories of functioning. For purposes of studying change patterns, mean factor scores representing family functioning at the beginning and the end of the study period were compared. These are shown in Exhibit 15.1.

EXHIBIT 15.1   FACTOR SCORES OF FAMILY FUNCTIONING AT THE START AND THE END OF THE STUDY (N=175)

FACTORS	Mean Score[a] Beginning	Mean Score End	S.D. Beg.	S.D. End	P
Interpersonal-expressive	62.75	60.69	8.50	10.77	.05[c]
Instrumental	61.50	61.93	9.50	10.22	N.S.
Economic	62.94	63.61	7.61	6.99	N.S.
Formal relationships[b]	66.81	67.20	4.66	4.13	N.S.
Health conditions	65.92	62.91	6.27	7.96	<.001[d]

[a]Mean factor scores are the sums of subcategory scores divided by the number of categories in the factor and multiplied by ten.

[b]Based on only 116 cases because of missing information.

[c]On the basis of a two-tailed t test where t = 1.98.

[d]$t = 3.92$.

Data in Exhibit 15.1 convey part of a picture which is more complex than that which is revealed by the total functioning score of the 175 families in the longitudinal study. Beginning and end scores in the dominant interpersonal-expressive factor, which is composed of eight subcategories, indicate changes that are statistically significant at the 5 percent level. That is to say, during the research period interpersonal relations between parents, parents and children, as well as nuclear family, relatives and friends showed a measure of deterioration despite the fact that disturbed functioning was more heavily concentrated in instrumental areas at the outset of the study (we shall return to this point in Chapter 16). In contrast to this, instrumental functioning (composed of five subcategories) covering tasks aimed at maintaining the physical aspects of family life as well as economic functioning (made up of four subcategories) show a slight but statistically not significant improvement. The factor formal relationships (with two subcategories) also shows a small but insignificant rise, while the one variable factor labeled health conditions registers statistically significant negative change at the 0.1 percent level.

A roughly comparable picture is communicated when movement in functioning is analyzed by the conceptual areas (main categories) of family functioning. Change scores here are represented by values with a theoretical range from 1 (or -6 negative change) to 13 (or +6 positive change), with a score of 7 denoting zero movement. The following are the mean scores and standard deviations (in parentheses) for each area of family functioning:

Family relationships and unity	6.86	(1.32)
Individual behavior and adjustment	6.89	(1.18)
Care and training of children	6.33	(1.24)
Social activities	6.98	(1.03)
Economic practices	6.93	(1.07)
Home and household practices	6.97	(1.40)
Health conditions and practices	6.86	(1.17)
Use of community resources	7.12	(0.79)

The composite picture is one of slight, but not statistically significant, negative movement except for care and training of children (t = 5.03, p< .001 using a two-tailed test). It should be remembered that the judgmental weighting employed in the rating of subcategories results in slightly different group scores — whether for an area or factor — than does the extraction of mean factor scores, which gives each subcategory equal weight. Allowing for this difference in method of calculation, we find that scores for main categories also show that there is more extensive negative movement in areas with interpersonal-expressive components — especially care and training of children, and family relationships and unity — and in health conditions and practices — with lesser negative or slight positive change in the others. It will be recalled that the above conceptual groupings do not combine, as do the factors, types of functioning by the nature of the activity (e.g., instrumental and expressive) but bring together functions having a common goal, such as the care of children or the maintenance of family health. This accounts for the fact that more factors show slight positive movement than do main categories, for the positive changes in the subcategories in the area use of community resources, for instance, were distributed among the instrumental, expressive and formal relationship factors.

All in all, however, the quantitative change in areas of functioning is characterized by minor modifications in the level of role and task performance, except in care and training of children. Deterioration here was mainly in the spheres of training and emotional care (physical care showed a very small negative change), suggesting that the care and rearing of children tends to be an area of problems at this life-cycle stage. The increase in disturbed functioning in this area can be viewed as a handicap which is inherent in the process of children growing older, presenting parents with new and somewhat bewildering situations that may be difficult to handle. The demands of a crib-bound infant or a toddler are, after all, less complex than those of a preschooler.

Although the span of time over which the longitudinal study extended was less than four years, we can still ask whether the change recorded was uniform over the entire period or took on different forms. In order to accomplish this we compared family functioning scores for each family at the beginning, at the midpoint and the end of the study. The midpoint was designated as the time about halfway through the research period and it was determined separately for each case, not for the group of study families as a whole. Omitted from this comparison were 38 families whose evaluation of functioning was of the before-after type — that is to say, they were not interviewed during the course of the study. The question that needed to be answered first, before inquiring into the more detailed nature of change, was whether the method of seeing families only at the start and the end of the project instead of several times during its course tended to influence the findings on movement. Such a comparison revealed no systematic bias as a result of the different methodologies.[6] Thus, we have confined the study of the temporal components of change to the 137 families with three or more contacts with an interviewer.

The beginning/midpoint/end comparison of social functioning scores for these families shows an almost uniform but rather unexpected pattern. The total family functioning score and seven out of eight main category scores of social functioning show more negative changes during the first half of the study period than during the second. The beginning to midpoint decline in the level of social functioning is represented by a score of 28.24, which is statistically significant (t = 3.53, p < .001 with a two-tailed test) for overall family functioning as well as for the main categories care and training of children (t = 5.00, p < .001) and individual behavior and adjustment (t = 2.08, p < .05). Exhibit 15.2 shows the changes in main category scores from the beginning to the midpoint and from the midpoint to the end of the study.

The beginning to midpoint study period is characterized by a family functioning deterioration — significant in two areas — except for use of community resources. By contrast, the second half of the study period

EXHIBIT 15.2: CHANGES IN MAIN CATEGORIES OF SOCIAL FUNCTIONING FOR 137 FAMILIES BETWEEN THE BEGINNING, MIDPOINT AND END OF STUDY

AREA OF FAMILY FUNCTIONING	Scores—Beginning to Midpoint		Scores—Midpoint to End	
Family relationships and unity	6.77	(1.21)[b]	7.15	(1.03)
Individual behavior and adjustment	6.73	(1.07)[c]	7.22	(1.02)
Care and training of children	6.34	(1.09)[d]	6.95	(1.02)
Social activities	6.84	(0.91)	7.18	(0.93)
Economic practices	6.77	(1.11)	7.09	(0.97)
Home and household practices	6.90	(1.09)	7.06	(1.19)
Health conditions and practices	6.86	(0.99)	7.01	(0.90)
Use of community resources	7.09	(0.78)	7.07	(0.64)

[a] A score value of "7" represents zero change.
[b] Standard deviations are in parentheses.
[c] Significant beyond 5 percent level.
[d] Significant beyond 0.1 percent level.

shows a slight improvement, none of it significant, in all areas of social functioning except care and training of children. This area registers a continued deterioration, although the rate is reduced in role and task performances. The change scores, it will be recalled, indicate direction — around the zero change value of 7 — relative to the starting position at each interval. The combined value of change for the entire research period was reflected in the change scores for that time span presented earlier. Thus, we find that during the first half of the research period the social functioning of the 137 multiple-contact project families showed a greater decline than during the second half, with the exception of one area, use of community resources, which indicated that in both periods there was an approximately equal gain.

Factor scores, as would be expected, reveal a similarly fluctuating pattern with the modifications resulting from a different alignment of subcategories as a result of the factor analysis. This is shown in Exhibit 15.3.

We observe in Exhibits 15.3 and 15.4 that beginning-to-middle factor score differences show greater negative movement or less positive change than middle-to-end score differences with one exception. The factor of formal relationships had data on only about half the cases and showed a slight, statistically nonsignificant, rise-decline pattern. The significant negative changes on the interpersonal-expressive dimension and in health conditions occurred during the first rather than the second half of the research period. The families' instrumental functioning, denoting ways of managing the home and providing physical care for

EXHIBIT 15.3: FACTOR SCORES OF FAMILY FUNCTIONING AT THE START, MIDDLE AND END OF THE PROJECT FOR FAMILIES WITH MORE THAN TWO RESEARCH INTERVIEWS (N=137)

| FACTORS | Mean Scores | | | P | |
	Beginning	Middle	End	Beg.-Middle	Middle-End
Interpersonal-expressive	62.57	59.86	60.85	$<.02^b$	N.S.
Instrumental	61.51	61.68	62.14	N.S.	N.S.
Economic	62.77	62.18	63.41	N.S.	N.S.
Formal relationships[a]	66.42	67.61	67.34	N.S.	N.S.
Health conditions	65.91	63.21	62.70	$<.01^c$	N.S.

[a]Based on only 67 cases because of missing information.
$^b t = 2.34$ (two-tailed test).
$^c t = 3.21$ (two-tailed test).

EXHIBIT 15.4: CHANGE PATTERN BY FACTORS IN THE SOCIAL FUNCTIONING OF 137 FAMILIES

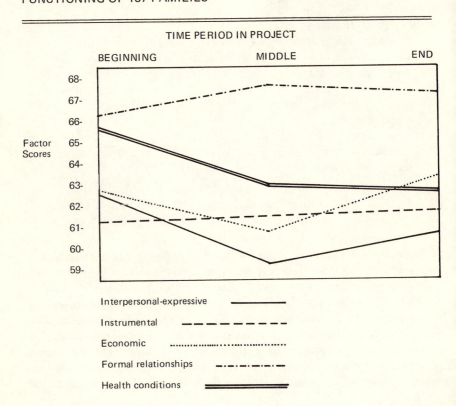

TIME PERIOD IN PROJECT

BEGINNING   MIDDLE   END

Factor Scores

Interpersonal-expressive   ————————
Instrumental   — — — — — — —
Economic   ....
Formal relationships   —··—··—··—··—
Health conditions   ══════════

family members, registered very slight improvements during both study phases.

Summarizing the data from Exhibits 15.2 and 15.3 we find that the areas of functioning comprising interpersonal-expressive roles, including the emotional care of children[7] and the family's general state of health, all of which showed a decline in functioning over the three-to-four-year period, were the ones which revealed the main downward trend during the first half of that time span. Instrumental and economic functioning and behavior involving formal social relationships (church activities and formal social activities) fluctuated slightly, and the level of adequacy was somewhat but not significantly lower at the project's beginning than at its termination.

An initial suspicion that the down-and-up change pattern constitutes an artifact of measurement because more sensitive and presumably more negative information may have been transmitted by the respondent after the first contact was dismissed for two reasons. First, as a result of prior experience the principal investigators were fully aware of this possible pitfall in the measurement procedure and had been carefully instructed from the very beginning to update the narrative account of the beginning situation whenever pertinent information became available in later interviews. Second, a comparison of beginning/middle/end main category functioning scores for the above 137 families with the scores for 177 experimental group families not dealt with in this study[8] showed very similar movement patterns.[9] Two findings regarding the treatment group families need to be mentioned in elucidation of this point. In spite of differences between treatment and control groups that could be ascribed to intervention, the change patterns of the two were more similar than dissimilar.[10] The risk mentioned above relative to data for the 137 control group cases, of beginning information being misplaced, does not apply to treatment group families. The beginning profile of family functioning had generally been updated completely a short time after the initial research interview as a result of multiple contacts between family and project staff. We are led to conclude, therefore, that the change pattern thus identified represents not a measurement artifact but a condition inherent in family development for the period under study.

The researcher who is confronted with data which either run counter to or are outside the framework of a hypothesis is faced with the need to furnish an explanation. In this instance we are dealing with a situation where the general hypothesis of declining adequacy in family functioning did not take into account a predominant trend of downward and then upward movement. Instead, implicit in this hypothesis, but not spelled out specifically, was an assumption of a modal change pattern for the half-periods, corresponding to the changes for the whole period. This assumption, which was not treated as a hypothesis (that is to say, as a subject originally seen in need of formal testing), was not borne out, but rather an up-down pattern of change was discovered. It was thus necessary to extend the inquiry into the more specific nature of the change patterns in young families during the early life-cycle stages.

In order to accomplish this goal we carried out a detailed analysis based on the total scores of each profile of social functioning of the 137 families with more than two research interviews. With the exception of three of these cases, each family in this sub-analysis had four or more evaluations with a range between four and ten and a mean number of 5.4 (S.D. 1.3). Although the number of contacts on which the longitudinal assessment is based vary, it may be assumed that the fairly close spacing of even the least frequent interviews (once a year) furnishes a picture of change that is in accord with that provided by more frequent contacts.

The charting of scores for each interview made it possible to identify three major empirical types of change patterns, each of which can again be divided into two to three subtypes.[11] The above typology takes the form of labels attached to the family groups rather than to their patterns of functioning. The three basic types were: (1) straight-liners, or families whose mean level of social functioning did not change or changed very little; (2) steady changers, who moved consistently either up or down; (3) zigzaggers, cases showing an erratic pattern of up-and-down movement.

The three main types, their corresponding subtypes together with a brief operational definition of change patterns are given below:

1. *Straight-liners:* change between the first and last evaluation is 3 scale points or less.
   a. No-changers: families whose social functioning scores are equal throughout or fluctuate within one scale point from the starting position.
   b. Hoverers: cases whose scores fluctuate between 2 and 3 points from the starting position.
2. *Steady changers:* change is 4 or more scale points in one direction.
   c. Climbers: scores rise from the beginning to end (allowing for one deviation).
   d. Skidders: scores fall from beginning to end (allowing for one deviation).
3. *Zigzaggers:* change is 4 or more scale points but of a fluctuating nature.

e. Zigzaggers-up: ending more than 1 point higher than the beginning position.

f. Zigzaggers-even: ending at the same level or within 1 point of the beginning position.

g. Zigzaggers-down: ending more than 1 point lower than the beginning position.

The percentage distribution of 137 families according to the foregoing typology is as follows:

Straightliners	*Percent*
a. No changers	8.8
b. Hoverers	21.2
Steady Changers	
c. Climbers	14.6
d. Skidders	21.9
Zigzaggers	
e. Zigzaggers-up	10.2
f. Zigzaggers-even	12.4
g. Zigzaggers-down	10.9

Given the three basic change types, we observe, first of all, that the number of families in each group is roughly equal in size, with the steady changers having a small lead (36.5 percent) over the zigzaggers (33.5 percent) and the straight-liners (30.0 percent). The no-changers represent the smallest minority, and the modal patterns of movement in family functioning over a three-to-four-year period are "skidding" and "hovering" at the same level. When combining subcategories according to the overall direction from the beginning to the end, we find that those which terminate at the same level at which they started (no-changers, hoverers and zigzaggers-even) have the lead (42.4 percent) over those whose overall direction of movement was on a downward slope (skidders, zigzaggers-down — 32.8 percent) and those who moved in an upward direction (climbers, zigzaggers-up — 24.8 percent). Given the present definition of change, which assigns a degree of latitude to the "no movement" position (it includes cases that end up a point higher or lower than the starting position),[12] we find that only one-quarter of the families improved their overall social functioning, while three-quarters either registered only minor changes in total score or had lower scores at the end of the study.

The preceding set of data together with the beginning/midpoint/end analysis of total family functioning and its components shows that the typical family does not stand still but changes its position over time regarding the way it carries out socially expected tasks. Within the configuration of fluctuating movement some dominant patterns can be identified. One of the most important of these — though not isolated in the above typology because midpoint functioning is not identified within the moving pattern of social functioning — is the mean tendency for young families to function most adequately shortly after the birth of the first child, least adequately at the time he is about two years old and at an in-between level at the point when he is ready to enter kindergarten. The predominant down-up pattern thus is not equally balanced. Families at the very end of the research period do function less well than at the beginning as was shown by the comparison of beginning and end scores (see Exhibit 15.1 and the paragraphs following it). Moreover, we also learned (see Exhibits 15.2 and 15.3) that the down and up components of the down-up pattern are not completely consistent but embrace variations relative to the way the change variables were organized. The predominant downward trend of the first phase is not seen in instrumental functioning, formal relationships and use of community resources. The general upward trend of the second phase is modified by formal relationships, health conditions and care and training of children, all of which either continue a downward trend or reverse an early upward trend. Still, the modal first phase pattern for factors as well as main categories is a decline which substantially exceeds the subsequent rise in degree of social functioning adequacy. Though this movement pattern lacks a high degree of uniformity, it does run counter to a previously stated hypothesis of overall negative change during the research period and therefore requires an explanation.

Longitudinal studies, which relate various aspects of family life to life-cycle stages, do not generally break them down into short phases corresponding to those used in the present research. Feldman, however, discovered, in an inquiry concerning couples' satisfaction with different stages of the family life cycle, that parents rated the first year with the infant as more satisfying than either the childless (before the arrival of the first child) or preschool stage.[13] Wesley Burr's study of middle-class families indicated a decline in satisfactions with tasks, children, sex, companionship, etc., between stages 2 (very young children) and 3 (oldest child of school age — stages defined by the author which do not fully correspond to the Duvall stages used in this study), with an upturn in the satisfaction curve at stage 3.[14] In the present study, however, both stages cover relatively large time spans, and the exact point of change in satisfactions cannot be pinpointed.

A qualitative review of events, tasks and roles of the young couple shows, nonetheless, that a finding of declining adequacy in family functioning after the infant stage followed, some two years later, by a partial reversal of this trend, is not farfetched. Childbirth and early parenthood are surrounded by a romantic aura similar to that attached to the honeymoon. The demands of a normal infant after he adjusts to a routine of feeding and sleeping are not excessive. The shift in the family's social constellation from a dyad to a triad, requiring multiple adjustments in relationships, responsibilities and power structure, has not yet occurred. The parents' mobility, though more restricted than before birth, is not yet as limited as when the child begins to walk and needs perpetual supervision. If the family faces a space problem it does not become acute until the child gets older and he and the parents need the privacy of separate bedrooms. As a result, the economic pressures to acquire larger quarters with suitable sleeping and play space are less at the infant than at the toddler stage. Above all, problems of discipline and control are absent until the child turns into a social being, capable of independent behavior.

The middle stage of the research, it may be assumed, was characterized by the very handicaps and burdens that were absent or present but to a muted extent during the infant stage: more demands upon the parents' time, greater financial responsibilities, decreased mobility, major readjustments in the husband-wife relationship and the emergence of problems in the child-rearing area. Second pregnancies or births were characteristic during this mid-evaluation period. An advanced stage of pregnancy or the need to care for a baby while on older child is underfoot or perhaps still in diapers are conditions likely to put a major strain upon the family system. This latter point is actually documented by our data which show that families who had more then one child during the time of the study — compared to those who had but one child — showed a relatively greater decline in social functioning during the first than the second half of the project. Differences, though small, are consistent for total scores and factors.[15]

If the preceding developments explain a deterioration in social functioning during the first half of the research period which is significant in some areas, to what can be ascribed the improvement, however small, during the second half? A plausible explanation is that, following efforts to come to grips with the problems of the middle period, the families were probably able to develop routines for coping with the problems. Perhaps equally important is the fact that the development of the first child into a preschool youngster and the growth of many of the second children into toddlers (only one-quarter of these study families had more than two children) simplified and perhaps reduced the scope of child care. To the extent that the family developed successful mechanisms for dealing with the problems of the infant growing into a toddler, we expect that these served to ease the transition for the second and subsequent children, and were beneficial to the overall social functioning of the family.

We do not know whether the small relative improvement (which in the case of care and training of children and the factors formal relationships and health conditions means lesser or small deterioration) during the second research phase constitutes a short- or long-term trend. The evidence from most longitudinal studies which address themselves to the issues of satisfaction, companionship, intimacy and related variables (see Chapter 2) indicates a long-term trend, spanning the major portion of the child-rearing period, toward less satisfactory conditions. On the strength of these findings we hypothesize that the minor improvements in family functioning during the preschool period constitute a short-term trend to be followed by a further decrease in functioning adequacy as school-age children present more problems, as economic pressures mount as a result of increased family needs, and as husband-wife roles become more segregated and less egalitarian.[16]

An interpretation of beginning-to-end scores hinges, of course, in part on the meaning that can be read into the changes occurring between the midpoint and the end. Since over half the families show a fluctuating pattern of social functioning when the units of observation are relatively short time periods (four months to a year) it comes as no surprise that an analysis of the longer time spans of 15 months to two years also show fluctuations which tend to remain hidden in trend analysis based on life-cycle stages. We feel that secular trend analysis is complemented by short-term trend analysis, for the latter maximizes the chances to establish empirical and theoretical links between significant events in family development and changes in social functioning. Short-term trends, on the other hand, can only be meaningfully interpreted when they can be analyzed within the context of long-term movement in family functioning.

Using change in functioning during our research period as the dependent variable, we are saying that, during this span of time, extending from the stage when the first-born is either an infant or beginning toddler to the point where he reaches the age of four or five, net changes in the families' social functioning are likely to be affected by certain familial characteristics. The particular selection of a termination date for the research leaves open the question of whether the results would have been substantially altered by an extension of the study period. On the basis of identified patterns (a mean decline statistically significant on some dimensions of functioning followed by a much smaller mean rise, not significant on any dimension [see Exhibits 15.2 and 15.3]) and findings from other studies, one would tend to view the net modifications during the study period as a link in a chain of a gradual and continuing but fluctuating trend toward less adequate family functioning.

SOME CORRELATES OF CHANGE IN FAMILY FUNCTIONING

With these reservations concerning the interpretation of our change data, we undertook to identify some of the correlates of the functioning change which occurred during the study period. The analyses are confined to total score, main categories and factors. The first two were cross-tabulated by positive, zero and negative change. Total score distributions for the total sample of 175 families indicated that 39.4 percent of the cases changed in a positive direction, 13.7 percent did not change, and 46.9 percent moved negatively. The three basic factors (factors 4 and 5 are not included in this analysis because together they comprise only three variables) were broken down in five positions—two levels each of positive and negative change and a middle no-change position. In order to avoid including those variables with only a tenuous relationship to change we decided to base identification of major correlates (total score, main categories and factors) on a statistical significance at the 5 percent level and a gamma coefficient of ±0.30 or more.

Surveying the relationship between our social and ethnic status variables and change in family functioning, we find that most correlations are of a very low magnitude and statistically nonsignificant. Ethnicity and social class bear no clear-cut relationship to the way the family changed in the course of the research project. Even the marital status of the woman (the comparison is confined to black women because few OWs in the sample were white) bears only a weak relationship to the various dimensions of family functioning except for the care and training of children. More families headed by unmarried mothers showed negative movement (59 percent) in that area of social functioning than families headed by two parents (32 percent). This relationship is statistically significant (gamma = +0.41, X^2 = 8.79, 2 d.f., p<.02). The same holds true for families who had more children during the study period, where the number of children is also associated with negative change (gamma = +0.32, X^2 = 15.75, 4 d.f., p<.01).

The out-of-wedlock status, we observe, imposes multiple handicaps upon the social functioning of families (see Chapter 8), but its effect is not measurable in statistically significant terms during a limited time period except on child-rearing practices as was shown above. The negative consequences are greatest in training methods and emotional care (gamma = +0.52, X^2 = 11.83, 2 d.f., p <.01) but reach a significant level also in physical care of the child (gamma = +0.33, X^2 = 8.61, 2 d.f., p<

.02). Also, families who give birth to more children have greater difficulty in the care and training of children (gamma = +0.32, X^2 = 15.74, 4 d.f., p< .01). We judged that the diverse and complicated arrangements that unwed mothers had to make for the care of their children, often requiring changes from one sitter to another on short notice, were less conducive to the socialization of children than the provisions made by married parents. The presence of several children probably also represents a deficit from the instrumental point of view. The family with more children has a harder time if for no other reason than that limited economic resources must be stretched farther. In line with this observation we note with interest that the number of children has a significantly negative effect on change in overall family functioning (gamma = +0.30, X^2 = 12.18, 4 d.f., p <.02). This relationship reflects a cumulative change of most areas in the same direction, but the area correlations, except for care and training of children, fall short of the significance criteria laid down above.

Study families who had more than two children during the research period spaced them very closely, and we hypothesize that this imposes great burdens on the mother, strains economic resources particularly in lower-class families and makes demands on the husband-wife relationship, which would be notably reflected in the family's less adequate social functioning. Exhibit 15.5 details the significant relationship between change in overall family functioning and number of children born.

EXHIBIT 15.5: RELATIONSHIP BETWEEN NUMBER OF CHILDREN BORN AND CHANGE IN TOTAL FAMILY FUNCTIONING[a]

| NATURE OF CHANGE | NUMBER OF CHILDREN BORN % CHANGE | | | |
	1	2	3 or more	Mean %
Positive	46.4	40.8	27.9	39.4
Zero	19.7	14.5	4.7	13.7
Negative	33.9	44.7	67.4	46.9
Total	100.0	100.0	100.0	100.0
N	56	76	43	

[a]Gamma = +0.30; X^2 = 12.18; 4 d.f., p <.02.

Percentage differences in change in social functioning indicate that the gap between families who had three and more children (20 percent of the families had three, 5 percent had four children) and those who had two is greater than between families with two children and families with one child. This supports the hypothesis that close spacing is a particularly critical factor. However, in making this statement it should also be remembered that the number of children a family bears is related to their social status and their level of functioning at the start of the study (see Chapter 10). Thus, three or more children were born to 13 percent of Class 1-4 families, to 19 percent of Class 5 families, and 35 percent of class 6 families (X^2 = 6.50, 2 d.f., p<.05). They were born to 14 percent of the white and 27 percent of the black families (X^2 = 3.95, 1 d.f., p <.05). Three or more children were a slightly more (but not statistically significantly) frequent occurrence for Negroes at each class level than for whites. And having three or more children was also correlated with less adequate social functioning (X^2 = 4.57, 1 d.f., p<.05). In short, close spacing could be viewed as being partly a function of being lower class and/or having more problems with regard to fulfilling socially expected roles and tasks. Of course, recognizing this does not explain the relationship between child spacing and change in functioning. It merely shows that some families are more likely than others to have their children at close intervals. One might deduce that close spacing by socially handicapped families is likely to aggravate an inherently disturbed situation. Such an explanation, admittedly, is somewhat speculative in light of the fact that social and ethnic status factors by themselves showed no consistent relationship to change in functioning.[17]

The original level of overall family functioning, surprisingly enough, is negatively and significantly related to total change score (gamma = -0.33, X^2 = 27.51, 6 d.f., p<.001), to the instrumental factor (gamma = -0.35, X^2 = 55.85, 12 d.f., p<.001) and to the economic factor (gamma = -0.30, X^2 = 54.22, 12 d.f., p<.001.)[18] This is in accord with an earlier discovery (see Chapter 12) of greater gains in self-support for the less adequately functioning families than for those who function well. In other words, the initially more poorly functioning families made greater gains in total social functioning than those identified as being less handicapped in the beginning, and improvements took place mainly in the instrumental and economic dimensions of family life. Even number of children did not seem to affect this upward trend. A ceiling effect of the family functioning scale may contribute to some extent to this relationship since 12 percent of the families in the original study group functioned adequately in all areas.[19] It is more likely, however, that what we are observing in these young families are the effects of social pressures that work in the direction of greater conformity of those who are behaviorally deviant.

The question of child spacing relative to change in family functioning requires exploration over a longer span of the family life cycle. Luckey and Bain, in a study of 80 couples who had been married an average of slightly over 13 years, did not find marital satisfaction related to child spacing.[20] By contrast, Hurley and Palonen found evidence that the higher the ratio of children per years of marriages the less satisfactory the marital experience.[21] Similarly, Frederick L. Campbell, using a sample of 1,242 women in the Detroit area, concluded that "the rate at which children are added to the family simply compounds the disruptive effects of increasing size."[22] Both increasing size and close spacing tend to reduce egalitarianism. As children are added to the family the wife takes on an ever larger share of the home duties, though Campbell observed that with the coming of the fourth child, when tasks become overwhelming, husbands tend to relieve their wives of part of their work.[23] Family growth by itself led to a more symmetrical distribution of decision-making, with husbands becoming more involved in child-oriented decisions and women exerting more influence in social decisions.[24] However, wider spacing patterns hold advantages for women, for the long periods between children enable them to take the most active part in the three areas of economic, social and child-oriented decision-making.[25]

Christensen, in surveying the research on the relationship of number and spacing of children to marital success, concludes that the dozen or so studies on the subject have produced contradictory results because research, by and large, has failed to take into account and treat as an "intervening" variable the parental values of husbands and wives.[26] Christensen is able to argue his case cogently by showing the varying results coming from samples whose value system with regard to having children is known to differ. In defense of our own findings we would simply add that the negative association of number and, by implication, the spacing of children to family functioning needs to be interpreted as applying to a young urban, predominantly lower-class and nonwhite population.

PREDICTING THE DIRECTION OF FAMILY DEVELOPMENT

Prior chapters have furnished us with manifold evidence that the level of a family's social functioning at the start of the life cycle is closely correlated with social and ethnic status factors as well as the social functioning of the parents' families of orientation. Efforts directed at predicting the functioning of young families at the outset of the study may be said to be supported by the discovery of substantial and significant relationships among the aforementioned factors. The same is not true, however, for predicting the direction of development after the first child is born.

We must keep in mind, of course, the fact that we have been dealing with a short period of time in the total family life cycle which precluded the chances to identify long-term trends in family functioning. It is also clear that we can only draw uncertain inferences about the relationship between the short-term trend we have studied and a long-term trend examined by others. The exploration here will have to confine itself to changes during the period studied.

Beginning attempts to predict change in social functioning during the early stages of the family life cycle took the form of identifying a group of study families whose overall movement during the period was clearly in a negative direction. These families' characteristics were then compared with those of the remainder of the families who had shown more positive change. This mode of analysis differed from the previous exploration of correlates of change by not including in the negative change group all the cases which showed negative movement of 1 scale point or more but only those which exhibited more decisive negative change. Accordingly, the latter group comprised any family with a total negative change score of 4 points or more, or families with a beginning score of 52 to 54 who moved at least 3 scale points in the negative direction, or families with an initial score of 51 or below who registered a minimum of 2 points of negative change. The rationale for this breakdown is the argument that families with a lower degree of social functioning adequacy find negative change of a lower magnitude potentially as threatening to their well-being as greater change is to those termed most adequate.

These 53 negative change cases were compared with 122 families who registered more positive change, on the following demographic and background variables: social class, ethnicity, marital status, beginning level of social functioning by total score and factors, social class of families of origin, and level of social functioning of families of origin. Of these variables only ethnicity and the social functioning of the maternal (but not paternal) family of orientation are significantly related to substantial negative change in family functioning during the course of the project. White families were less likely than black families to manifest negative change of several scale points ($Q = -0.40$, $X^2 = 4.38$, 1 d.f., $p < .05$). The small size of what might be termed the disorganization-prone group precluded an analysis of change by ethnic factor with class held constant. Moreover, the absence of a significant relationship (gamma = -0.13) between social class and change would have diminished the value of such an undertaking. The overall functioning index of the maternal family of orientation, composed of the expressive and instrumental components of social functioning of the maternal family of origin (for details see Chapter 7), was significantly related, but only at a moderately high level to tangible negative movement during the course of the research project (gamma = -0.39, X^2 = 8.36, 2 d.f., p <.02).

The sum and substance of this effort to predict early change in family functioning must be an admission that, although group trends for the period under consideration can be identified, we are not able to predict which families will move clearly in the direction of social malfunctioning during the early stages of development. Ethnic status and social functioning of the maternal family of origin furnish some clues on direction but they actually explain only a small portion of the variance of change. A large part of the problem, as we stated earlier, is the low magnitude of the change during the second and third stage of the family life cycle. This made it difficult to isolate a large enough statistically significant group that exhibited a change pattern which could be termed malfunctioning-bound. The picture might well be different, and this is suggested by some of the more long-range studies cited in the literature, if the period of observation were extended to cover two subsequent stages of the Duvall life cycle, namely those called "families with school children" and "families with teenagers."[27] These are the phases most often selected as cut-off points in the determination of long-term longitudinal trends.

Despite the appearance of randomness in the early change in functioning patterns, we have been able to uncover a number of regularities which testify to the worthwhileness of this kind of short-run exploration. Perhaps one of the most intriguing findings was the negative relationship between beginning functioning and overall change during the early child-rearing period. This contradicts a widespread notion that a poor start is a one-way ticket to family disorganization. Although we have shown earlier that gains made by families in the face of deprivation fail to overcome the already-existing handicaps, the foregoing findings seem to suggest that developmental forces operating within the family furnish valuable supports for efforts to improve family well-being. The term "support," however, conveys a critical notion in relation to such efforts. Such supports are not enough in an environment where social status and economic opportunity are as closely interrelated with family functioning as in the present research setting.

NOTES

1. Duvall, *op. cit.*, p. 8.

2. George Sternlieb, *The Tenement Landlord*, New Brunswick, N.J.: Rutgers University, Urban Studies Center, 1966, pp. 22-39.

3. These are group percentages that do not reveal the nature of the shifts. For data on changes in OW status see Chapter 8.

4. The most negative movement score in this study group of 175 families was −29, corresponding to a value of 1. The most positive change score was +19, representing a value of 49.

5. t = 1.51, p < .20 using a two-tailed test.

6. Testing for statistical significance of differences appeared inappropriate in this case because few differences at a statistically significant level appeared even for the changes from the beginning to the end of the study. Instead, it was necessary to compare the 38 before and after cases with the 137 families interviewed three and more times during the course of the study on the direction and magnitude of the differences in change scores. The change score for total family functioning was 28.76 for the before and after group, 29.04 for the rest of the families. The mean difference for the eight areas was .18. The before-after group registered higher change scores in three areas with a mean differnce of .16; the multiple contact group showed higher change scores in five areas with a mean difference of .18. In short, there is no evidence that the interview methods which were used accounted for change score differences.

7. The training and emotional care of children accounted for most of the negative change (6.21) in care and training of children (see Exhibit 15.2), while physical care showed only a small decline (6.87) during the total research period.

8. Geismar, Lagay, Wolock, Gerhart and Fink, *op. cit.*, pp. 67-72.

9. In this study treatment cases showed either a *relatively* greater decline or lesser positive movement during the first than the second period in all eight areas and in total family functioning scores.

10. Geismar, Lagay, Wolock, Gerhart and Fink, *op. cit.*, Chapter 6.

11. This scheme was first presented in Geismar, Lagay, Wolock, Gerhart and Fink, *op. cit.*, pp. 103-107 (Reproduced with permission of The Scarecrow Press, Inc.).

12. The decision on cut-off points for defining no change is admittedly arbitrary. In the remaining change analyses we have chosen for statistical reasons — to permit a further breakdown of families moving up or down — to define the no-change category as cases who ended up in the same position in which they started.

13. Harold Feldman, *Development of the Husband-Wife Relationship*, p.22.

14. Wesley R. Burr, *op. cit.*, pp. 33-36.

15. Gammas correlating number of children born during the project (two or more children versus one) and change in social functioning for the periods beginning-middle and middle-end were as follows. Total score: -0.25 and -0.03; factor 1: -0.09 and -0.05; factor 2: -0.33 and +0.19; factor 3: -0.06 and -0.05. The three factors comprise 85 percent of the variables in the factor analysis. Factors 4 and 5 had not been included in this change analysis.

16. Jan Dizard, *op. cit.*, pp. 15-21.

17. The number of families with three or more children is too small to carry out analyses with a third variable held constant.

18. See also Chapter 12 showing comparable results in an analysis with two degrees of freedom.

19. Fifty-eight percent or 52 families at or near the top (scores 54-56) in beginning functioning moved in a negative direction, 27 percent held the line, and 15 percent showed some upward involvement. Thus the scale ceiling did not prevent families from continued functioning at the beginning level or making some improvement in social functioning.

20. Eleanore Braun Luckey and Joyce Koym Bain, "Children: A Factor in Marital Satisfaction," *Journal of Marriage and the Family*, 1970, 32 (February) pp. 43-44.

21. John R. Hurley and Donna P. Palonen, "Marital Satisfaction and Child Density Among University Student Parents," *Journal of Marriage and the Family*, 1969, 31 (August) pp. 483-484.

22. Frederick L. Campbell, "Family Growth and Variation in Family Role Structure," *Journal of Marriage and the Family*, 1970, 32 (February) pp. 45-53; p. 52.

23. *Ibid.*, p. 49.

24. *Ibid.*, p. 51.

25. *Ibid.*, p. 50.

26. Harold T. Christensen, "Children in the Family: Relationship of Number and Spacing to Marital Success," *Journal of Marriage and the Family*, 1968, 2 (May) pp. 283-289.

27. Duval, *op. cit.*, p. 8.

16.

The Young Urban Family in the Context of Family Study

This book has sought to convey the significance of early life cycle stages for an understanding of the family as a social institution. Role and task patterns near the start of the family life cycle have been identified, and the degrees to which they contribute to family well-being have been assessed. The relationship between the family's major structural characteristics and its social functions has been examined in an effort to pinpoint factors predisposing the family toward varying levels of social functioning. Attempting to cast light on the nature of development during this formative period, family change patterns and their correlates have been identified. In addition, the choice of setting and the resultant composition of the research population, predominantly nonwhite and lower class, offered an opportunity to study the type of family which is becoming the core element in many large, urban American communities.

In the previous chapters the quantitative side of attitudes and behavior has been highlighted. This approach, aimed at testing a number of theoretical propositions, was made possible by the availability of a reasonably representative sample of young families.

In the selection of problems, analysis of data and discussion of findings, our emphasis has been on understanding the nature of the social functioning of young families at a middle-range theoretical level. We stressed the discovery of those factors in family life and background which are related to adequate or inadequate functioning and, within the limits of sample and time span, to changes in that functioning. We did not use the implications of the knowledge acquired by this study for either higher level theory building or for the formulation of family programs and family policy. Efforts such as this, collecting extensive knowledge about the young family, must precede attempts at theory construction. The policy issue of professional intervention to improve the social functioning of young families,[1] has already been examined in a companion study which utilized the same research population. This book is a gathering of new data about young families, a contribution to the growing body of family theory.

When Presvelou reviewed American and European sociological literature over an eight-year period, he found two shortcomings: (1) empirical research, on the whole, restricted itself to testing theories on mate selection; and (2) young families, considered primarily a closed system, had only a few areas of their internal dynamics analyzed while external dynamics were completely ignored.[2] This study differs from the modal patterns cited by Presvelou, but seeking a new approach limited the principal investigator's opportunity to test hypotheses derived from prior empirical research. Furthermore, variations in conceptualization not only between the present study and other studies, but also among other research endeavors pose problems when we attempt to replicate findings. Despite these difficulties, we found it possible to connect the present research with a variety of past efforts in the realm of family study.

Two key concepts used in this analysis, family functioning and family developmental stages, should be considered for their utility, both from the point of view of research strategy and the significance of findings for the development of theory on young families.

The social functioning of the family is not one of the "traditional" variables considered in the sociology of the family. The reason for this is that family research over the past four decades has been wedded to a few preferred concepts such as happiness, stability, adjustment and power. Occasionally, objections will be raised to the quasi-normative nature of social functioning, but this challenge lacks solid ground since sociological research does not eschew measurement relating behavior to norms, whether these be of a family, neighborhood, community or nation.

The variable of family functioning, though developed and standardized for more heterogeneous population groups, proves to be sufficiently sensitive to discriminate significantly among various types of family statuses and structures as well as sets of attitudes and orientations. The three factor-analytic subdimensions — interpersonal-expressive, instrumental and economic — identify the most common denominators in family role and task performance, thereby reducing the complexity of the data analysis. The rather close correspondence between the empirically derived factors and the conceptual areas or main categories constitute one means of validating the family functioning scheme.

The developmental life-cycle stages concept explains some important variations in social functioning over time. Above all, use of this concept demonstrates that time is a central correlate of a family's level of social functioning. One of the limitations in this study was the shortness of the time span covered (a mean of 38 months). A microscopic longitudinal approach such as ours suggests two far-reaching refinements in analysis: (1) the Duvall family life-cycle stages[3] need to be broken down, perhaps into the 24 category system proposed by Rodgers[4] or even in a more refined manner to account for the combination of exact ages and number of children; (2) each family's developmental pattern needs to be pinpointed in terms of such a system in order to establish a typology that fits specifically the span of each family career studied. The latter arrangement would have overcome the problem we encountered of variability in family age, a result of our using a 16-month period in order to constitute a sample (see Chapter 3).

We found that the "developmental" approach to the study of the family furnishes a suitable framework for analysis of social functioning. The bulk of the foregoing presentation, comprising a cross-sectional analysis of family functioning, provided a structure in which the relationship of that variable could be tested against a series of relevant concepts. However, the introduction of the time factor laid the groundwork for moving the analysis from the co-variant to the antecedent-consequent level.[5] As we said before, the main drawback in the longitudinal study was the short time span covered and the lack of refinement—needed in microscopic analysis—in life-cycle categories. At the same time, the intertwining of the social functioning and developmental approaches point the way toward the establishment of life-cycle schemes which take into account the needs of long-range as well as short-term longitudinal research.

In spite of these reservations regarding the design of the study, *555 Families* emerges with several revealing conclusions that require testing in other urban settings:

1. The young urban family, contrary to the stereotypes created by some of the writings on urban problems and decay,[6] is a fairly well-functioning entity. Family units handicapped by illegitimacy and absence of the father, though functioning in a significantly less adequate manner than those with two parents, do not emerge as a very disturbed group. (The mean percentage of families headed by unwed mothers which functioned at a marginal or lower level in the eight categories of social functioning was only 15 percent at the start of the study.) Even Class 6 black families, probably the most disadvantaged group in the sample, functioned substantially above the marginal level (the mean percentage functioning at the marginal or lower level was 15 percent). During the two life-cycle stages following the birth of the first child these families more or less hold their ground (unwed mothers encounter

more problems in the area of child care), and the lower-class families, predominantly black, show even slightly greater gains than those of the higher classes, especially in economic functioning. Unwed mothers improve their financial and housing status at a rate about equal to black married mothers, but the lowest status and most handicapped study families at the beginning of the study register relatively greater improvements in their economic situation than other families.

What emerges here is a profile of limited malfunctioning of even the socially most deprived families and some evidence of strength early in the family life cycle exhibited in improved functioning, particularly in the economic realm. However, as we have pointed out repeatedly, these gains do not go very far toward narrowing the large gap existing at the time the the first child is born between the deprived and the socially privileged family. Nonetheless, they are contrary to a widespread notion of early social deprivation leading steadily to a sharp deterioration in family adequacy.

2. Social class and ethnicity are significant determinants of a family's beginning status. Above all, the index of a family's social position correlates highly with most types of family role and task performance. Because Negro and white families distribute themselves differently in the social class hierarchy, the question of black-white differences has to be posed generally in terms of the ethnic differences once the class factor is held constant. These controlled comparisons often show that being Negro or white has a relatively insubstantial effect on the way tasks are performed. For instance, the adequacy of use of community resources is very similar for black and white families, and the former group actually makes more extensive use of them. On the other hand, white parents at every status level share the task of disciplining children much more extensively than do Negro parents. Also, in most areas of social functioning whites perform somewhat more adequately than blacks when class is specified, although the differences in magnitude are small when juxtaposed with uncontrolled comparisons. In the economic area it has been shown that holding class constant does not nullify the differences in job opportunities. The researcher's inability to control for social and opportunity structure may be at the root of many of the black-white disparities, although other differences such as parental task sharing or use of birth control may be subcultural, in the form of differing conceptions about family life.

The salience of the social status factor in many forms of human behavior has been long established. The strong nexus between the American system of social stratification and the social functioning of families, particularly young families, is still in the realm of knowledge "in becoming." While other investigators have concentrated mainly on behavioral differences, with little regard to the functional consequences,[7] the present inquiry concentrated largely on some evaluative dimensions relevant to social policy, particularly health-welfare and conformity-deviance. The notion that the social class structure should circumscribe the quality of early family life to such a large extent is as much out of line with the American credo as is the race problem. Two questions suggest themselves as subjects for further research: Is the close relationship between the social structure and family life an American urban phenomenon, or is it characteristic of industrial society in general? If the latter is true, what are the implications for programs to modify family life, particularly those that put their main emphasis on such narrow-gauged services as counseling, homemaking and family-life education?

3. The foregoing data and other data cited in the study illustrate some of the difficulties inherent in the facile application of the "subculture argument" to explain differences in behavior between status and ethnic groups. A convincing case for such an explanation must rest upon proof that groups differ genuinely rather than spuriously (i.e., as a result of factors other than group characteristics) and that differences are rooted in the values as well as the behavior of those compared. The difficulty in explaining subcultural differences, as shown above, may lie in the methodological problems in equating groups such as black and white families with respect to their position in the American class system. An example of failure to show that dissimilarities in behavior patterns are grounded in values and beliefs was furnished by the findings that differences in short-run birth rates of three social classes are not paralleled by comparable differences in mothers' preference on family size.

Where variations in social functioning and attitudes among status and ethnic groups can be shown to be related to certain social and economic characteristics and where evidence is lacking that differences are part of an integrated system of beliefs and behavior, the "subculture argument" is devoid of a theoretical basis and does not further productive inquiry.

4. The young urban family does not present a sharp profile of social functioning; that is, the degree of adequacy in the various areas of family functioning does not vary greatly for the average family. This is in contrast to some clinical populations whose social functioning shows a steep slope with greatest disturbances concentrated in interpersonal-expressive areas.[8] The instrumental dimension of family functioning, comprising the physical arrangements and activities for the welfare of the family, emerges as only slightly more troubled than the interpersonal-expressive one. Among sub-areas with mean functioning below

the near adequate (6) level, housing appears as more of a problem than marital relationship and income (see Chapter 5). In contrast, project families as a group experienced greater negative movement during the study period in the interpersonal-expressive dimension of social functioning (see Chapter 15) than they did on the other major dimensions of family functioning.

Keeping in mind the often-stated reservation that changes measured during the study period may not represent a long-term trend, we note, nevertheless, that the above observation conforms to some earlier findings on the subject. The notion advanced here, based on a comparative analysis of family profiles[9] and scalogramming social functioning,[10] is the thesis — still in the nature of an hypothesis needing extensive testing — that family malfunctioning proceeds from the interpersonal-expressive areas to other dimensions of social functioning.

This hypothesis does not assume a cause-and-effect relationship between interpersonal-expressive malfunctioning and overall family disturbance, for the roots of the latter and eventual family disorganization may be found in many areas. In a city such as Newark they are likely to be in poverty and psychosocial deprivation. The hypothesis merely suggests that families which experience increasing problems do so above all in their interpersonal relations. In this process of deterioration in family functioning there is, no doubt, a reciprocal interrelationship among the areas, but decline over time is likely to be more pronounced in the areas subsumed in this study under the interpersonal-expressive factor. The long-term result in families exhibiting such change patterns is a social functioning profile similar to those identified in the studies of seriously disorganized families. [11]

5. The quasi-microscopic approach to the change in family functioning — made possible by relatively frequent contacts with the families — revealed a fluctuating pattern of movement over time. Like individuals, families do not move on an even keel but experience changes in behavior in response to a multitude of physical and social stimuli. For the bulk of the families the overall net change during the research period was inconsiderable and leaned slightly in a negative direction but with differences by internal components of functioning (see Chapter 15). That would suggest that a measure of built-in stability, in the form of a continuity in social roles and tasks, is quite characteristic of young families.

Within the fluctuating change patterns some modal trends could be identified. One, already mentioned and giving at least partial support to the study hypothesis, is the movement in the direction of less adequate social functioning. The second, unanticipated but discovered in the course of data analysis, is the downward-upward pattern during the timespan covered by the research. Possible explanations for this short-run trend were discussed in Chapter 15. This finding highlights a point that is likely to be overlooked in research which spans long time periods, as many of the longitudinal family studies do. The life-cycle stages out-lined by most investigators do not necessarily represent periods which are homogeneous as far as family functioning is concerned, and intra-stage differences, as our analysis showed, may even be greater than those which occur between stages. The crucial point in intrastage analy-sis is, of course, the identification of significant events and developments associated with family functioning. It is not inevitable that these be landmark occurrences, such as the birth of the first child or his entry into school. They may be more latent experiences such as the cumulative effect of caring for several children while pregnant or the assumption by the mother of such potentially conflicting roles as child-rearer and wage-earner.

6. Intergenerational continuity, not only in social status but also in family functioning, was clearly demonstrated through a comparison of the young family units with their respective families of origin (see Chap-ter 7). While facts concerning the limited status mobility in modern American society have been known to the field of sociology,[12] informa-tion about the high degree of continuity in social functioning represents an extension of knowledge in the field of family study, though it is not totally unexpected. The meaning of social continuity has to be inter-preted in the context of people's objective situation and their goals and aspirations. Thus, status immobility for a predominantly lower-class population such as the one studied here is no asset in a society where the common goal is improvement in economic and social status. Continuity in family functioning may mean an extension of relative stability from one generation to the next as in the case of the study population, or it could signify a continuance of social disorganization where the subjects are handicapped families.

The positive element in functioning continuity emerges in settings such as the one studied, where relative intergenerational stability in family life, backed as it was by extensive kinship ties, constitutes a pro-tective shield against the hazards resulting from unwed motherhood, economic deprivation and life in the deteriorating metropolis.[13] At the same time, we need to remember that the absence of upward mobility in family functioning complements the lack of status mobility and can be viewed as the intrafamilial side of the larger social situation in which certain segments of the population find themselves bogged down in a way of life they do not desire.

In conclusion, we need to stress that the sociology or social psychology of young families is not a subject separate from family study but is an effort to focus on significant aspects, namely the structures, roles, interactions, functions, attitudes, values, etc., of parent-child groups at a formative period in the family life cycle. The study of young families provides the link between premarital functioning and the operation of the fully developed family system. Research on young families permits an exploration of relationships to families of origin, of early child-rearing attitudes and practices, and of beginning family interactions and transactions, all of which have bearing upon subsequent family functioning but are extremely hard to document retrospectively.

Though the study of family development can benefit considerably from longitudinal research, it cannot serve as the sole method of data collection because it is time-consuming and expensive. Tested alternative approaches, such as the segmented longitudinal technique (where several segments of the life span are studied over a limited time period) or the intergenerational panel (combining longitudinal interviewing with retrospective histories of the parent and grandparent generation) [14] will permit the use of larger samples and reduce the problems of attrition which plague genuine longitudinal research.

Of course, this cross-sectional study of 555 families and the longitudinal analysis of 175 family units, though reasonably representative of their larger universe, tap only a small segment of the population coming under the heading of the young urban family. As we reflect on the findings, such as the high measure of social functioning continuity between the grandparents' and parents' generations or the high intraclass similarity in responses regarding community change, we cannot help but ask whether the specific conditions prevailing in Newark at the time of the study were not a major factor contributing to the results. Issues such as these carry their own impetus for fostering cross-validation research.

NOTES

1. Geismar, Lagay, Wolock, Gerhart and Fink, *op. cit.*

2. C. Presvelou, "Images and Counter-Images of Young Families or the Dynamics of Family Living in Society," in Presvelou and DeBie, *Images and Counter-Images of Young Families*, pp. 19-35; p. 25.

3. Duvall, *op. cit.*, p. 8.

4. Roy H. Rodgers, *Improvements in the Construction and Analysis of Family Life Cycle Categories*, Kalamazoo, Michigan: Western Michigan University, 1962 pp. 64-65.

5. Reuben Hill, "Contemporary Developments in Family Theory," *Journal of Marriage and the Family*, 1966 (February) pp. 10-26; p. 16.

6. For a contrary view more in line with the findings of the present study, see John Mo-

gey, "The Negro Family System in the United States," in Reuben Hill and Rene König (editors), *Families in East and West*, The Hague: Mouton and Co., 1970, pp. 442-453.

7. For a systematic treatment of the relationship between social class and family life, see McKinley, *op. cit.*

8. Geismar, "Family Functioning as an Index of Need for Welfare Services."

9. *Ibid.*, p. 104.

10. Geismar, La Sorte and Ayres, "Measuring Family Disorganization."

11. Geismar, *Patterns of Change in Problem Families*, p. 5; Geismar, "Family Functioning as an Index of Need for Welfare Services," p. 104; Geismar and Krisberg, *The Forgotten Neighborhood*, p. 330.

12. Leonard Reissman, *op. cit.*, pp. 293-374.

13. Several studies which have identified diverse benefits of intergenerational continuity were based on population samples representing stable families. See Joan Aldons, "The Consequences of Intergenerational Continuity," *Journal of Marriage and the Family*, 1965, 27 (November) pp. 462-468.

14. Hill and Rodgers, *loc. cit.*, pp. 203-207.

Appendix 1

Two Case Studies

What can the following two case studies add to 16 chapters of writing about the young urban family? The foregoing presentation sought to be predominantly quantitative, depicting the demographic characteristics, the patterns and changes of family functioning, and the interrelationships among selected variables. All of these were aimed at acquiring knowledge and testing theoretical propositions. In this manner of displaying data results, which is inevitably highly focused as well as fragmented, the total family as a unit of interacting personalities tends to get lost.

These two case studies are designed to furnish the reader with a more qualitative and integrated picture of two young Newark families. The author tried to pick families that are reasonably representative of the total study population. The selection process took the form of taking at random out of a pool of computer-drawn cases families with four or more narrative profiles each, characterized by the following salient modal variables of the study population: being Negro, belonging to the lower socioeconomic status group, having a certain number of children born, demonstrating a level of family functioning which is near adequate or above marginal, manifesting minor changes in social functioning during the study period with a trend toward less adequate functioning, particularly at the midpoint of the study. One of the families chosen is headed by two parents, the other by an unwed mother. Families headed by unmarried mothers represent roughly one-third of the research population.

In several other respects the case studies do not follow the median or modal characteristics of the longitudinal study group. The likelihood of pulling a completely representative case out of a sample is exceedingly small. More important than true representativeness, which could only be achieved by portraying a synthetic unit, is the fact that the two cases are real family groups whose characteristics and social functioning convey vividly relationship patterns, material conditions, values and aspirations of young families living in the metropolis.

The names of the families and their members, addresses, birth dates and places of employment have been changed to preserve their anonymity.

THE ARNOLD FAMILY

Mr. and Mrs. Arnold have known each other for many, many years, since they lived in the same housing project and attended the same schools. Charles dated one of Thelma's friends for a short period, but started going steady with Thelma when she was 16 years old. The couple attended school events, saw movies and went to parties, where both of them liked to dance.

Their first child was born before the Arnolds married. Charles had not asked Thelma to have sexual relations with him until they had been going together a year. She, however, was afraid, and easily convinced him to wait. Then, when the couple was alone in her apartment, with only her younger sister around, their first child was conceived. Thelma has said that she doesn't know how it came about, but she loved and planned to marry Charles and, above all, was curious. Friends had told her something about sex, but she knew nothing of birth control methods. She was frightened at first, and did not enjoy sexual relations. Despite her fear, the couple continued their physical relationship once a week at most, in her home. Gradually she came to enjoy her husband more, and now they are both very pleased with sex, in which they engage three or four times a week.

The young couple was married at home by Thelma's Baptist minister when their first child was six months old. The reason they gave for waiting was that they both had to graduate from high school and save money before the marriage. It was actually Charles, a year behind Thelma in school, who convinced her to wait. Thelma lived with the baby at her parents' home before the wedding, working as a salesgirl and paying her mother for babysitting. Charles came to see her almost every day. In the years of their relationship there had never been a time when the two had not planned to marry.

Thelma's folks expressed no disapproval over her out-of-wedlock status. They seemed happy over the couple's apparent love for each other but were extremely anxious that the marriage ceremony actually take place. Charles was considered a "good catch" because of his quiet ways and job ambitions, and they did not want to be left with an extra child to care for.

After the wedding Thelma became pregnant with their second child. Her husband was delighted, for they both loved children, and she enjoyed perfect health in both pregnancies, during which she attended the City Hospital Clinic. At the suggestion of the clinic staff, Thelma planned to take birth control pills after delivering her second child. Because of their limited funds she and her husband could not see having a third child very soon, and Thelma felt the pills were the most convenient and least embarrassing birth control method. The Arnolds planned to have one more child eventually.

The couple and baby, Joseph, moved in with Charles' parents immediately after the wedding, with an apartment promised them in the housing project in about four months. They were very excited about the prospects of having a place of their own, saved enough for the first month's rent and bought furniture in anticipation. They managed occasionally to go to movies and even to bank for the children's future education, although they owed a good deal on their new furnishings.

Thelma felt shy and uncomfortable with Charles' parents although she termed them kind and sweet. Charles' parents owned a two-family dwelling and so had enough room for the new couple and baby. In addition to the new living arrangements, Thelma and Charles had to adjust to seeing each other daily, to accommodate to changes of mood, and to be quiet when the other did not want to talk or be bothered. On the whole, however, Thelma termed them alike, without conflicts and very considerate of one another. He, for instance, took her out sometimes, though she insisted she had become accustomed to staying home, just because he considered it good for her to leave the house. They did not keep anything from each other and she, though she seemed to defer to him, appeared to have an equal say in family matters.

Thelma and her grade-school educated parents moved from the South when she was a child. She was the fourth of five children. For 14 years the parents have lived in the same housing project, her father employed as a baker and her mother keeping the home. Their children lived and were employed around Newark, with Thelma the only unwed mother of her or her husband's family. Her parents emphasized the need for the children to finish high school, obey orders and be friendly. They were very quiet and religious people, attending church regularly. Thelma could not remember her parents ever fighting.

Charles had but one sibling, a sister still in high school. His parents had also come from the South. Mr. Arnold, Sr., was an illiterate factory worker who did odd jobs for a furniture company. His wife, who had finished grade school, was a domestic worker. During the period when they were living together she sometimes helped Thelma care for the baby.

Religion was very important to the young couple. They tried to live according to the teachings of the church, which was evidently central to their lives. For recreation, Charles engaged in sports with friends. They both wanted to save for a home of their own, preferably in a "nice" area similar to the one where his family lived.

But money was very tight. Charles had only begun working full time, earning $60 a week. Before that he had been employed according to the firm's need, with layoffs between short periods of being either full- or part-time. Although he liked his job and the people he met in the food processing plant, he felt it was temporary because the income was so inadequate. The job's only advantage was the lack of pressure, which made it easy for him to attend night school classes. Although he had graduated from high school he took evening courses preparing him for college, where he hoped to study business administration. Thelma was vague about the courses he was taking, although she encouraged him because it made him happy, and also because she liked the idea of his wishing to better himself.

Joseph was a normal baby, tall and slim, who had walked well at the age of ten months and enjoyed regular food by one year. Both mother and father gave him a great deal of care and attention. He loved his paternal grandmother's German shepherd with whom he played, he enjoyed his tub baths and had a large number of clothes. He responded to a stern "No," but Thelma was unsure how discipline would be handled at a later stage. Most important to her was that he be polite and study hard.

A private physician gave them regular medical checkups but they saw a dentist only when they were severely bothered. Thelma continued to attend City Hospital clinic for prenatal examinations; she and Joseph were there for four days after his birth. The baby attended the Baby Keep Well Station where he had all his immunizations. All were reportedly in good health. This family paid careful attention to hygiene and good nutrition.

Thelma was very pleased with the response of the Housing Authority, which offered them an apartment within a few months. But she could not see herself going to any other social agency and asking a perfect stranger for help. That would go against her whole rather reticent personality.

In their free time the couple usually stayed near home, visiting Thelma's family infrequently because of her advancing pregnancy. On weekends they took the baby to the park for picnics and on Sundays they usually went to church.

Terence, the youngest child, was also born at City Hospital, and the two of them, active and demanding attention, seemed to change Thelma's outlook. Though her house was immaculate she let the children play in wet, incomplete and dirty clothing. She did not give them time or attention and looked forward to the periods when she could get away, leaving the boys with her mother, usually, but with others when possible. The boys resembled their father more than their mother, tall and rather thin. Neither one presented problems, although the oldest did not eat well and they both were ardent thumbsuckers. The parents had decided they did not want more children, and Thelma was taking birth control pills regularly. The time to theorize about discipline had gone. She slapped the children with her hand to enforce her rule and, when angered, talked sternly in loud tones which the little boys dared not ignore.

At this stage of their marriage Thelma began to express openly her negative feelings toward her husband. Her display of emotion may have been the result of having two small children or perhaps her husband's plan to attend a Southern college. When they had first married she had hidden such emotions, she freely admitted, but now she more openly expressed them to her husband. Even though this sometimes precipitated an argument — usually over small and silly things such as going to the store — she felt that this was probably the best way to handle her feelings.

Thelma could not admit to having a negative relationship with Charles' mother, but the older woman supported her son's plans to return to school, and she was going to support the family while he was away. Charles would only see his wife and children on holidays. When Thelma complained about his going away he silenced her by explaining that this was the only way to better himself and thus do better for the family. Since he had applied for admission late and had left his job on the strength of being accepted, he had to find other employment when he learned that he would not enter until the summer. He did not particularly like his new job.

At his new work he netted a little over $70 a week. Twenty dollars of this went for food each week, and $60 a month for rent, which was soon to be raised. They had straightened out the furniture payments so that they now had to pay only $34 each month on that bill. Thelma got a weekly allowance of $10 which she spent, although she could not account for the items. Money meant a great deal to her; she indicated that one of the things she liked best about her husband was his generosity toward her.

Her annoyance with her husband extended to his noninvolvement in housework. He had been raised to consider this women's work, and formerly she had not expressed anger. Now she was irked that only in extreme cases such as illness would he help. Although she had insisted before that they did little drinking, she now indicated that it was his behavior when he was drunk (but she again insisted that this happened very rarely) that she disliked most about him.

Her preoccupation with housework and children seemed to change their leisure habits. Thelma did not feel that they had enough time to attend church, and the family no longer went to the park either, although she could not quite explain why.

Thankfully they had no illnesses; they used a dentist only when severe pain made them seek an appointment. Since they had to wait until they had the money to pay a dentist they tolerated bad teeth until they accrued sufficient savings.

When Terry was a year old Thelma began working nights, earning $67 a week as a full-time technician in a radio parts factory. For seven months she worked, and cared for the children and house during the day. Finally she quit to have a cyst removed from her breast. Actually, she was thankful, for the work was getting to be too much for her. After the operation she had to see the physician every three months because the condition was probably hereditary and might be adversely affected by her taking birth control pills. While she was in the hospital her mother cared for the boys, and during her short recuperation Charles helped her with the housework which was very unusual. She did not find work immediately but collected unemployment compensation, thinking that in the future she would have to work but not at a full-time job.

Meanwhile Charles got ready to go South to college. After his bags were packed and just as he was ready to go to the station to take a train, he received a telephone call from the college advising him to enter a trade school rather than continue in college studies. Terribly disappointed, he refused to talk about his reactions and/or his future plans with his wife, but he did not go ahead with any trade school ideas. His mother, who was so intent upon his rise, was also bitterly disappointed. However, another child at the time was preparing for college and she shifted her attention and emotions to her. And yet, after dreaming these dreams all his life, Charles could not root them out, but talked of rising through the ranks to a better job in the plastics organization where he found employment.

He netted $79 a week at the plastics firm. The rent was raised to $71 a month. The couple continued to pay for the furniture and had plastic covers made, with payments of $10 a month on them. Thelma thought they spent $15 a week on food, but this is questionable for it would have been less than they had spent during earlier stages of their marriage. As before, they had no car or telephone, and they had just opened a savings account, with a balance, she embarrassedly related, of $5.00.

Not only had schooling fallen through; money continued to be a problem and the children were hyperactive. Joseph, the older, no longer listened to his mother and loved to roam. Terry, the younger, was extremely destructive though he stayed close to his mother, and smashed everything he could lay his hands on. Thelma had taken to beating them with a strap for discipline, although her husband felt she was too lenient. She characterized both boys as being very bad, and let them run around in dirty clothing although her apartment was immaculate. At night she told Charles that she was too tired for sex, an excuse which made him very angry. All in all, the marriage seemed joyless, like a life sentence that had to be carried out. Thelma looked old and drawn. When she talked about eventually having a few more children because of her love for them, the interviewer was surprised, for the sentiment did not correspond to the real situation involving money, time, energy and warm, loving feelings.

The Newark riots of 1967 brought catastrophe. Charles was wounded in the abdomen and the left leg when a white man fired two shots one evening after curfew when Charles was about three miles from the heart of the riot area. Charles was taken to a nearby hospital, and he was listed in critical condition. Fortunately he recovered rapidly, and left the hospital in seven days, though he could not work for about four months. The family was incensed at the injustice of the shooting and the severe financial strain it placed upon them. The senior Arnolds gave some financial support while Charles was unable to work. Thelma worked in a factory while Charles cared for the children. His place of employment felt he must have been involved in the riots and put pressure upon him, causing him to resign. When he was well enough to look for other work, he was consistently refused employment on the basis of involvement in the riots. Finally he found his present job as a draftsman. In the interim when he was not yet working and Thelma had left her job, she applied to the Welfare Department and received assistance for two weeks until her husband's disability payments began to come through. She was very surprised at the ease of getting this help and the fact that the department gave them no difficulty at all.

They felt lasting resentment at what they considered unjust treatment resulting from the riots. They joined the United Community Corporation, the only formal association they had had outside the church, and began attending weekly meetings. Often they want to a playhouse which presented primarily the plays of the militant Newark black playwright, Leroi Jones.

In their daily life, however, the anger did not cause much difference. Thelma became pregnant again, perhaps because she wanted to leave her job, but that is conjecture. She worked as a machine operator until the advancing pregnancy made it too difficult. Before leaving, she signed up for an OEO-sponsored program to teach her clerical skills but had to abandon thoughts of entering the program during pregnancy. She planned perhaps to enter it later after the baby's birth, thinking her mother would care for all of her children. She claimed that this training would make her self-sufficient when her husband went to college as he had once planned, but Charles had no specific plans which he had shared with her in this area.

Actually, there was a question about the amount of communication the two engaged in. The pregnancy had not been planned. Thelma had unilaterally discontinued use of the birth control pills and, though she gave as an excuse pain in her abdomen and leg, acknowledged that she enjoyed her condition and looked forward very much to having a baby girl. Her husband was very upset, for he had long considered two enough for them financially. Thelma thought that he had by then accepted the situation and was looking forward to having a girl for a change.

Aside from plans for the future or the pregnancy, the two had general problems in talking to each other. Thelma had once said she was getting over holding in anger and frustration; she later spoke derisively of her husband "talking all the time"; and at the state of the third pregnancy she admitted that at times she deliberately said nothing when he wanted to talk, just to be mean. On the whole they quarrelled very seldom, but when they did it usually centered around finances or his sitting with the children so she could visit girlfriends.

For her such visits were a new experience. Two very close girlfriends lived nearby and she saw them perhaps four or five times a week. The couple still saw a great deal of both sets of parents. When they wanted to do something big they occasionally went with other couples to New York to the theater.

Thelma seemed very happy and relaxed during that period, neat, well dressed and contented. The boys were often over at her parents' home. The older boy was a confirmed roamer who liked to be with the big boys but still sucked his thumb when he watched TV. Charles was finally getting Joseph's last name changed to his, for it had been legally registered under his wife's maiden name since the boy had been born out of wedlock. The younger one, Terry, still was a mama's boy, liked music, and was as particular about his clothing as his father. They both had rather poor appetites but Thelma gave them vitamin supplements every day. They slept well, were weaned and toilet trained normally, and Thelma kept them well dressed, causing her a large wash all the time. For discipline Charles beat them, and Thelma interfered when she thought he was hitting them too hard. Though she also relied on spankings, she attempted to find other ways of chastising, such as sending a child to bed early, but Charles called her too soft with them. Obviously the two could not agree on methods of punishment. Charles spent very little time with them aside from this disciplinary role. He was away most evenings and weekends and only occasionally took them with him on Saturdays or Sundays, although he always oversaw their haircuts. Sometimes in the summers, Thelma took the boys to the nearby city park.

As before, the house was very clean, and wall to floor draperies had been added to the windows. Thelma shopped weekly with a prepared list and bought her meats where savings were to be found. They had a telephone at $7.20 a month and insurance at $7.40, but their rent was still $71 a month and their food bill had remained the same. Charles was making $110 a week in his new job as a draftsman and Thelma received unemployment compensation. They had no savings account and no charge accounts at any of the stores.

For her third baby Thelma used private prenatal care and planned to deliver at a private hospital where she was covered by Blue Cross and Blue Shield. Other medical or dental care was sought only when specific problems arose, for the boys had had all their immunizations and all were in good health.

On the whole, this was a happier period for Thelma. She considered her husband a rather good provider, although she sighed for things she wanted but could not have, and, after hesitating, stated that she would probably marry her husband again but at a later age, after she had the free time and ability to travel. There was no time in their lives to entertain even thoughts of such frivolity.

THE WEBSTER FAMILY

Lillian Webster gave birth to a son in the spring of 1965, just three months short of her eighteenth birthday. Craig, her chubby little boy, never saw his father, for there never had been any thought of marriage. Lillian and George had gotten together alone in her aunt's apartment, a favorite spot for their high school friends. One afternoon when the couple was alone they had sexual relations. They had gone together for about five months. Lillian explained that they had engaged in intercourse for the fun of it, but she swore that it happened only once, and that she had thought she really loved George. So why not—especially since she had gotten both emotional and sexual satisfaction from the act. Two months later, before she knew that she was pregnant, she discontinued going to her aunt's, then stopped seeing George altogether. Her feelings for him had suddenly changed, although she could not quite explain how.

George was not the first boy Lillian had known sexually. She had been intimate once before with a boy she was dating in the projects close to her brother's apartment where she was living. What she knew of sex or of birth control she had picked up from her older sister and her own peers. Of course, the fact that she might become pregnant had never entered her mind.

Lillian's family, her siblings and cousins, were not too upset when she told them of her pregnancy, confirmed in her fifth month by the City Hospital Clinic. Her aunt, however, was angry, for she thought of herself as being partially responsible. Additionally, she was hurt because the two youngsters had violated her trust in them.

The question of her parents' reactions did not come up in interviews, for both had died in the South. Lillian came from a rural background, and her father, a semiliterate farmer, had been the first to die. After selling the farm, her mother had kept the family together in a country home, supported by welfare. Religious herself, making sure the children attended regularly, all social activities centered around the church. Mrs. Webster was dedicated but not overly strict, and Lillian was grief-stricken when her mother had a stroke and died.

A few months later in 1961, Lillian came to Newark, where she and other siblings lived with a married brother in a housing project. Older siblings were employed around the city, some married and others single. On holidays the whole family would get together, but no cultural forms reminiscent of their parents and their southern heritage seemed to have come with them up North. Lillian could not remember being in church for more than a year before Craig was born. Her main form of recreation was going to movies or carnivals, and her only date had been the boy close by, already described.

The married brother, with whom she continued to live until shortly after the birth, became legal guardian for the baby. Lillian never met the putative father's parents, and she did not even know if they had heard of her pregnancy. When the pregnancy had been confirmed she had contacted George, but at first he did not believe that the coming child was his. She thought that she finally convinced him; however, no further contact and no support agreement was made. At that time, George, like Lillian, had one more year until graduation from high school.

At first the girl was resentful over the pregnancy, but in the last months this changed to a happy acceptance, and Lillian has not shown little Craig any resentment. The only difference the pregnancy seemed to make was her inability to graduate from high school with her class. Everything was normal. Not even morning sickness bothered her, and the delivery followed the same pattern.

In a few months the new mother moved in with her older sister, a pretty girl with a five-year-old son also born out-of-wedlock. While Lillian was quiet and shy with strangers, placid in nature, liking quiet people and occupations, looking younger than her years, her sister seemed more sophisticated, very pretty, the decision-maker for the two. They got along very well, sharing work and meals and expenses, for the older sister also received welfare. Lillian took care of the older child plus her own on the weekends when her sister dated, while in return her child was cared for when she went to school. Four nights a week she attended high school equivalency classes, hoping to finish that last grade which she had missed. Her plan was to get a secretarial position when she completed her schooling.

The apartment she shared was in a tenement in a ramshackle neighborhood, commercial as well as residential, inhabited mostly by blacks. Large inside, it had been rented furnished and was very clean, with two bedrooms and adequate sanitation facilities. Small appliances, however, were missing except for an iron, and the living-room furniture and linoleum were worn and torn.

Going to school took many evenings; child and house care took most of the day. The baby received a great deal of love both from Lillian and her sister. At first the older boy resented the attention received by the baby, but he learned to play well with him and stopped his initial teasing behavior. Still, although she got on well with her sister and nephew, Lillian was very lonely. She was not aggressive and had little opportunity to meet boys. There were no dates after the baby's birth. It might be nice, she thought, for George to see and get to know his son, and also for her to meet with him, be friendly and get to know him better. In reality her only contacts were visits to members of the family and friends from the project.

Although she had taken public classes in child care, Lillian allowed the baby to sleep with her in the same bed. She always felt that somehow the welfare checks could not be stretched enough to buy a crib. Craig hated vegetables, and consequently his diet consisted mainly of starch with some protein. Lillian did not discipline him while he was still a baby, though she did put him in bed when he cried too much. At nine months he crawled but stood only with support. And although he did not yet talk, he loved music, bouncing and laughing when he heard it. She did not attempt toilet training.

At this stage Lillian worried whether the welfare check would cover the extra clothing she wanted to buy the child for the holidays, the crib and baby walker. For herself she was sorry she could not afford a sewing machine, more books and a typewriter. The check of $130 gave her just enough to get by with her share of the rent $34 per month and food $15 per week. Although she had no debts she also had no savings and no insurance. Medical care had always been public but she had no complaints about it, since neither she nor the child had any health problems that first year.

She had already given some thought to the baby's schooling. Like her mother, who thought highly of education, she considered it an asset, a means to get good employment. Her dream was to have Craig go to college. As for herself, she wanted a secretarial position after graduating from the equivalency course, although she had no previous job experience. She hoped to be independent and no longer in need of welfare help (which she was grateful to have) as soon as possible. From the community she had one wish — day care facilities for the working mother.

In the year that followed, 1965, Lillian moved with her sister to another apartment. Although she had mentioned vaguely the wish to move because she liked new places (but not out of Newark), it was really not a step forward, for they had to take one room less. The house was large and clean, at one time very fashionable. A big double bed had to be moved into the corner of the living room, which also boasted some torn modern furniture and a television set. There was no set housekeeping schedule, but Lillian did most of the cleaning and used the washing machine in the building. Her sister was now working as a domestic at various houses during the week. She did the shopping and cooking which waited until she returned from work. Their diet was high in carbohydrates and starch with some protein, but Lillian was very vague about the kind of meat they ate, although she did mention that the baby would only eat chicken.

Lillian seemed very fuzzy about money and the division of sums spent for rent and food out of her welfare allowance. Perhaps she gave her sister whatever was asked for whenever it was requested. But there is also the possibility that the older girl still received welfare assistance though she was working and Lillian may have been exhibiting more of a guarded attitude than vagueness. The monthly welfare check to Lillian and her child was $141 which, the mother said, "pays for everything but I have to stretch it every day."

As before, she took long walks with the baby but not to the park any more, although she did not know why. Although there was a municipal pool not far from her house, she did not use it or even seem to know about it. Craig was clean and well-cared for but still chubby, perhaps because of his diet. He had learned to use crying for what he wanted, and Lillian began to discipline him by spanking. Still, she was very affectionate and warded off the older boy who sometimes became obstreperous. She had decided to wait with toilet training until after the holidays, for she hoped then to be able to afford a potty seat. The beginning attempts without the seat had been unrewarding.

Craig had been in good health during the year, although Lillian had had some very minor illnesses and three teeth had to be extracted. She had been rather apathetic about seeing to the baby's attendance at a Well Baby Station. When she had gone there the first month of Craig's life they had told her to wait until he was a little older. She did not call them again until almost two years had passed, and by then they had lost the boy's birth certificate. They told her to get another. She said she planned to apply for a duplicate from the hospital, but in the meantime Craig had had none of the shots usually given to babies and had not yet been seen by a physician.

The young nephew had been in a car accident and had spent a month in the hospital. When he finally returned home he had a very noticeable limp. Lillian didn't seem to know whether he was to be seen by a physician about this nor did she know what the boy's mother thought about the subject, but she knew that he was scheduled soon to have a tonsillectomy. He, not worried about limps and tonsils, was very anxious to get back in the first grade where all his friends were.

Lillian was not particularly happy about her situation. As before, her main recreational outlet was her close family. She did not see or get support from the putative father, and the horizon was empty of prospective boyfriends. She was so quiet she gave the impression of being unsure of herself. When the social worker called she volunteered very little information and spent the time watching television. In the winter she sometimes went to the movies with her girlfriends, and in the summer she and the baby accompanied her older sister, boyfriend and son to Palisades Amusement Park.

Schooling had stopped. For one semester she had gone evenings, but when she was required to repeat the course, she did not go back. At the same time she had cut her hand on glass and had caught a bad cold, and this always entered her mind when she thought or told of dropping out of school. At times she talked aloud of attending the school near her home in the day, and other times she considered taking a correspondence course. But one thing she knew. She would not want the kind of work her sister did. And her strong concern about community day care centers continued.

During the next year, 1966 to 1967, Lillian seemed to lose more and more interest in keeping herself neat and clean. Some of this had been apparent the year before in her unkempt hair, but as the baby got older the mother became careless about her personal hygiene and her clothing, at least in the daytime. Craig, however, was clean, and Lillian insisted that his wardrobe was adequate. He was taller than last year, a friendly little boy who liked playing with other children. His mother's method of disciplining was to holler at him. He was toilet trained and slept well at night. Because there were no children in the neighborhood for him, Lillian spent a great deal of time at a sister's where there were many children to play with.

The girl's apathy extended beyond herself. Although she now had a steady boyfriend who came around every night, took her to parties and bars, she knew very little about him. Lillian thought he worked in a factory but was not sure. She thought that perhaps he made about $80 a week, but this was a guess. She did know, however, that he was ambivalent about marriage, and she thought that perhaps in a year he might be ready, or at least she said so when she was asked. Her own family would be happy if they would take such a step, she added.

There were many perhapses in her conversation. Perhaps she and her sister would find another apartment in place of the one they had; perhaps she would finish the high school education she had once counted on. All of these conjectures were far in the future.

She had followed through about little Craig's health, though. She herself would not see a dentist because of the pain, but she had gotten the baby's shots taken care of and even administered vitamins as the doctor suggested. All Craig suffered from were frequent colds.

They lived in the same place, and the same financial and living arrangement were in force between the two sisters. The older woman had the same boyfriend, and Lillian's nephew had slowly gotten over his limp so that there was no trace of it. Lillian had enough from her welfare check to go to the movies or buy clothes sometimes.

By 1968 the older sister had moved out. Since Lillian was unable to pay the rent, she also moved. Her first two-room apartment cost her $100 a month, but she finally returned to the project near her family, where she had three bright rooms for $98 plus utilities. The area and the apartment were clean and well kept, although she had sparse furnishings for the place. Lillian felt that her welfare allotment, $199 a month, was adequate for her needs. Although she had no system for managing money, she claimed that she had no outstanding big bills.

The same boyfriend was now a fixture in her apartment. Craig called him Daddy, and Lillian's friend took Craig on errands and to the park. All three went to visit the boyfriend's parents. When asked point-blank, however, Lillian no longer talked about the maybe of marrying him next year. She did not want to marry, she said, because she "is not ready for marriage." If asked whether the young man had ever proposed, Lillian became evasive.

In the housing project the close family maintained its active interest in each other. Craig had many cousins and friends with whom to play; he seemed active, friendly and curious, and was anxious to enter kindergarten in the fall. His appetite was good, his mother said; he went to bed whenever he wished to, staying up late watching TV, for he slept on the living-room couch. Lillian called him a bad, bad boy, but when asked to explain further, she said, "I don't know; he's just bad." He seemed normal in all ways but one — his speech was impossible to understand.

During the day Lillian visited with family and girlfriends. On weekends she went out with her boyfriend to the movies or to visit Roselle or Metuchen to see each other's relatives. The couple had met in a bar and occasionally they went to bars for recreation. As before, all her associations were informal, with family and friends and boyfriend — she had no formal associations, not even the church.

Lillian seemed to be less apathetic than before. Her appearance and clothing were clean, although her dress was unironed. Just as she no longer talked of marrying, she no longer speculated about going on with school. Lillian seemed now to be able to distinguish between what she was going to do in reality and what she would have liked to do in her imagination. She seemed to be able to accept her own situation and to build her life around her nature, rather than invent excuses and dream worlds for herself.

Appendix 2

Family Functioning Interview Schedule

A. FAMILY RELATIONSHIPS AND FAMILY UNITY

1. *Marital Relationships*

a. History

Circumstances leading to marriage: how did you meet? when? where? was there a formal engagement? what made you decide to get married? how did both sets of parents feel about the marriage? when were you married? where? who performed the ceremony?

Postmarital adjustment — first years: where did you live? how far from husband's or wife's parents? how often did you exchange visits? how did you get along with parents and inlaws? job situation; financial resources; emotional and social adjustment; sexual adjustment and relative importance of sex in married life; use of birth control; how many children do you desire? how would you prefer (have preferred) to space them?

Early image of marriage: agreement or discrepancy between image before marriage and actual experience; degree of realism of premarital image; knowledge of sex before marriage; source of such knowledge; premarital sex experience.

Arrival of first child: planned versus unplanned pregnancy; physical and emotional health of mother during pregnancy; husband's and wife's attitudes toward child during pregnancy and after his (her) arrival.

b. Present Functioning

Degree of love and compatibility: how well do the partners get along generally? agreement or disagreement in tastes, interests, views, temperaments.

Closeness of emotional ties versus estrangement and conflict: what kind of emotional relationship? what does wife expect and what does she get regarding tenderness, demonstrated affection, considerateness of feelings, moods, irritations, off-days, temper? what does husband expect of wife? what does he get?

Interdependence and independence between partners: degree of sharing; talking out feelings; agreements and disagreements, both regarding marriage and outside affairs.

Sources of satisfaction and dissatisfaction: inside and outside marriage, regarding friends, relatives, job, social and cultural pursuits; family goals: what do spouses want on a long-term basis?

Agreements and disagreements: their sources; who makes decisions? about what? what are the results? is there a division of labor? what is its nature and how satisfactory is it? any other differences, disagreements or problems? how are they handled?

Sexual adjustment: frequency of sex relations; how important and how satisfying to each?

Responsibility for financial support: who bears it? how well is it met?

Extramarital relationships: how long in progress? how casual or intensive? is marriage partner aware of it and how has he or she reacted?

Mutual role expectations: what does the wife see as her husband's and her own duties and responsibilities? how does the husband see this? do their views agree or differ? what are the effects?

Part played by separated partners: if couple is separated, give detailed description of present relationship; extent to which legal obligations are met.

2. *Relationship Between Parents and Children*

Degree of affection between children and parents.

Display versus concealment of emotions: how are they displayed — holding and cuddling, playing, etc.? amount of care and helping done by the husband, if any; how satisfying to each partner is arrangement for care and discipline?

Degree of respect of children for parents.

Parents' respect for children's rights: how much understanding does each parent have of infantile behavior, i.e., the demands and needs of young children, especially when it interferes with parents' comfort and freedom?

Indifference or rejection.

Favoritism shown by parents.

Companionship and shared activities: what kind of activities does each parent share with the children?

3. *Relationship Among Children*

Degree of closeness, loyalty, affection among children.

Pride in siblings' achievements.

Playing patterns, sharing of possessions.

Cooperation versus resentment.

Areas of agreement and conflict: fighting, teasing, bullying.

4. *Family Solidarity*

Sense of family identity: cohesiveness versus individual solitude and isolation of family members; do the members of the family generally "go it" together or is there a pattern of going separate ways?

Reciprocal values, goals and expectations: values shared versus values that divide the family.

Family traditions and ritual, shared customs: what, if any, are family traditions? this might include what may have been adopted from their own parents and is still shared with them.

Degree of affection and emotional warmth versus conflict and indifference among family members.

Pride in family, pulling together in times of stress.

Shared activities: meals, recreation, travel; planning for common goals.

Nature of decision-making process: is it individual or group?

The use of cultural media such as movies, T.V., radio, books, magazines, etc., as part of family life.

5. *Relationship With Other Household Members*

Nature of relationships with household members (specify who they are) who are not part of the nuclear family.

Degree to which other household members share in or are excluded from family life.

Benefits and problems inherent in a combined living arrangement: who benefits and who is harmed? in what manner? effect of arrangement on family's economic situation, sense of identity.

B. INDIVIDUAL BEHAVIOR AND ADJUSTMENT

Under separate headings cover the behavior and adjustment of: (1) father, (2) mother, (3) oldest child at home, (4) second oldest child, (5) third oldest child, etc. For each individual list birthdates after first name and date(s) of marriage where applicable. Divide the narrative on each family member into two parts: (1) history and (2) present functioning.

1. *History*

Structure of family of orientation; nativity of parents; religion of parents; amount of education of parents; size of family; one or both parents in the home; number of siblings; ordinal position of respondent; out-of-wedlock children.

Social and emotional atmosphere of parental home; affection and solidarity versus conflict; marital relationship of parents; relationship to parents; sibling relationships; health of parents; separations or other crises in family; basic values of the home (religious, ethical, levels of aspiration).

Socioeconomic status of parental home: occupation and income; regularity of income; work patterns; type of residence (rural-urban); characteristics of neighborhood; pattern of social activities.

Education, training and job experience of husband and wife prior to marriage; type of schools attended; reasons for leaving school; occupational training; jobs held before marriage; talents and hobbies.

Social adjustment before present marriage; type of adjustment at home and after leaving home (if applicable); social, emotional and health problems; delinquency and other deviant behavior; social activities and leisure; patterns of dating; social status of siblings.

2. *Present Functioning*

a. Factors To Be Considered for Parents (family of procreation)

General characteristics: appearance, mannerisms, personality traits, ideas, values, attitudes, interests, education and intelligence levels. Give brief physical description of each parent.

Social behavior: adaptive behavior, social skills, relationships with people and institutions; social conformity versus deviance; handicapping traits and attitudes; law violations; drinking, drug addiction, deviant sexual behavior; other forms of deviant behavior.

Mental-physical state: personality structure, mental health, emotional disorder, internal conflict, mental retardation, chronic and/or serious disease.

Role performance: as spouse, breadwinner, homemaker, neighbor, member of the community, participant in trade and professional associations, member of clubs, lodges, special programs, etc.; nature and degree of role involvement; acceptance vs. rejection by role partners; personal competence for role playing; degree of satisfaction derived. Draw on agency records, psychiatric evalutions, police and probation records as well as your own observations.

b. Factors To Be Considered for Children

General characteristics: same as for parents.

Social behavior: same as for parents.

Mental-physical state: same as for parents.

Role performance: as child in home setting, sibling, pupil, member of peer groups, play groups, etc.; nature and degree of role involvement; acceptance vs. rejection by role partners; personal competence for role playing; degree of satisfaction derived. Draw on school and camp reports, psychiatric and psychological summaries, test results, police and probation records, as well as your own observations.

C. CARE AND TRAINING OF CHILDREN

1. *Physical Care*

Physical appearance.

Supply and condition of clothing.

Nutrition.

Attention given to cleanliness, diet and health needs.

In the case of infants, give the schedule of the mother's care.

2. *Training Methods and Emotional Care*

Affection, indifference, rejection, rigidity, overpermissiveness.

Kind of punishment used (or contemplated in the case of an infant): appropriateness of discipline to behavior; discipline by whom, for what? consistency of discipline, family rules; agreement between parents over exercise of discipline; approval of good conduct (whether given).

Encouragement of independence versus fostering of dependence.

Differential treatment of siblings.

Behavior standards set by parents.

D. SOCIAL ACTIVITIES

1. *Informal Associations*

Relationships with parents, in-laws, friends and neighbors: their nature and frequency.

Social outlets of family members.

Antisocial acts: their nature and motivation.

Identification with larger groups, i.e., neighborhood, community.

Socialization experience for children beyond the nuclear family.

Ways in which free time is spent informally.

2. *Formal Associations*

Membership of family members in organized groups (social, economic, political and recreational).

Attitude toward organized groups and activities (include unions, lodges, religious groups, etc.).

Type of activity in groups: nominal memberships versus leadership or committee memberships.

Degree of satisfaction derived from formal associations.

E. ECONOMIC PRACTICES

1. *Source(s) and Amount of Family Income*

   Employment, public assistance, insurance, support from relatives.

   Adequacy of income relative to family's needs.

   Satisfaction with income.

   Necessities provided?

2. *Job Situation* (applies to family members who contribute substantially to support of family)

   Nature of work, employment practices.

   Behavior on job, attitude toward employment.

   Relations with boss and co-workers.

   Satisfaction or dissatisfaction with job.

   Suitability of job for person's capabilities.

   Frequency of job changes.

   Reaction of wife and children to job situation.

3. *Use of Money*

   Ability to manage money: who manages the money? who decides on expenditures? agreement versus disagreement over money management.

   Budgeting: haphazard or systematic? use of banks, methods of saving, insurance.

   Priorities for spending money: realistic regard to basic necessities.

   Amount and nature of debts, reason for debts.

F. HOME AND HOUSEHOLD PRACTICES

1. *Physical Facilities*

   Type of home, age, ownership (public, private), number of rooms, arrangement of rooms, privacy, crowding.

Physical condition of home.

Characteristics of neighborhood: types of buildings and their age; conditions of buildings and yards; nature of street scene: traffic, people on the streets, cleanliness, etc.

Adequacy of basic household equipment: furnishings for sleeping, bathing, refrigeration, cooking, sanitation.

Attitude toward home: attention to making it attractive versus neglect.

2. *Housekeeping Standards*

Management of household chores: how assigned, executed?

Ways of serving meals and adequacy of diet; timing and regularity of meals.

Buying patterns: food, clothing, recreation, car, furniture, etc.

Neatness of home: pride versus indifference regarding management of the household.

G. HEALTH CONDITIONS AND PRACTICES

1. *Health Conditions* (include a paragraph on each family member)

Health of family members: adequate, normal functioning? problems, diseases, handicaps, debilitating conditions, mental illness?

2. *Health Practices*

Medical care obtained or avoided?

Use of preventive resources: well-baby clinics, T.B., x-ray.

Care exercised in following medical instructions?

Disease prevention practices; physical hygiene practices.

Dental care: regularity, hygiene.

H. RELATIONSHIP TO SOCIAL WORKER[1]

1. *Attitude Toward Worker*

Opinions expressed by client family; attitudes reflected in their behavior; is family cooperative, indifferent, hostile, suspicious, etc.? Which family members reveal what kinds of attitudes toward professional intervention?

2. *Use of Worker*

Manner in which client uses worker: for advice, guidance, concrete help, dealing with problems, venting feelings, manipulation, etc. What does client expect from worker?

I. USE OF COMMUNITY RESOURCES

1. *School* (include primary, secondary and adult education)

Value parents place on education, their attitudes toward the school.

Interest they take in children's school activities, contact with school personnel.

Children's attitudes toward school, achievement, attendance, behavior.

2. *Church* (check "not appropriate" if no contact or nominal tie only)

Membership and attendance; denomination.

Type of participation; services, Sunday school, church clubs, etc.

Satisfaction derived from attendance.

Agreement of parents on children's participation.

Influence of church membership on family solidarity.

3. *Health Resources* (include only physical health)

Type of services used: public; private; clinics; outpatient departments, etc.

Knowledge about and attitude toward resources: cooperative; apathetic; suspicious; hostile; resentful, etc.

Use of agencies: appointments kept or missed; medical advice used or disregarded.

4. *Social Agencies* (include panel and correctional services such as probation and parole, housing authorities, employment agencies, public welfare, family planning services, social adjustment ser-

vices — general and sectarian, mental health and hygiene clinics, etc.)

Knowledge about and attitude toward agencies; well or poorly informed; favorable attitudes; hostile; resentful; apathetic; defensive, etc.

Use of agencies: source of referral; family seeks help; is cooperative; uses agency appropriately; is overly demanding; refuses to accept agency services; etc.

5. *Recreational Agencies* (include clubs, community and neighborhood centers, organized playgrounds, public and private recreation programs and services, recreation camps, etc.)

   Knowledge and use made of recreational agencies by children; frequency and regularity of use.

   Parents' use of and attitude toward recreational facilities for children and adults.

NOTES

1. Only applicable where evaluation is part of an intervention study.

Appendix 3

Sample Validation Study*

ASSESSING BIAS:
A COMPARISON OF TWO METHODS†

Evaluation of research designs employing probability sampling, particularly those based on samples of individuals rather than households, has repeatedly disclosed relatively large discrepancies between design objectives and actual performance.[1] The failure to secure substantial portions of a random sample raises obvious questions regarding the sample's representativeness and consequently the validity of the measurements obtained.

PROBLEM

In the sampling effort reported here[2] 49 percent (N = 585) of the potential respondents randomly selected from a vital statistics listing of all young primiparae in a particular urban area could not be interviewed because of removal to an unknown address.[3] During initial interviewing, resources were not available for a major effort to locate these lost respondents. Therefore, after an attempt had been made to secure a lost respondent's new address through (a) the mails,[4] (b) a search of the

* Reprinted from *The Public Opinion Quarterly*, Vol. 33, Winter 1969-70.© 1970 by Columbia University Press (reproduced with permission of the author, Bruce W. Lagay, and the journal). The author is associate professor in the Graduate School of Social Work, Rutgers University.

† The research reported here, supported by Grant #190, Welfare Administration, U. S. Department of Health, Education and Welfare, has been adapted from a more detailed paper entitled "Finding Lost Respondents: A Field Procedure for Locating Inaccessible Respondents When Assessing Dependent Variable Bias in an Incompletely Constituted Random Sample," and is available upon request from the author.

current telephone directory,[5] and (c) one field visit to her former neighborhood, the case was set aside as not located.

This decision necessitated taking steps to ascertain the amount and direction of bias it had produced. Two approaches were used. The first, hereafter referred to as the check data method, set out to explore the demographic compatability between individuals included in the sample and those who had been excluded. The second, referred to as the dependent variable method, sought to locate and interview a subsample of those individuals originally excluded and to compare them with originally interviewed respondents with reference to the major dependent variable under study.

METHOD

Both approaches to bias measurement utilized the same 10 percent randomly chosen sample (N = 59) of families originally not located (N = 585), and compared it with a group of 59 cases randomly chosen from those families who had been located and interviewed (N = 559).

The check data method. Birth registry and census materials were used to obtain check data on race, occupation, rent, and legitimacy of birth. Information for neighborhood and dwelling unit comparisons was obtained through field visits to the former addresses of all 118 families in both subsamples.

The dependent variable method. The effort involved in locating lost respondents was considerable. In all, there were over 420 contacts with informants, mostly telephone, though the mails and some field visiting were also employed.

To a large extent the success of a tracking effort depends on the individual(s) carrying it out.[6] The development of initial leads to respondents is the most challenging aspect of tracking. In some cases, clues to initial sources of information were suggested by respondent characteristics. For example, the listing of a respondent's husband's occupation on birth records might lead to an employer, a union, or a licensing body; a former address in a public housing project or in an urban renewal area to the housing authority; or an out-of-wedlock birth listing to welfare department files.

Discovery of a telephone company publication in which subscribers are arranged by address rather than name permitted calls to tenants at the respondent's former address or to neighbors at adjacent addresses. These contacts often suggested subsequent tracking strategies. For example, if knowledge of the imminent birth of a second child was uncovered, a check with the bureau of vital statistics and then the well-baby clinics was made; knowledge of a serious illness suggested a check with city hospitals and clinics; ownership of a car, a check with the motor vehicle registration bureau; a history of debts, contact with credit departments of stores, and so forth.

Leads culminating in a respondent's new address were obtained from relatives and former neighbors in 27 instances, from health, welfare, or other public agencies in 12; from retailers in 5; from superintendents and landlords in 4; and from employers in 3. Fifty-one families, or 86 percent of the 59 lost respondents, were located in this fashion, and dependent variable measurements were obtained from 41 of these.[7] These 41 cases represent 69 percent of the total subsample of 59 originally lost respondents, or 77 percent of the total eligible sample.

RESULTS

The check data method. An analysis of selected demographic check data did not show striking differences between families in the bias study subsample and those in the originally interviewed subsample. Chi-square coefficients obtained suggested that those differences which were present were probably due to chance, and offer little reason to believe that exclusion of the unlocated families has biased the original sampling of dependent variable measurements (see Appendix Table 3.1).

The dependent variable method. The dependent variable used for comparison was the social functioning of the family, as measured by the St. Paul Scale of Family Functioning.[8] Assessment is made in 8 major areas[9] and 24 subareas of family functioning along a scale ranging from 1 (inadequate) to 7 (adequate), with a score of 4 representing marginal functioning. The family's scores in each of the 8 major areas of social functioning are then added, yielding a total score of family functioning.

A comparison of family functioning scores for the two subsamples is presented in Appendix Table 3.2.

Examination of the percentages recorded in Appendix Table 3.2 indicates a difference in dependent variable score distributions between the two samples. Both chi-square and rank-sum tests applied to these data indicate that the two groups differ significantly. Thus, the dependent variable method of bias measurement demonstrates the existence of a significant positive sampling bias, undetected in the foregoing check data comparison.

A more comprehensive assessment of dependent variable bias would demonstrate not only the existence and direction but the amount of bias present. However, the dependent variable in this study does not presently lend itself to other than ordinal handling. This means that corrective adjustments to the over-all dependent variable measurements must be stated in essentially qualitative terms.

APPENDIX TABLE 3.1: CHI-SQUARE COMPARISONS BETWEEN SUB-SAMPLES OF THE ORIGINALLY INTERVIEWED AND ORIGINALLY NOT LOCATED FAMILIES ON SELECTED DEMOGRAPHIC VARIABLES

DEMOGRAPHIC VARIABLE	x^2	d.f.	P
Race	.20	1	$<$.70
Legitimacy of birth	.33	1	$<$.70
Type of dwelling[a]	2.14	2	$<$.50
Type of neighborhood[b]	1.08	2	$<$.70
Racial composition of neighborhood	.88	2	$<$.70
Condition of neighborhood[c]	.00	1	$<$.99
Occupational status of husband (when present)[d]	.70	3	$<$.90
Median dollar gross rent of census tract	4.75	3	$<$.20 $>$.10

[a]Types of dwellings were: private apartments, private home converted to apartments and other.

[b]Types of neighborhoods were: residential, residential-commercial and other.

[c]Condition of neighborhood: good or deteriorated.

[d]Occupational status was computed through an adaptation of Hollingshead's Two-Factor Index of Social Position. Breakdown used: middle-middle and above, equivalent to Hollingshead's occupational factors I through IV; lower middle = V, lower = VI and lower-lower = VII.

APPENDIX TABLE 3.2: FAMILY FUNCTIONING SCORES OF ORIGINALLY INTERVIEWED AND ORIGINALLY NOT LOCATED FAMILIES

FAMILY FUNCTIONING Scores[a]	Subsample of Originally Interviewed Families (N = 59)	Subsample of Originally Not Located Families (N = 40[b])	Total (N = 99)
56-53 (high)	72.8%	37.5%	58.8%
52-48	17.0	30.0	22.2
47-13 (low)	10.2	32.5	19.0

[a]Distribution for rank-sum test has been collapsed to conserve space.

[b]One additional case was dropped from this analysis because of incomplete information.

NOTES

1. Frederick F. Stephan and Philip J. McCarthy, *Sampling Opinion*, New York, Wiley, 1958, p. 323.

2. See Ludwig L. Geismar and Jane Krisberg, "The Family Life Improvement Project: An Experiment in Preventive Intervention," Parts I and II, *Social Casework*, Vol. 47, November and December, 1966.

3. Representativeness, though desirable, was not a prime requisite for the success of this longitudinal project's experimental-control design.

4. Address changes when known to postal authorities can be obtained from them by stamping "Address Correction Requested" on a letter sent to the potential respondent or arranging directly with the post office to make a clerical search of their files for address changes and removals.

5. The commercially sponsored city directory was four years old and of no value in locating lost respondents.

6. Appreciation is due Mrs. Sara B. Holzer, research interviewer, whose imaginative and unfailing efforts developed and executed the tracking procedures.

7. There were 4 refusals and 6 cases which failed to meet the sample definition. The latter group of disqualified respondents was produced by errors in vital statistics reporting and should never have been included in the universe from which any of the samples were drawn.

8. See Ludwig L. Geismar and Beverly Ayres, *Measuring Family Functioning: A Manual on a Method for Evaluating the Social Functioning of Disorganized Families*, St. Paul, Minn., Family-Centered Project, Greater St. Paul United Fund and Council, Inc., 1960.

9. The eight major areas are: family relationships and unity, individual behavior and adjustment, care and training of children, social activities, economic practices, household facilities and practices, health conditions and practices, and use of community resources.

Coding Scheme for Validity Testing of Family Functioning Data

1. *Physical Well-Being* of (1) Husband, (2) Wife, (3) Child(ren)

   Good — Absence of serious or frequent illness or chronic condition, absence of physical handicaps of a disabling nature.

   Fair — Mild chronic illness or physical handicap present not hindering a person's daily functioning.

   Poor — Serious or frequent illness, chronic condition or serious physical handicap which prevents effective functioning.

2. *Emotional Well-Being* of (1) Husband, (2) Wife, (3) Child(ren)

   Good — Person's adjustment to environment and ability to form interpersonal relationships is adequate; person is flexible and reality oriented in interaction with people, has positive self-image, feels able to cope with and succeed in life situations.

   Fair — Some problems in adjustment to environment are apparent but not of such a severe nature as to cause serious malfunctioning; some feelings of inadequacy and insecurity present.

   Poor — Poor adjustment to environment; limited ability to form interpersonal relationships; psychosis or extreme neurosis present; person feels unable to cope with life situation.

3. *Satisfactions* (1) Intrafamilial, (2) Extrafamilial, (3) Instrumental and (4) Sexual

   High — Pleasure gained from interaction with others and from the performance of tasks within the family and on the outside.

Medium — Limited enjoyment from interacting with others or from the performance of tasks.

Low   — General dissatisfaction with interaction in the family and outside the home, lack of satisfaction from the performance of tasks.

4. *Role Allocation in* (1) Child Rearing, (2) Household Tasks and (3) Financial Management

The question posed is, Who carries out what tasks? Are they carried out singly by one parent, jointly by both parents, allocated to someone outside the family or accomplished by some other arrangement?

5. *Goals, Values and Beliefs in the Areas of* (1) Education, (2) Priority of Purchases and (3) Religion

The question to be answered is, Who believes what? Do the marriage partners express similar or dissimilar preferences and goals in the three areas designated?

6. *Decision-Making in* (1) Economic Management, (2) Child Rearing and (3) Social and Recreational Activities

Information sought here covers the question, Who decides what? Regardless of what the parents' wishes and goals may be, who are the people in the family or outside of it who make decisions in the above areas? Are decisions made by one person or are they made jointly?

Appendix 5

Husband-Wife Agreement on Six Family Life Variables

VARIABLE	Ratio of Agreement	x^2
Physical well-being of		
Husband	.80	6.64
Wife	.83	8.06
Child (ren)	.93	15.64
Emotional Well-being of		
Husband	.78	5.40
Wife	.83	8.06
Child (ren)	.75	4.32
Satisfactions		
Intrafamilial	.75	4.32
Extrafamilial	.70	2.56
Instrumental	.80	6.64
Sexual	.68	1.86
Role allocation in		
Child rearing	.90	9.62
Household tasks	.90	9.62
Financial management	.83	8.06
Goals, values, beliefs		
Education	.90	9.62
Priority of purchases	.78	5.40
Religion	.78	5.40
Decision-making		
Economic management	.73	3.38
Child rearing	.78	5.40
Social and recreational activities	.78	5.40

Mean Ratio = .80, S.D. = .067.
For $p = .05$, $x^2 = 3.841$.

Matrix of Pearsonian Correlations Among Total and Main Category Family Functioning Scores at Start of Project

PART 1

	Indiv. Behavior	Care and Training of Children	Social Activities	Econ. Practices
Family relationship	.807	.596	.651	.548
Individual behavior		.664	.716	.635
Care and training of children			.513	.530
Social activities				.511
Economic practice				
Home and household practices				
Health conditions and practices				
Use of community resources				

	Household Practices	Health Conditions and Practices	Use of Community Resources	Total Scores[a]
Family relationship	.386	.436	.441	.705
Individual behavior	.517	.513	.546	.779
Care and training of children	.520	.615	.587	.666
Social activities	.378	.411	.443	.678
Economic practice	.558	.579	.522	.703
Home and household practices		.568	.470	.686
Health conditions and practices			.659	.624
Use of community resources				.578

For statistical significance at the .001 level correlation coefficient must be at least .32.
N = 555.
[a]Total scores for purposes of machine analysis were divided into four score groupings.

Appendix 7

Rotated Factor Matrix of Family Functioning Subcategories[a]

| VARIABLES | Factors | | | | | Communalities |
	I Interpersonal- Expressive	II Instru- mental	III Economic	IV Formal Assoc.	V Health Cond.	
Marital relationships	0.723	0.028	0.405	0.142	0.347	0.829
Parent-child relationship	0.765	0.287	0.093	0.013	−0.063	0.680
Family solidarity	0.782	0.119	0.351	0.158	0.194	0.812
Relationship with other household members	0.603	0.355	0.131	0.187	-0.138	0.561
Indiv. behavior father	0.577	-0.012	0.598	0.209	0.269	0.807
Indiv. behavior mother	0.781	0.356	0.161	0.085	0.162	0.795
Physical child care	0.464	0.720	0.137	0.046	0.094	0.763
Training methods and emotional care	0.731	0.389	0.050	-0.098	0.040	0.700
Informal associations	0.655	0.179	0.293	0.281	0.153	0.649
Formal associations	0.196	-0.067	0.271	0.631	-0.110	0.528
Source and amount of income	0.243	0.425	0.655	-0.040	0.221	0.720
Job situation	0.132	0.140	0.821	0.200	0.043	0.753
Use of money	0.371	0.237	0.545	-0.146	0.156	0.536
Physical facilities of home	0.191	0.516	0.212	-0.247	0.466	0.627
Housekeeping standards	0.291	0.643	0.199	-0.117	0.393	0.706

| VARIABLES | Factors | | | | | Communalities |
| | I | II | III | IV | V | |
	Interpersonal-Expressive	Instru-mental	Economic	Formal Assoc.	Health Cond.	
Health conditions	0.105	0.189	0.126	0.163	0.650	0.511
Health practices	0.214	0.793	0.180	0.149	0.213	0.776
Use of church	0.057	0.175	-0.051	0.751	0.219	0.649
Use of health resources	0.178	0.839	0.115	0.212	0.035	0.794
Use of social agencies	0.213	0.449	0.498	0.168	0.266	0.595

[a]Use of school with loadings of less than ± .50 was dropped from the analysis.

Appendix 8

Variables in the Community Services, Resources and Facilities Substudy

---

I. PRIMARY PROVISIONS

A. *Income, Employment, Social Security*

Jobs; job training; job finding; employment insurance; workmen's compensation; social security; medical insurance; welfare.

B. *Housing*

Public housing; less costly private housing; open housing.

C. *Basic Socialization*

Schools for children.

D. *Health*

Hospitals, clinics, baby-keep-well stations; private medical and dental care.

E. *Social Adjustment*

Homemaker service; day care centers and nurseries; marriage counseling; parent-child counseling; counseling for the mentally ill; counseling for other problems; neighborhood centers; nursing homes for the aged; help for alcoholics, addicts.

II. SECONDARY PROVISIONS

F. *Social Control*

Reach City Hall with complaints; faster action by City Hall; police protection; free or low cost legal aid.

G. *Social Participation and Recreation*

Safe parks, playgrounds and community centers.

H. *Secondary Socialization*

Schools for adults.

I. *Derived Instrumental Needs*

Garbage collection; street lights; clean streets and sidewalks; public transportation; convenient neighborhood shopping.

Index